THE JAPANESE COMPANY

THE
JAPANESE COMPANY

RODNEY CLARK

YALE UNIVERSITY PRESS

NEW HAVEN AND LONDON

TO MY PARENTS

Set in Monotype Bembo and printed in the United States of America.

Library of Congress Cataloging in Publication Data

Clark, Rodney, 1945–
  The Japanese company.

  Bibliography: p.
  Includes index.
  1. Industrial management—Japan. 2. Industrial relations—Japan. 3. Industry—Social aspects—Japan. 4. Corporations—Japan. I. Title.
  HD70.J3C58   301.18'32'0952   78–65480
  ISBN 0–300–02310–3 (clothbound); 0–300–02646–3 (paperbound)

12   11   10   9   8   7

CONTENTS

List of Tables

List of Figures

ACKNOWLEDGEMENTS

This book was made possible by the generosity of the London Cornell Fund, which financed my research when I was a student of the School of Oriental and African Studies. I was greatly helped in writing it by Robert Fleming & Co., Limited, and its associated company Jardine Fleming. Fleming's continued to allow me access to their files and the use of their telex system even after I had left their employment, and frequently exercised their influence in Japan on my behalf. I owe a great debt to my friend Kurata Masaharu of the Mitsubishi Bank, and to his father, Kurata Kaoru, of the East Japan Corrugated Board Manufacturers' Association, who between them prepared my entry into a Japanese company and did so much to help me settle down in it. Kanamaru Mineo and Taeko offered me boundless hospitality, and solved all sorts of logistical problems for me while I was living in Yokohama. Very many people gave me help and advice in collecting information, and making sense of what I had collected. I am particularly grateful to my sister Penny, Miyo Docherty, Nagashima Nobuhirō, Nakaji Noriko, Greg Roszkowski, Tsurumachi Akio, and Peter and Yuki Vranic. Hirota Osamu of the Japan Institute of Labour hunted down elusive documents for me in Tokyo, and Setsuko Wright gathered quantities of material on my behalf at the British Museum. Of my former colleagues in the Fleming group, I should like particularly to thank William Garrett, with whom I began investment banking in Japan; Robert Thomas, who took considerable trouble to find answers to my many questions; and Patrick Gifford, for his enthusiastic help on countless occasions, and his rigorous review of drafts of Chapters III and VII. Richard Sims and Shimura Haruyoshi made many valuable suggestions for improving those parts of the book which deal with history and law respectively. Ronald Dore read two earlier versions of the work and saved me from a number of errors. Okamoto Hideaki spared me a great deal of time at various stages of the project, and I learned much from many stimulating conversations with him. Keith Thurley took a kind interest in my research from the first, and offered me useful advice throughout it. I am particularly grateful for his comments on the final draft. I should also like to thank my wife Stephanie for the patient care with which she

ɪ*

helped me prepare the book, and for all the encouragement she gave me while I was writing it.

Finally, I should like to express my great gratitude to the directors and employees of 'Marumaru', for their most generous hospitality and friendly indulgence towards the inquisitive stranger in their midst.

NOTE ON JAPANESE NAMES

Japanese personal names are written in the customary Japanese order, family name first, except when referring to the Japanese authors of works in English. In some cases Japanese companies are referred to by colloquial forms of their official English names—'Daiei', for example, instead of 'The Dai'ei, Inc.'. The official names are listed in the index. Macrons represent lengthened vowels. They have not, however, been applied to Japanese words which have passed into English, nor to better known place names.

References in the footnotes to works written in Japanese are indicated by an asterisk.

CHAPTER I

Introduction

The aim of this book is to explain how the Japanese company is run, and how its workings affect those associated with it, and the people of Japan in general.

In all those countries which permit their existence, joint-stock companies have achieved enormous importance. They organize the greater part of manufacture and commerce and employ much, perhaps most, of the population. They distribute wealth, making some people rich and leaving others poor, elevating whole regions to prosperity or denying them the means to it. Companies are themselves political institutions of some consequence, for within them men are as firmly subordinated to each other and to common ends as may be possible in the normal circumstances of a democracy; but companies also have political significance in the narrower sense that they are frequently engaged in national politics. What companies do, their decisions to open and close factories, their successes and failures in business, have consequences which governments cannot ignore and must try to shape or qualify. Conversely, companies cannot afford to remain indifferent to government actions, and often attempt to influence political activity. Companies also have intellectual, cultural and moral effects. They pay for and conduct much of the scientific and social research on which economies depend, and by which societies understand themselves and make ready for change. Company advertisements encourage ephemeral preferences, certainly, but also profound ideas. By direct sponsorship, and even more by their recruitment policies, companies have contributed to the development of systems of education and have helped establish the values given to different branches of learning. Finally, companies have introduced to each country new processes and ideas from others, and have been responsible for a flow of people between different parts of the world.

Within each country the joint-stock company is second only to the state itself among great institutions. In international affairs, the company has been able to play off any one government against others and so acquire considerable autonomy.

The reason why the company has achieved such influence is everywhere the same and is simply explained. The company is a legal fiction, a device by which a business is made independent of the individuals who found it. Someone who wants to start a company draws up an appropriate list of articles of association, arranges for the issue of shares in return for the share capital, the appointment of directors, and registration by the authorities, all in accordance with the law of the country in which the company is to be domiciled. From that moment on, for most practical purposes, the company is considered a separate and independent legal entity. Its assets are its own, and not those of its sponsors. It alone is responsible for its liabilities. It may enter into contracts, employ labour, or take legal action, without necessarily exacting any kind of commitment from its sponsors, or prejudicing the rights of any of the individuals concerned with it.

The best known of the advantages of incorporation is that the liability of investors in a company may be limited. People can put their money into a company and play a part in its management with the assurance that, if mistakes are made, and the company incurs serious losses, they will not be called upon to pay the creditors from their own pockets. The company will be put into liquidation and they themselves will only lose the money they paid for their shares. Limiting liability not only removes a formidable obstacle to commercial initiative, but also makes it easier for an enterprise to achieve a size incommensurable with the wealth even of the richest individuals. There are partnerships of considerable size like, for example, accounting firms, but it would require hundreds of obliging millionaires to stand surety for the debts of a car manufacturer or a shipping line. In practice, only a company can safely grow very big.

Another important advantage of the separation of enterprise from entrepreneur is that it is much easier for a company than for one or even several owner-managers of a business to enlist the support of outsiders. A company can offer not merely money but also some influence over its affairs to the different sorts of people whose help it must have. Employees can be attracted by the possibility that they will one day exert real authority in the enterprise, instead of being permanently subordinated to the owners. Those who provide a company with money, either as shareholders or as creditors of various degrees of priority, receive power over the company in proportion to the extent of their contributions and the risks they are taking. The outsiders, employees, contractors, bankers and investors, can judge the impersonal nature of a company, set out in financial reports and explanatory handbooks, more accurately than they can gauge the disposition of an entrepreneur. They can also enter into clear and contractual relations with it, and avoid the risk of at least some of the disturbances which can arise when individual people, with contrasting characters and different interests, commit themselves to one another.

A third advantage lies in the perpetual existence of the company. An entrepreneur will retire and die, but a company can go on indefinitely. Naturally, their durability adds to the attractions of companies as business partners and employers. Even more important, it enables companies to work on a time-scale far greater than their mortal rivals. Companies can recruit and train people to do jobs which will only become important after five or ten years have passed. They can conduct research unperturbed by the probability that they will not benefit from what they discover for decades. They can enter into forward commitments and undertake projects over such long periods that no individual could be confident of ever seeing the business through.

It must be admitted that these advantages, limited liability, impersonality and continuity, can be achieved by other means. The difficulties of unlimited liability can be overcome by insurance; contracts can be used to reduce the uncertainties of caprice and partiality; and continuity can be assured by the principle of heredity, so that a business remains 'in the family'. Nor are all companies automatically endowed with these advantages. A great many companies in all countries are merely small family firms which have adopted the form of the corporation so as to pay fewer taxes. Such family companies do gain something from the limitation of their liability, but they are far from impersonal and their continuity may be permanently in doubt. Nevertheless, incorporation is an excellent preliminary to the success of an enterprise; and the company is so much the most convenient form for commercial co-operation on a large scale and over a long period of time that, apart from the organs of the state itself, there are no alternatives to it.

If companies in different nations owe their success to the same elegant legal fiction it does not mean that companies are everywhere the same. Each country has added its own legal elaborations to the nearly universal principle of incorporation. But these are niceties, rarely of great significance. Far more important is the fact that as the company has risen to eminence in each of a number of different nations it has had to adjust to different pre-existing institutions and has been shaped by different circumstances. It has been influenced by—and, of course, has contributed to—economic conditions in a variety of ways. It has been allowed more or less political power. In different countries, and even in the same country at different times, its rules and practices have been challenged or supported by common opinion. Besides this, in all its local manifestations the company has been subject to what in this frame of reference must be accounted mere fortuities: scandals, wars, fashions, or the incidence of personalities. Even in such similar nations as the United States and Great Britain the company has quite distinct features: its formal organization, its treatment of employees, its relations with organized labour, its ownership, its political posture, its cultural connotations, are far from identical.

The Japanese company, in just the same way as the American or British, is the product of a particular history. In the next chapter, therefore, and before I discuss the company's present position in Japanese society, I shall briefly explain the historical context.

Thereafter I shall deal with the Japanese company as it exists today. I shall begin by describing the company's central part in the scheme of Japanese industry and commerce. I hope to show how the Japanese company, in spite of its constitutional similarity to companies in the West, is different from the Western company even as a unit of production or an instrument of business. Next, I shall anatomize the company. I shall consider its organization, the way it is managed, and the methods by which its managers are chosen and assigned their tasks.

The subject of the fifth chapter, how people join and leave companies, may not appear of sufficient consequence to be worth long discussion. It is, however, a topic of crucial importance, and for several reasons. It is commonly held in Japan that there is 'lifetime employment': that company employees should or may—or even actually do—stay with their companies for life, entering them from school or university and remaining with them until they retire. The idea that the Japanese enjoy 'lifetime employment' has even become familiar in the West, where newspaper articles refer to the practice, and there are television programmes about the allegedly permanent attachment of the Japanese worker to his employer. By looking at the labour market as a whole, and also at how people join and leave a single company, it should be possible to discover how far 'lifetime employment' really exists in practice.

Another reason for studying recruitment and resignation is because it provides us with a clue to the nature of authority in Japanese industry. The company, like any other co-operative venture with a specific aim, must be to some degree authoritarian. Someone must be able to get other people to do what has to be done. Yet at the same time the individual company is a voluntary association, which no one has to belong to. Knowing the kind of people who leave a company, and the reasons why they do, helps us to understand the principles on which its internal discipline is based, as well as the limits beyond which that discipline cannot be applied.

Yet another consideration is that the labour market is an important means by which companies collectively influence society. Let me give two simple examples. If companies give preference to applicants from certain schools then everyone will want to get into those schools and the education system may be changed. Or again, by requiring people to retire from work earlier and so forego high salaries and positions of responsibility, companies can alter the economic and political balance of the community. The influences that companies exert through the labour market are frequently indirect and subtle, like many 'market forces'; so much so that those making company policy may not realise what the results of the policy will be, and those subjected to the influences may not always be aware of them.

Finally, the study of the labour market reveals what is perhaps the most potent force for change in the organization of the Japanese company. Japan is growing older. The combination of a falling birth rate and a lengthening life span means that an increasing proportion of the population is beyond the present age of retirement; while the average age of those who are working is rising rapidly. Company policies and practices already show signs of accommodation to this demographic movement.

In the last two chapters I shall conclude the themes developed in the fifth. The questions of how far there is 'lifetime employment' and what the nature of authority is in Japanese industry can both be seen as parts of a more general question about the quality of the relationship between company and employee. Taking the example of one particular firm, I shall describe how employees see their employer and how they behave towards one another. In some ways their attitudes to the company and to fellow workers are peculiarly Japanese. This is not to say that they are unintelligible to a Westerner, but merely that they are the product of Japanese history and culture. But to a far greater extent their attitudes are conditioned by immediate circumstances: by the way the company is organized, the position each employee has within it, and the state of the labour market—just as one would expect of the attitudes of company employees in any country. If company life in Japan appears strange to

Westerners it is not so much because people are thinking in an impenetrably Japanese way but because the context for their behaviour, the organization of Japanese industry, is unfamiliar to us.

The other two themes, the influence of the company on society and the possibilities of change, constitute the subject of the last chapter. I shall try to determine how different sections of the community are affected by company practices. I shall then review the various factors both within the company and also in society that lend the company stability or are causing it to change.

Although, as the prospectus above makes clear, I shall be dealing with a number of important economic and social topics concerning the Japanese company, I will have to leave many things out. For any book of this length, which deals with an institution so central to modern industrial society, must be a compromise between surface and depth; and in order to give a little more time to some points I am going to curtail discussion of others. Three of these, which I shall scarcely mention in the body of the book, deserve an apologetic hail and farewell here.

I shall not be saying much about relations between companies and local and national governments, though obviously these are among the most important relations that companies have with institutions outside industry. To explain exactly how governments guide and influence industrial companies, and how companies involve themselves with the formation not merely of government policies but even of governments themselves, would take a book, or rather a number of books, for many have been written on the subject.[1] I would like, however, to correct a common misapprehension that Japanese industry and government are so close in their aims and workings that the whole of Japanese industry is under government control, or alternatively that Japan is to be likened to a single gigantic company: 'Japan, Inc.'

The idea of 'Japan, Inc.' is partly an extension from persons to institutions of the ill-informed judgement that all orientals look the same. It is also partly a rationalization of Japanese commercial success, which becomes attributable to an advantage no Western businessman enjoys: the unconditional support of a sympathetic government. It is an absurd over-simplification. Neither the Japanese government nor Japanese business are unitary bodies. The governing party is split into factions.

[1] For recent reviews and up-to-date references see G. L. Curtis (1975) and Philip H. Trezise and Yukio Suzuki (1976). Earlier important works include William W. Lockwood (1965) and Chitoshi Yanaga (1968).

Different ministries publicly adopt opposing policies and privately work to defeat each other. Business interests do not coincide. Declining textile companies call for protectionism, car firms for free trade. Dairy producers want one set of rules, margarine makers another.

There is no doubt that when industry can agree upon what it wants its demands are taken seriously in the various branches of government, possibly more seriously in Japan than in other countries—though no government on the planet fails to care for the needs of industry. Nevertheless, in Japan as elsewhere the government has to consider how its policies affect various other sectors of the community, many of which are represented by powerful interest groups. In recent years, at least, Japanese businessmen have sometimes had considerable difficulty in bending the government to their will. The business federations have failed, for example, to prevent the choice of a candidate they disapproved of as Prime Minister, and they have unsuccessfully opposed new taxes.[1] It can be argued that these are trivial set-backs; that business controls government because government is imbued with the values of business. Politicians think the same way as company presidents, and so do the latters' will in following their own prescriptions. In theory this argument is hard to refute. In practice there are few countries in the world in which political and industrial managers are of such different dispositions that a similar argument might not apply, at least in some degree. The superficial evidence therefore reasserts itself; companies and those who run them do have a substantial influence in politics, but there are important occasions when they do not get their way.

The converse proposition that the government controls business is equally a quarter-truth. In its handling of industry the Japanese government has two great advantages over Western ones. It has at its disposal a formidable store of information, for the Japanese are assiduous collectors of the most detailed statistics. It has also established a tradition of 'administrative guidance'. Ministries offer companies advice on matters of policy —whether or not to carry out a plan, how big a factory's capacity should be, what type of money should be raised for investment capital—and firms are on the whole ready to follow it. Most Western governments do, of course, attempt to influence business by similarly informal means, often quite successfully. On the other hand, the Japanese government has

[1] The Prime Minister was Tanaka Kakuei. See G. L. Curtis (1975: 40). The tax was the Special Company Tax, levied on larger and more profitable companies over a two-year period from March 1974. Details are given in the *Nihon Keizai Shinbun* (evening edition), 30 March 1974, p. 1, 'Kaisha tokubetsuzeihō ga seiritsu' (The Special Company Tax Law materializes).

to overcome certain disadvantages in imposing its will on industry. Government spending is a rather smaller proportion of the national product than in Western Europe, and there is little government ownership of industry; so that the Japanese government cannot use its economic power as easily as the British or French to get companies to comply with its requests. The considerable attachment that Japanese, patriots though they are, feel for their companies constitutes another obstacle to the exercise of government authority. When, for example, the Ministry of Finance requests that banks curtail their lending to some particular sector, there will be general compliance with the form of the request; but each bank will try to devise ways of lending indirectly to companies in that sector so that when restrictions are removed it will have a competitive advantage.

Let me end this denial of the existence of 'Japan, Inc.' by quoting two cases of difference between government and industry. The Ministry of International Trade and Industry has, over the past decade, attempted to create a single major Japanese computer company to challenge IBM out of the many rival manufacturers presently making computers on what is by world standards a small scale. The rearrangement of the industry has taken a long time, and even now is unfinished.[1] The difficulty the Japanese government has had in persuading electronics firms to pool resources and subordinate themselves to what the government supposes to be the national interest compares strikingly with the ease with which the British government established International Computers in similar circumstances. The second case comes from a related industry and concerns Casio, now perhaps the largest calculator manufacturer in Japan. In 1972, when it was a rather less significant firm, Casio challenged the same Ministry's attempt to impose on the electronics industry a scheme for limiting exports to Europe. Casio did so by applying to the Fair Trade Commission, a quasi-judicial body, for a ruling that the Ministry's scheme constituted an unfair practice.[2] Such open opposition to the government is rare, for Japanese companies usually prefer subtly to pervert or circumvent 'guidance' they do not like; but no harm seems to have come to Casio for asserting its independence.

[1] Eugene J. Kaplan (1972: 42–54).
[2] Strictly speaking Casio, together with one other company, appealed against the Japan Machinery Export Association, the body administering the scheme to limit exports under Ministerial guidance. Within a few weeks the Ministry of International Trade and Industry was to enter the fray directly. *Nihon Keizai Shinbun*, 14 June 1972, p. 6, 'Dentaku yūshutsu sūryō kisei: sengyō nisha ga "matta"' (Calculator export volume rules: the two specialist firms 'waited').

A second, equally important subject I shall be dealing with only cursorily is the foreign relations of the Japanese company. Everyone knows how Japanese companies have altered world trade. They have all but monopolized the export markets in calculators, cameras, motor cycles, ship-building, television sets and similar products. They are perhaps the leading influence on the international traffic in many important commodities. Originally mainly traders, in the last few years Japanese companies have been investing abroad, on the one hand to assure some degree of control over the production of the commodities on which the Japanese economy depends, and on the other to avoid having to pay high wages at home and penal tariffs in export markets. Japanese companies control paper mills in Canada, cattle farms in Australia, oil rigs in Indonesia, electronic component plants in South East Asia, Italian fine chemical works, Irish textile producers, American food firms, Brazilian steelworks, British ball bearing factories, and Indian shipyards.

In the future the flow of investment and of techniques and people from Japan to the foreign subsidiaries of Japanese companies is likely to continue apace, and the Japanese may displace Western firms from new business sectors. Already there are signs, as Japanese banks, engineering consultancies, trading houses and property companies do more and more business abroad, that the dominance that the United States and Great Britain have established in the world trade in 'invisibles' may one day disappear.

I have chosen to put this subject aside partly because it is too big.[1] It is also very much a political topic—or perhaps it would be more accurate to say that the political consequences of Japanese trade practices are more immediately apparent than, for example, the social consequences, some of which will only become manifest over many years. Since I shall be giving little space to the domestic politics of Japanese business, it seems at least consistent in imperfection to exclude its foreign politics as well. Another excuse for such a large omission is that the Japanese economy is still very little dependent on foreign trade, at least by comparison with the major European countries. Even though the Japanese companies that are active abroad are of such significance in world affairs, most Japanese firms have only indirect foreign connections. They buy foreign goods or sell abroad through intermediaries, usually trading companies. Although their managers are well informed by the newspapers of what is happening outside Japan, and may well have been on trips to study American and European factories, foreign affairs are not likely to be a serious preoccupation for them.

[1] A good brief survey is M. Y. Yoshino (1976).

A third feature of the Japanese company I shall not greatly emphasize is the relation between management and union within it. I shall explain later on why union-management relations are of less significance in Japanese industry than in American and European. Even in America and Europe I have the impression that academic observers are more interested in union-management relations than their importance in the life of the workplace justifies. Consider how little work has been done, for example, on the problems of salesmen, who constitute so large a proportion of today's work forces, by comparison with the work done on unions. Another reason for lightening my concern with this issue is that two excellent recent books on Japanese industrial organization, R. P. Dore's *British Factory—Japanese Factory* and Robert E. Cole's *Japanese Blue Collar*, have both made union-management relations a central part of their discussions.[1] Finally, I have already said elsewhere[2] most of the little I have to add to their accounts of the subject and the numerous books on Japanese labour unions before them.[3]

My last preliminary is to correct any impression given by the title of this book that there is only one kind of Japanese company. Japan is certainly a more homogeneous society than any of the larger Western nations. Everyone speaks the same language and usually only that language, reads the same newspapers, watches the same television programmes, goes to the same kinds of school, and obeys the same laws. Nevertheless, there are considerable regional differences, as one would expect in a country fifteen hundred miles long. Add to these the differences in industrial traditions, the size of companies, the nature of their businesses, and the qualities of the people involved in them, and it is evident that companies vary enormously. A vast steel producer, with tens of thousands of employees and several blast furnaces distributed over the country, is obviously not going to behave in the same way as a small establishment, still essentially controlled by the founding family, making and selling Japanese confectionery in one or two remote prefectures. A rapidly growing electronics firm may have little in common with a sugar company permanently on the brink of insolvency. No one would mistake the employees of a bank, the self-confident elite of Japanese commercial society, for those of a coal mine, conditioned by strikes, industrial decline and regional dereliction.

[1] R. P. Dore (1973) and Robert E. Cole (1971).
[2] R. C. Clark (1975).
[3] Among them Alice H. Cook (1966) and Solomon B. Levine (1958) and (1967).

The same qualification applies with even greater force to 'the Western company' with which I shall occasionally compare the Japanese one. To talk of 'the Western company' is to ignore entire political entities and whole cultures as well as the varieties of business. More than this, to compare 'the Japanese company' with 'the Western company' is to imply that most Japanese companies, however much they differ from each other, are nevertheless easily differentiated from Western companies, even though these are even more heterogeneous. The justification for this assumption will become clearer in the course of this book. It is that the history and the present organization of Japanese companies differ more or less consistently in a mass of details from the history and organization of companies in each of the major Western powers. Though the points of difference may only be minor and the differences themselves slight when considered separately, taken together they suggest the antithesis of a Japanese and a Western company system. It must nevertheless be admitted that the assumption is difficult to prove; and its convenience does not uphold its validity.

The only way to handle the great diversity of the Japanese material is knowingly to make precarious generalizations. Sometimes I will be able to adduce statistical evidence for my grosser statements, and sometimes to cite the work of others. But in discussing many subjects I shall be relying largely on my own experience, and I owe the reader an explanation of what this is.

I began the research for this book with the sociological study for a period of fourteen months of a single company, which I have called Marumaru. Thereafter I spent nearly four years in Japan as an investment banker. My work required me to interview the managements of perhaps two hundred companies, and to make detailed analyses of at least twenty; and by doing business in Japan I saw aspects of the Japanese company which had been hidden from me as an academic researcher. I have not, for reasons of confidentiality, been able to make direct use of the information I acquired as a banker in this book, and much of the material I present will be taken from Marumaru. Nevertheless, what I have seen of other Japanese companies persuades me that though Marumaru is not the paradigmatic Japanese company it is not wholly unrepresentative of the firms of Japan. Most of the observations I made at Marumaru might have been made in dozens of other companies. It has to be said, however, that the Japanese companies I know, even superficially, constitute only the tiniest sample of an immense universe; and I know too many strong, large and successful companies, and too few small and feeble ones, to make it easy to achieve a balanced view. Describing so large and so rapidly changing a subject is inevitably an invasion of Russia. The vastness of the territory is bound to be deceptive, and time will take what conquests there are away.

CHAPTER II

The Historical Influences on the Company

The history of the company in Japan is that of the successful adoption of a Western institution during a period of unprecedented economic and political change. More than this, it is in many respects the history of the changes themselves. Whereas in Britain and the United States the company only came to prominence as a means of organizing business after considerable industrial development had already occurred, in Japan the company arrived almost at the moment when the country can be considered to have entered the modern world, and it was adopted immediately in order to make the growth of industry easier.

THE MERCHANT HOUSE

It is best to begin by explaining how commerce was organized before the company was known in Japan, in the Tokugawa period (1615–1868), when the country was ruled by the hereditary regents, or Shoguns, of the Tokugawa family. During much of the period Japan was sealed off from the rest of the world, for the Shogunate severely restricted foreign trade. The principle of government could be described as feudal—though it was a feudalism different in many ways from the European type. The country was divided into domains, each ruled over by a lord who owed allegiance to the Shogun. There were four main social orders. The highest of these (except for a small number of Court nobles attendant on the impotent Emperor) was that of the warriors or samurai. Their function was to administer the state. The second and largest order was that of the peasants, whose honourable task was to provide the wealth of the nation and the means to support the samurai. Below these stood the artisans. The last of the four orders was that of the merchants, condemned to inferiority in Confucian theory because they merely distributed goods that others had produced.

In spite of the low position assigned to them the merchants achieved considerable economic power. Japan was a populous nation with three very large cities, and the scale of agricultural production and urban demand was able to sustain businesses of substantial size. At the height of the feudal period merchants were financing the production of wood, oils, cotton, fruit and above all rice in enormous quantities, arranging their transport to the great cities from distant domains, storing them, selling them, and engaging in speculation and money-lending on the proceeds.

Enterprises of this magnitude obviously required the co-operation of many people. To obtain it, and to ensure the continuity of their businesses, the Japanese merchants, like their counterparts in pre-industrial Europe, relied on the institution of the family. The family in Tokugawa Japan consisted essentially of a group called a 'house' (ie), the word referring both to a physical entity and to the people associated with it, as in the English 'House of Windsor'. The membership of a house varied greatly, but it might consist of a househead and his wife, their elder son and his wife, and the younger unmarried sons and daughters of the househead. Usually the eldest son would succeed to the headship on the death or retirement of the current head, while the young sons would leave to found their own establishments, and the daughters would marry into other houses. The house was a political, economic, and legal unit. Every Japanese in each of the social orders was required to register as a member of a house, and was legally subordinated to the househead. It was the house rather than its members that owned property; the househead merely managed the property for the sake of the house, its current members, its generations of ancestors, and its unborn posterity. Like the medieval city— and, of course, the modern joint-stock company—the Japanese house was a corporation: an enduring body with rights quite separate from the rights of the individual people who comprised its membership at any time.

The house was equally a corporation in each of the four orders of Tokugawa society. Among the samurai, for example, hereditary offices became the right of certain houses, and a peasant house would have the right to farm (and the duty to pay taxes on) a particular piece of land. In the merchant order the house system meant that families did not so much own businesses, as with the European business family: the house itself was the business. The enterprise and the family were united in the same corporation. The head of the house would live on the premises of the business, and his wife and children would naturally be with him to help him run it. The assets of the business would be at the same time the property of the house, for which the househead was responsible both to outsiders and to the other house members, past, present and future; and the liabilities of the business were the obligations of all the house members jointly.

A successful enterprise would soon need more people than could be provided by a single house. It was possible, of course, to give the younger sons of the househead the money to set up 'branch' houses which would operate as business affiliates of the main house, under the same house badge. Another expedient was for the househead to adopt the young men who married his daughters and engage them in the business. Even so, more people would soon be needed. Outsiders had to be taken in. They were taken in, however, not as salaried employees but as young apprentices for whom the househead was in some degree *in loco parentis*.[1] Apprentices would enter a merchant house at about ten years of age to be taught reading and writing as well as business procedures, and to begin simple and often menial work in return for board and lodging. The treatment of an apprentice at this age would not be substantially different from the treatment of a younger son of the house; indeed the apprentice might even be a cousin or some more distant relation of the househead, while the younger son of the house might be learning his business in another house. The apprentice was expected to stay with the house for a long time, becoming first a senior apprentice and a clerk and then, if he merited it, chief clerk and even general manager. The longer he stayed and the more responsibility he was accorded in the affairs of the house the nearer his status became to that of a true, genealogical house member. He might be married to a daughter of the house and treated almost as one of the family—though distinctions were usually preserved between family and staff. Even if the apprentice did not rise so high within the house he could expect, after ten or more years of service, to be given the money to start a branch house under the house badge—though, again, his branch was hardly likely to be as big as that of a younger son. In short, outsiders were recruited into the business house in return not for contractual rewards, but for the benefits of a long, possibly even life-long association with the house in a relationship which was always analogous to, and sometimes almost identical with, that of a family member.

This type of organization, in which the whole enterprise could be seen as a fictitious family, was not only suited to the social conditions of feudal Japan but also to the kinds of business the merchant order was permitted to undertake. Merchants were allowed only to trade, to distribute commodities, and to lend money—though some merchants did enter into manufacturing in the late Tokugawa period. Business of this sort depends

[1] See J. H. Wigmore (1969: 83–8).

on two things: the ability to inspire enough trust in suppliers and money-lenders to obtain short-term trading credit; and knowledge of a market in one or more products. Trust is a resource that only time and habit can create, and a family business is at no great disadvantage in developing it. On the contrary, in the Japanese merchant house business experience, family honour, and legal co-responsibility were engaged together to reduce the creditor's risk. At the same time, trust within the enterprise was enhanced by the metaphor of kinship and by the familiarity (in both the archaic and modern sense of the word) that came from long apprenticeships. Apprenticeship was also, of course, the means of inculcating in the work-force the other essential, specialized knowledge.

The principles of organization of the merchant house would have been difficult to apply to enterprises requiring large quantities of long-term capital: canal building or dock construction. Public works on this scale were usually accomplished by political means in feudal Japan, domains or villages being required to cut channels or set up irrigation systems. The homogeneous membership of the merchant house with its uniform ranks of clerks was also more easy to assimilate to a family than the more heterogeneous collection of unskilled labourers, craftsmen of various types, and managers needed in a manufacturing firm. In fact, the organization of manufactures among the artisan order in feudal Japan depended very much more on contractual relationships. Skilled workmen might move from firm to firm in search of experience and better pay, and unskilled labour might be recruited on a short-term or seasonal basis.[1] I should also add that some merchant houses went a long way towards dispensing with the idea of firm-as-family. As a shop prospered the owners might decide to live in a separate house and commute to work. The budgets and accounts of shop and home would be kept apart, and the day-to-day running of the business would be left entirely to clerks, who would be far more nearly paid employees than members of the family.[2]

The merchant houses were organized into guilds.[3] Originally formed to regulate the trade in some commodity, a guild would frequently achieve a monopoly and then have that monopoly confirmed by the government in return for payments of money. The guilds governed themselves, though under official supervision. Their constitutions varied, but a guild might consist of as many as several hundred houses, and might be sub-divided into unions, each dealing with transactions in a specialized

[1] R. P. Dore (1973: 378–9).
[2] Nakano Takashi* (1962: 26).
[3] This account is largely based on J. H. Wigmore (1969: Chapter VII).

part of the whole business of the guild: cypress or cedar trading, for example, in the timber guild. Both the guild and its constituent unions would have directors who were appointed, perhaps by rota, from the member houses. The economic contributions of the guild, which became apparent by default when guilds were temporarily abolished in 1841–2, were to lay down the rules of trade, to facilitate credit, and to promote business confidence and the stability of the market. While doing this, however, the guilds prevented competition and frequently manipulated prices. The guilds also contributed to the support of the individual member houses. The houses of a guild agreed, for example, to refuse employment to apprentices or clerks who left the employ of other houses in the same guild. (The very fact that such agreements were made suggests that relations within the houses were not always ideally family-like.) The guild would also help to regulate the creation of branch houses by older member houses.

By the middle of the nineteenth century, after two hundred and fifty years of power, the Tokugawa Shogunate was experiencing serious political and economic difficulties. The feudal social order was breaking down, and there was increasing agitation for a restoration of the Emperor, for whom the Shogun was theoretically merely deputizing. At the same time the Western powers, armed with scientific weaponry which the Japanese could not match, were demanding that the policy of isolation should be ended, and that Japan should open her ports to foreign trade. The weakness of the government was reflected in the decline of the merchant houses. The merchants depended on the regime for their monopolies of domestic trade; and because of the policy of isolation they had been unable to gain the measure of independence of domestic affairs that comes with overseas interests. When the Tokugawa Shogunate finally collapsed few of the merchant houses were able to transform themselves into the modern industrial organizations that were to flourish in the new state.[1]

Though the merchant house cannot be accounted the direct ancestor of the modern company, it has had an influence on the industrial organization of Japan. Perhaps its greatest contribution has been ideological. It offered an historical precedent to sustain certain ideals which only became fashionable after the Tokugawa regime had ceased to exist: that employees should stay with one organization for life, and that their relations with their employees should be in some sense similar to those within a family.

[1] Or so the orthodox account goes. For a different view see Kōzō Yamamura (1974: 163–87).

The merchants have also had practical influence. The merchant order provided many of the entrepreneurs of the new regime, especially those engaged in banking,[1] though not as many as the samurai. Moreover the successors to the merchant houses are still active today. They take the form of wholesalers and regional distributors dominating a complicated distribution system which has helped shape the Japanese market in a great many commodities and manufactured goods.

THE MEIJI GOVERNMENT AND EARLY INDUSTRIALIZATION

In 1868 the last of the Tokugawa Shoguns formally relinquished his authority over Japan in favour of the young Emperor Meiji. Shortly after its accession to power the new government began a programme of dismantling the feudal system, with its classes of society and its fiefs, and replacing it with the institutions of a nineteenth-century Western state. Within a dozen years of the Restoration a start had been made in the construction of modern systems of national and local government, finance (under the Tokugawa taxes had been payable in rice), land ownership, law and justice, and education, as well as the recruitment of a modern conscript army. These transformations took place with what appears in retrospect to have been remarkable smoothness. For this there were a number of reasons. The accession of the Emperor had been a restoration, not a revolution, and the great changes wrought by the Imperial government could be made to appear less apocalyptic by presenting them as contributions to the continuity of an Imperial power validated by antiquity. Many of the changes had been prepared for or even prefigured in the last days of the feudal regime. The Tokugawa education system, for example, by means of which Japan had achieved a high level of literacy, gave a fine start to its successor, a modern school and university system which was, however, less popular than its predecessor in some respects. There was also a general awareness of Japan's military helplessness and scientific and social backwardness by comparison with the great powers of the West, and consequently considerable approval for measures intended to make Japan strong, rich, and modern. In any event, the last and most serious rebellion against the new authority was defeated in 1877. From then onwards, no matter how much political and administrative changes might generate controversy among the governing minority of officials and educated people, there was no doubt that they could be made to stick.

[1] Kōzō Yamamura (1974: 165–78).

One of the highest priorities of the new government was to encourage modern industry, which was rightly seen as the source of the superior power of the West. The obstacles to the development of industry were obvious. There had been an economic decline concomitant with the political weakness of the Tokugawa government, and commerce was languishing. There was scarcely any modern industry, though the Tokugawa government had established a shipyard, and one or two of the domains had set up factories. Very few Japanese had the scientific and technical knowledge to operate modern equipment. Any Japanese goods that were produced would have to compete with foreign manufactures which could not easily be excluded from the Japanese market, because of the unequal treaties Japan had earlier concluded with the Western powers. The government was short of money. Yet besides raising industries it had to build the armed forces to prevent invasion and also compensate the former samurai for the loss of their privileges.

The countervailing advantages were mostly to be found in Japan's educated, disciplined and homogeneous population. There was a peasantry which not only fed the nation and provided, through its cottage industries, a great proportion of the first exports, but which was also patient and enduring enough to bear much of the fiscal burden until at last modern industries came into being. There was a commercial system which, though antiquated and much diminished from its former strength, still united the entire country and knew enough techniques of finance and distribution to be able to adapt to industry as it grew. There was a ruling elite with an appetite for new ideas and with the courage to risk putting them into practice. Above all, there was an awareness by men of all classes—and perhaps especially by those of no certain class, the interstitial half-samurai who provided so many of the entrepreneurs of the Meiji period—that change was essential and that, far from being harmful, change would bring opportunities for individuals and for the nation as a whole. But these advantages, now so obvious, took a long time to become apparent. In the first fifteen or twenty years of the Meiji period the growth of industry was slow.

During these twenty years the Japanese economy and government was sustained largely by the peasantry.[1] In 1873 the Meiji administration

[1] It is difficult to make precise estimates of the contribution of the peasantry to the Meiji economy because figures for land under cultivation and crop yields are very unreliable. Especially at the beginning of the Meiji period landowners reported low figures for both in order to escape taxation. As time went on the degree of understatement became less marked, and as a result there appears to have been an enormous increase in agricultural production. For a discussion see James I. Nakamura (1965).

replaced the peasants' feudal rice dues with a land tax of three per cent. of the assessed value of the land. This provided more than half of all government revenue in the period 1879–88, and perhaps as much as two-fifths of the revenue during the entire Meiji period.[1] Besides having to pay the land tax, the peasants were also liable to pay the commodity taxes, duties and income taxes which gradually replaced the land tax as the main sources of government revenue. A considerable proportion of the money raised from the peasants was used to compensate the samurai for the loss of feudal privileges, and some at least of the compensation money was invested in industry. In addition, the peasants were responsible for the bulk of Japan's first exports. After an outbreak of silkworm disease in Europe had allowed Japanese silks to enter foreign markets, raw silk became the chief Japanese export, accounting for forty per cent. by value of all exports between 1868 and 1893.[2] Silk and silk products continued to be important exports into the 1930s.

Within the breathing space afforded by the peasants, modern industries were created, largely by the state. The establishments inherited from the Tokugawa government—mines, shipyards and engineering workshops— were expanded. New ventures were attempted not only in heavy industry but also in light industries such as cotton spinning, silk filature, cement and glass. Modern communications were established. A post and telegraph service was set up and a railway was built between Tokyo and Yokohama in 1870–2. These investments, together with the less spectacular work of road building, irrigation, and port construction, were of enormous importance in facilitating the later development of the economy.

Although the government had, of necessity, to take the lead in establishing industries, there were both ideological and practical reasons why further industrial development was to take place in private hands. In the Western world, to which Japan looked for an example, it was the age of *laissez-faire* and capitalist achievement. The idea that governments should operate industries for the national benefit had not become widespread. Meanwhile the success of private enterprise, and its evident contribution to national interests, was everywhere apparent. In Britain, America, France and Germany great companies were running blast furnaces, cotton mills, dye works and paper factories, while other companies owned the railways, shipping lines and canals by which the products of these first were moved to every part of the world, including Japan. The Japanese could not fail to be aware that the fruits of the

[1] Harry T. Oshima (1965: 357–61).
[2] William W. Lockwood (1954: 336).

civilization to which they now had to aspire, the marvellous products and processes of the enlightened West, were largely produced by individuals and groups independent of governments, working for their own gain. In any case, Japan itself had a long tradition of private enterprise, though of a less progressive kind. It was perfectly natural, therefore, to suppose that once the government had given it an initial impetus, and provided that appropriate changes in attitude took place among those engaged in business, private industry could develop in Japan to the national benefit, just as in the West. The alternative, that the state alone could not only start industries but also maintain them, was an idea ahead of the times. If the Meiji government did consider it seriously then it certainly rejected it in practice. Government officials frequently emphasized that the new ventures they were sponsoring would one day be handed over to the people, or to those among the people who were prepared to run them.[1]

The government's withdrawal from direct participation in industry was hastened by increasing financial difficulties. From the beginning the new administration had suffered from a shortage of revenue and an excess of liabilities, and it had resorted to the printing press. By 1880 a crisis was imminent. Government paper (in which the ex-samurai were paid) was worth only half its value in specie. The rice price was twice what it had been three years earlier. The solution, devised by the new Finance Minister, Matsukata Masayoshi, was to raise taxes on commodities, and suspend further industrial investment in order to reduce the current budget deficit. In addition he arranged that the existing government industries, most of which were unprofitable, should be sold to private buyers. The proceeds were to be used to buy specie as the reserve for a new Bank of Japan, which would then issue notes which, unlike the government notes up till then, would be convertible into gold.

The sale of government industries took place at prices much lower than the capital invested in them—though not perhaps lower than people were prepared to pay for them[2]—and many of the buyers were friends of senior officials and previous beneficiaries of the government.

From now on, except for a brief period around the turn of the century, when the railways were nationalized and a state-owned iron works established, the government was not to initiate industrial projects on

---

[1] Byron K. Marshall (1967: 17–19). Thomas C. Smith (1955: 92–5) advances evidence that *laissez-faire* ideologies were rapidly losing their appeal just when the government began transferring factories to private hands.

[2] Thomas C. Smith (1955: 89–92).

its own. Instead it was to encourage industrialization by aiding private entrepreneurs.

What sort of men were the private entrepreneurs to whom the government offered its help? It is difficult to say, largely because they have been obscured from us by official eulogies and by their own writings, in which they interpret their motives and actions in terms of the ideologies of the time, notably patriotism, the cult of the modern, and an altruism based on Confucian theory. They were, moreover, a heterogeneous assortment of people, their most salient common feature being low origin, usually peasant with mercantile associations and samurai pretensions. They tended to owe their success to two factors, determination, frequently in pursuit of their own profits, and good contacts in government. It is possible, perhaps, to divide them roughly into two categories, 'merchants of fortune' and 'government protégés', according to which of the two factors predominated in their careers.[1]

One of the most successful of the merchants of fortune was Iwasaki Yatarō, founder of the Mitsubishi group of enterprises.[2] Born the son of a peasant in 1834, he bought samurai status with the help of his relatives. He entered the bureaucracy of his domain, and rose in the course of an irregular career to become its financial agent and procurer in the last days of the feudal system. When the domains were abolished in 1871, he received in payment for an earlier loan to the domain a certain amount of money and a number of the province's business assets, including ships. By dealing in these, and by currency arbitrage, he made himself a fortune. With this as his capital he entered the coastal shipping business, edging out his competitors by undercutting their fares. He gained greatly from the Formosan Incident, an ill-considered punitive expedition against the island of Formosa in 1874, for which he was asked by the government to provide ships; the contract having come his way because of his cultivation of the then Finance Minister, Ōkuma Shigenobu. From now on his shipping line was to receive a large number of direct and indirect subsidies from the government in order to help it defeat foreign competition. Iwasaki used some of the money he was given to enter businesses associated with shipping, such as warehousing and insurance. By 1877 his firm,

---

[1] I owe these categories to Johannes Hirschmeier and Tsunehiko Yūi (1975: 95–103). They add two further categories of 'image builders' and 'men of the spread-effect'. Among the former they include Fukuzawa Yukichi, who was not really an entrepreneur, and Shibusawa Eiichi, who was certainly an image builder but whose government connections make him a 'protégé'. The 'men of the spread-effect' are the entrepreneurs of slightly later periods and of peripheral areas, who need not concern us here.

[2] This account is based on Kōzō Yamamura (1974: 143–53).

Mitsubishi Shōkai, controlled eighty per cent. of Japanese shipping, and he himself had become a powerful but much resented public figure, befriended by cabinet ministers and attacked in the newspapers for unscrupulous business practices. In 1880 the rival group of Mitsui decided to challenge his monopoly of the seas, not merely for commercial reasons but also because the political supporters of the Mitsui group were the rivals of the politicians who patronized Mitsubishi. The fierce competition which followed between the shipping lines of the two groups ended in 1885 with a merger between them to form what is now one of the world's largest shipping companies, N.Y.K. Mitsubishi Shōkai was the biggest shareholder of the new line, and so could have been said to have won the battle with Mitsui. But Iwasaki died shortly after the merger at the age of fifty-two.

There were several other entrepreneurs of Iwasaki's type, who received help from the government and who represented themselves as serving the national interest, but whose prime motive was profit. One was Yasuda Zenjirō,[1] the founder of the group of companies bearing his name. Another was Asano Sōichirō,[2] the son of a physician, who started his career peddling charcoal, turned to making cement in 1881, acquired the government's Fukugawa cement factory in 1884, and ended as the head of a large complex of enterprises in many different industries.

In the second class of entrepreneurs the balance of personal acquisitiveness and government influence was reversed. Men like Minomura Rizaemon[3] were not indifferent to profit, and were unquestionably possessed of great business acumen; but their achievements were mainly due to excellent relations with the government. Minomura was a man of obscure origin who had become the steward of the merchant house of Mitsui in the turbulent last days of the feudal regime. He had been invited to take the stewardship when he was associated with another firm, a method of recruitment unprecedented in the history of the Mitsui, but justified by Minomura's abilities and also by his connections with the commissioner of finance in the Tokugawa government. Minomura was responsible for guiding the house through the difficult period of the Restoration and for preparing it for spectacular accomplishments in the new era. His greatest asset as steward was, perhaps, the support of some important officials of the Meiji government, and especially Inoue Kaoru, an influential statesman who took a close interest in the affairs of the

---

[1] Details of Yasuda's life are given in Kōzō Yamamura (1974: 153-9).
[2] G. C. Allen (1962: 87).
[3] John G. Roberts (1973: 64-72).

2

Mitsui group. Inoue consolidated Minomura's power within the firm, supported the reforms of the Mitsui organization which Minomura undertook, provided him with opportunities for new business, and may even have saved both him and the entire firm by forewarning him on one occasion of a change in government policy.

The best known of the politically favoured entrepreneurs was an associate of Minomura, Shibusawa Eiichi.[1] Shibusawa was born in 1840, the son of a farmer. Though an eldest son and heir, he abdicated his family responsibilities and joined a movement aimed at destroying the Tokugawa government and driving out the foreigners from Japan. On realizing that the Tokugawa regime was still too powerful to overthrow, Shibusawa abandoned the movement and instead joined the government as a junior samurai. He found favour with Tokugawa Yoshinobu, the heir to the Shogunate, and was made a member of a party accompanying the Shogun's younger brother to Europe in 1866–8. It was during this tour of the West that Shibusawa came to appreciate the extent to which industry was the source of European power. When the news came that the Tokugawa regime had fallen and that power had been restored to the young Emperor Meiji, Shibusawa returned to a Japan in which his future might have been expected to be dismal. In 1869, however, he found himself appointed head of the Taxation Bureau of the new government. He served in the Treasury for four eventful years, his responsibilities including the reform of the currency and the preparation of the new tax system. In 1873 he resigned from government service over disagreements about policy, and began a career as entrepreneur *pro bono publico* and publicist of the benefits of modernization and industry; a calling which made full use of his wide political acquaintance. Among the firms he helped to establish were: the First National Bank (with Mitsui and one other merchant house), 1873; Ōji Paper, 1875; Osaka Spinning Mill (later Tōyōbō), 1882; Japan Brewing Company (later Dai Nippon Beer), 1885; and Tokyo Artificial Fertilizer Company, 1887. In all he is said to have organized, directed, or advised five hundred companies. He also founded the first business association, the Takuzenkai, predecessor of the Tokyo Bank Association, and was instrumental in the setting up of the Commercial School, from which Hitotsubashi University was derived. When he was not engaged in these practical measures Shibusawa spent his time lecturing and writing. His influence on business ideology and the development of joint-stock companies in Japan was immense.

It is evident from these brief biographies that relations between the

[1] A good brief account of his life is Johannes Hirschmeier (1965).

government and private entrepreneurs were very close and frequently beneficial to the businessmen. Presented with opportunities, subsidized, and spared the rigorous taxation applied to the peasantry, the entrepreneurs were able to create commercial empires of considerable size. In the early years of Japanese industrialization, private enterprise, while remaining private, was underwritten by the state in a manner quite without parallel in England, where the Industrial Revolution took place almost without government help, or the United States, where the distrust of central government and the size of the country precluded government interference in private business. State patronage did not merely affect the material advance of Japanese industry; it also contributed to the ideas which animated it, some of which we shall now consider.

THE FORMATION OF A BUSINESS IDEOLOGY

The ideas about business and commerce which prevailed in the Tokugawa period were of Confucian inspiration. The division of society into graded orders was itself a Confucian commentary on the social significance of commerce and such industry as existed. The samurai were the highest order because they provided the blessings, and bore the burdens, of government. The peasants were the source of the national wealth. The artisans were inferior, but their status was validated by production. The merchants came last in the scheme of things because they neither governed nor produced wealth, but merely traded what others cultivated or made. Their place in society was the measure of an inferior though necessary role.

As money became more important as a means of commerce and the influence of the merchant houses grew in proportion, disrupting the neat pattern of transactions in rice and power that should have characterized the Tokugawa political economy, Confucian thinkers of both the samurai and merchant classes had to adapt their views to the changed circumstances. C. D. Sheldon discerns two main schools of thought among the samurai of the early Tokugawa period.[1] Some scholars considered that both the use of money and the concomitant power of the merchants should be curtailed by a return to a rice economy. Others suggested that the merchant's usefulness went some way towards compensating society for the objectionable nature of the profit motive on which the merchant acted; enjoining at the same time that the commercial activities which produced that profit should be controlled. Later samurai thought was

[1] C. D. Sheldon (1973: 132–43).

influenced by the habit the domains succumbed to of establishing monopolies over the trade in certain goods. Here the samurai were putting
themselves in a position where they, or at least the political order they
represented, was benefiting from trade. One justification of such arrangements was that samurai were inevitably involved in the economy, if only
as buyers, so that the extension of their economic activities was not
necessarily a fall from grace. There was also a development of thought
which paralleled European mercantilism, domains being exhorted to
produce and export goods to their neighbours in order to earn gold and
silver; and some thinkers applied the argument beyond the domain to the
whole country, and called for the encouragement of foreign trade.

The merchants' own response to the rise of the merchant class took the
form largely of a modest plea for the importance of trade and a mild
assertion that its benefits extended beyond the trader. To the moral ulcer
of personal profit could be applied the religious balm of Shin Buddhism.
The Shin sect, to which certain groups of merchants belonged, was
prepared to justify profits gained from unselfish motives, using arguments
which resembled those of Protestantism in the West: 'the basis of receiving this profit depends on profiting others. Thus both the business of
merchants and of artisans is the profiting of others. By profiting others they
receive the right to profit themselves. This is the virtue of the harmony
of *jiri-rita* [profiting self and others]'.[1] Despite the changes that did take
place in thought in the Tokugawa period, the samurai discovery of the
strategic importance of commerce, and the defensive exegeses of the
merchants, in the mid-nineteenth century it was still widely held that
business was an inferior occupation, especially mean when carried out for
personal gain.

For the new Imperial state these perceptions of commerce had obvious
disadvantages. If the government had been able or willing to undertake
all trade and industry itself then it would hardly have mattered if people
thought private business ignoble. But *laissez-faire* and government penury
combined, as I have explained, to persuade its rulers that Japan could only
industrialize through private enterprise. Clearly, views of business would
have to change if the country was to become rich and powerful. Changes
did occur, and remarkably quickly. The ideology of industry and commerce was altered in three ways, by the new ideas from the West, by the
exhortations of the government and evangelical ex-government entrepreneurs like Shibusawa, and by the example of the businessmen who did
achieve fame and who, whatever their real motives for enterprise,

[1] Robert N. Bellah (1957: 120), quoted in C. D. Sheldon (1973: 139).

managed to represent their activities as morally and politically enlightened.

In spite of the Tokugawa government's policies of excluding foreigners from the country and restricting foreign trade, the Japanese had been aware of Western ideas for centuries before the Meiji Restoration. The Dutch had been permitted to trade at Deshima, near Nagasaki, so that there had been opportunities for limited numbers of scholars to learn about the West. Towards the end of the Tokugawa period, and especially after the visits of Commodore Perry in 1853-4, the intrusion of Westerners, their artefacts and ideas on the Japanese became very much more marked and affected all levels of society. The reaction to Western influences, which were themselves very heterogeneous, varied greatly among different sections of the population, and included resentment, admiration, fear and even millenarian fantasy, though we tend today to take note of only the more rational and ultimately productive responses.

The extent and nature of Western technology, and frequently even its principles, had been known in Japan for a long time. The Tokugawa government itself supported institutions which translated and studied Western books on a range of subjects, and at least two of the domains had gone beyond mere book learning and set up laboratories for applied research in chemistry, metallurgy, and other sciences. The reason for this interest was, of course, political and military. From the early decades of the nineteenth century, when first the Russians and later the Americans and West Europeans came to Japan in warships armed with impressive modern weaponry, the Japanese had become increasingly aware of their military inferiority. The first Japanese visitors to the West were able to confirm what was already evident from what was known of Western technology and its military application: that the strength of a nation lay in its manufacturing industry.

Recognition of the importance of industry required by itself some adjustment of Confucian doctrines.[1] Yet it was even more difficult for a Confucian society to accept contemporary Western notions of how industry came to exist and of the place of business in the world. In the West at this time industry was considered the province of individual initiative, determination, and even avarice. The entrepreneur worked for himself, but the businesses and industries he created inevitably benefited the whole of society, inevitably not only because the factories he built and the goods he made contributed to the community as well as to him, but also because he helped to provide commercial competition, Adam Smith's 'invisible hand', which turned selfish action to the common good. A simple-minded

[1] The next few paragraphs are based on Byron K. Marshall (1967: 30-50).

transposition of this sort of idea to Japan might support the assertion, completely repugnant to Confucian moral values, that an unprincipled huckster who built a business did as much good for the world as a learned scholar-administrator.

Not surprisingly, this blatant individualism, which was in any case under attack in the West, did not pass with facility into the Japanese business creed. There was a school of Japanese individualists, the most notable of whom was Fukuzawa Yukichi, an influential publicist and educator, who advocated self-reliance and private initiative and who specifically attributed Japan's backwardness to the Confucian contempt for material things. It is probably significant that Fukuzawa was an academic rather than a businessman. Avarice in the public interest is more comfortably extolled by unacquisitive savants than by the people who are actually making money.

While men like Fukuzawa were advocating commercial endeavour for its own sake and for the sake of the benefits that would automatically accrue from it, the government and semi-official entrepreneurs like Shibusawa were offering other reasons why men (and particularly samurai) should engage in business. Their appeal was to nationalism and public spirit of a Confucian sort. The creation of industries was a service to the state and to the Japanese people. But it was essential that entrepreneurial activity should be undertaken in the right frame of mind. Though the entrepreneur, unlike the administrator, was handling material things, he should be no more materialistic than the latter, and his interest in money should not be selfish. Motives were even more important than results. As Shibusawa put it, 'To go bankrupt because of moral principle is not to fail, even though it is to go bankrupt. To become rich without moral principle is not to succeed, even though it is to become rich.'[1]

By this formulation personal profits were no more than fortuitously attendant on a business career. As Shibusawa, once again, explained it, 'My object does not lie in the increase of wealth, but from the nature of the business it so happens. That is all. Never for a moment did I aim at my own profit.'[2]

Under these influences public attitudes to commerce and its practitioners altered rapidly during the Meiji era. Businessmen were compared with samurai in the newly established business journals. Numbers of entrepreneurs were ennobled. When Iwasaki Yatarō, the founder of Mitsubishi, died in 1885, 50,000 people, including many of the great of the land,

[1] Quoted in Byron K. Marshall (1967: 39).
[2] Quoted in Byron K. Marshall (1967: 40).

attended his funeral.[1] It would, of course, be misleading to give the impression of a total reversal of the social order in favour of businessmen.[2] Government service continued to be considered more satisfactory than private business even by businessmen. Public opinion was not always blind to the excesses of the entrepreneurs—Iwasaki had been pilloried for greed only a few years before his sumptuous funeral. Towards the last years of the nineteenth century there was a reaction against the materialism and Western influence with which businessmen were inevitably associated. Nevertheless, a major change did take place, and some of the notions about industry that were established in the early years of the Meiji regime have endured in Japan to this day: among them the ideal of the businessman as the benefactor of the community and servant (though at a slight remove) of the state; and the precept that the business-man should be inspired more by altruism and high principle than profit.

THE RISE OF THE JOINT-STOCK COMPANY

These changes in the public regard for business took place at the same time as the introduction of the joint-stock company into Japanese commerce, and the two developments naturally had an effect on each other.

The theoretical advantages of the Western company as a means of amassing and putting to use large amounts of capital were clearly under-stood even in the last years of the Tokugawa regime.[3] As early as 1860 a man called Oguri Jōnosuke had gone to America to study commercial organizations. In 1866 the educator Fukuzawa Yukichi, who had himself been to the West, wrote: 'According to custom in the West, when a big enterprise extends beyond the power of one merchant, then five or ten people join together to do it. This is called a mercantile company. Such companies do every kind of business, building ships and trading with foreign countries, traversing the world over with express boats, setting up exchange houses and conducting business between the nations, building railways, factories and gas furnaces, as well as every kind of domestic commercial activity.'[4]

The first Japanese companies were established in 1867, the last year of

1 Kōzō Yamamura (1974: 152).
2 Though in expansive moments businessmen did suggest that such a reversal had occurred. Kyūgorō Ōbata (1937: 134).
3 Kanno Watarō* (1961: 219 ff.).
4 Quoted in Kanno Watarō* (1961: 221).

the Tokugawa Shogunate. Japan had been forced to open the ports of Hyōgo (now Kobe) and Yokohama to foreign commerce. To prepare for their opening the government had tried to compel the richer merchants to join together to form trading companies. These did not, however, survive the fall of the government which sponsored them. In 1869 the new Meiji administration tried its hand at coercing the merchants into forming companies. This time the companies lasted three or four years, constant government interference and management inexperience of foreign trade being two of the important reasons for their failure.

A third difficulty, and one common to both the Tokugawa and early Meiji companies, was that their principles of organization, which were imported from the West, were at variance with those of the merchant house. In the house a team of managers ideally patterned on the family owned the property and ran the business together under the direction of a single head. The company required co-operation between houses. The only Tokugawa economic institution which extended beyond the house was the guild, and it is not surprising that merchants frequently confused the new, officially sponsored companies with the old guilds. The similarity of company and guild was even present in the company organization. Instead of a system of shareholders, directors and managers there was a hybrid arrangement.[1] The original promoters of the company chose from among their number three General Directors, who then took turns at presiding over the firm. They were assisted by thirty Stewards, also chosen from the promoters, six of whom were on duty in any month as supervisors of the various departments. These rota systems were, of course, very cumbersome. In practice decisions were often taken by the permanent clerks in the departments, who thus became analogous to managers in a modern company.

Though they were commercially ineffective and short-lived these early companies were of some significance. They constituted a new type of collective enterprise which, though primitive, prefigured the share-issuing limited liability companies which built the Japanese industrial economy. Both the Tokugawa and early Meiji companies raised capital from numbers of different people instead of depending on a single pre-existing group. The Meiji (though not the Tokugawa) companies were independent legal personalities, with rights and duties separate from those of their promoters.[2] The Meiji companies issued a form of certificate in return for the investor's capital. The negotiability of the certificate was

---

[1] Kanno Watarō* (1961: 260–1).
[2] Kanno Watarō* (1961: 278–85).

limited, but it was unquestionably a precursor of the share. The companies also allowed for a partial separation of ownership and management.[1] They were, in short, prototypes which, for all their defects, offered useful experience not only to the merchants who ran them but also to the government and the public at large.

In spite of the lack of success of the trading and exchange companies, the Meiji government continued to propagate the idea of a company as a form of business organization with almost missionary zeal. Explanatory pamphlets were published to help promoters of companies, and government aid for a venture would be made conditional on its incorporation.[2] The company was extolled not merely for its financial and administrative advantages but also simply because it was modern and Western. The Japanese seem to have over-estimated the extent to which contemporary Western industry had been developed by companies[3]. They might have been less enthusiastic if they had realized how little the company had contributed to the Industrial Revolution in England, and how difficult the progress of company legislation had been in the West. Apart from being efficient and modern, the company was also seen as constitutionally virtuous. This is how, in 1876, Minomura Rizaemon explained why the Mitsui firm was becoming a company:

To insure our security is to adopt a co-operative system in business. There are several forms of such a system, but the best of them all is an anonymous company, by which it is meant that the company is named after the work it aims to carry on, instead of having the names of the persons involved in it. The transaction of business and the performance of duty are decided by conference according to the laws and regulations recognised by the government of the country. The whole procedure precludes privacy and guarantees fairness. This is the best procedure and to adopt the best is to keep up with the march of time. Therefore, we now drop the name of Mitsui Gumi and change it to Mitsui Ginko. Moreover, the relationship between the employer and the employee should be changed to that of partnership, aiming at co-existence and co-prosperity—namely to let all the members share profits as well as

---

[1] Kanno Watarō* (1961: 284–5) suggests that the system of General Directors and Stewards constitutes a move towards this separation, though these offices were filled by the promoter-investors. Elsewhere (260), however, he describes how decisions were frequently left to clerks. The separation of ownership and management is more evident in the latter circumstance.

[2] Yūi Tsunehiko* (1977: 326).

[3] *Ibid.*

happiness. Such is the outline of the prospectus for founding Mitsui Ginko.[1]

If the company, offering as it did security, impersonal fairness, modernity, concord and co-prosperity, were so beneficent an entity, it followed that service to one was an act that profited the community as a whole. Indeed, working for a company was almost as public-spirited as working for the government itself. Shibusawa put the point in a manner that would have meaning for any Japanese university graduate today who had just failed the civil service entrance examination:

> Private enterprises do not confer such high honour as work in the political arena, nor do they produce such a sense of pleasure, but the work of a joint-stock company has some honour, some responsibility, and also some self-interest, so that it is not without attractions for men of ability. At the same time, if by means of joint-stock companies we can secure the prosperity of production and trade, we may thereby expect to promote the wealth and power of a nation.[2]

After the demise of the early trading companies in 1871 a number of new companies with more modern constitutions and limited liability were formed. Most of these were banks, though the Kansai Railway Company (1871) was the first to issue unit shares, and the Kabuto-chō and Kakigara-chō Rice Exchanges were established as joint-stock companies, a development illustrating the prevalent confusion between new companies and old guilds.[3] The predominance of banks was partly due to government policies and partly to the power of example; banks can easily be formed by men of standing in a community—though they are not so easy to keep in being. The early banks were unstable because their notes could immediately be converted to gold,[4] but after the banks were relieved of the burden of convertibility in 1876 their number grew until there were no fewer than 143 in 1882.[5]

The deflation of 1882-6 caused the bankrupty of a number of insecure companies, but thereafter conditions were more favourable for enterprise and there was a striking growth in the number and size of companies. The paid up capital of Japanese companies, which had been 139 million yen in 1886, reached 357 million yen in 1896 and 940 million yen in

---

[1] Quoted in Kyūgorō Ōbata (1937: 111).
[2] Eiichi Shibusawa (1909: 470).
[3] T. F. M. Adams (1964: 23).
[4] For a more detailed explanation see G. C. Allen (1962: 43).
[5] T. F. M. Adams (1964: 13).

1906.[1] With the rise of new industries manufacturing and commercial companies became more common, and banks relatively less important. The authorized capital of banks, expressed as a proportion of all authorized corporate capital, fell from 54.2 per cent. in 1887 to 36.4 per cent. in 1894.[2] The influence of the banks nevertheless remained paramount: for the capital of the industrial companies came from the banks. The banks subscribed to share issues, and they also lent money to prospective investors on the security of the shares—besides, of course, lending money directly to the companies. Banks were to become the source of funds for groups of companies associated with families or entrepreneurs, groups like Mitsui, Mitsubishi, Yasuda and Asano; control over the groups being exerted partly through the banks and partly through group holding companies.

The rise of the joint-stock company was also associated with legal progress. During the first thirty years of Meiji rule commercial legislation consisted of *ad hoc* regulations and special enabling acts, while lawyers and politicians influenced by different national schools wrangled over the preparation of a comprehensive Commercial Code.[3] It was only when one was finally promulgated in 1899 that it became relatively easy for private individuals to form and manage companies. The so-called New Commercial Code of that year defined companies, accorded them legal personality as a matter of course, established the duties of directors, and provided for easy dissolution. The Code also allowed companies to opt for limited liability without the need for special arrangements. The Japanese government had been uneasy about allowing private entrepreneurs to limit their liability, because of the scope such limitation gave for irresponsibility.[4] Until 1899 it was a privilege specifically bestowed, rather than a right to be claimed by any company with the appropriate qualifications. Perhaps the greatest difference between the history of commercial law in Japan and in the West was that in Japan the law was created to serve rather than master the company. The moving spirit of company legislation was not so much, as in England and America, to curb private influence or prevent fraud, but to establish laws that would earn international respect and at the same time promote modern institutions.[5]

[1] T. F. M. Adams (1964: 29, 49).

[2] Masaki Hisashi* (1973: 9).

[3] For a general account consult Ryōsuke Ishii (1958: 592–8, 696–701).

[4] Yūi Tsunehiko* (1977: 329). Japanese scholars appear to differ over precisely which early companies had limited liability. Imuta Toshikatsu* (1968: 179), for example, contradicts Yūi by asserting that the first bank was a limited company.

[5] cf. William W. Lockwood (1954: 565–6).

There was one important feature of the company which the Meiji Japanese adopted from the West with less assurance; and in respect of which their capacity for emphasizing the purposeful and positive was not greatly exercised. This feature was the share. The share has Jekyll-and-Hyde qualities: it is a clever instrument for the accumulation of capital and a means of speculation; a certificate of democratic ownership and a casino chip. A number of circumstances combined in early modern Japan to accentuate the chancy and disreputable aspects of shares and dealings in them.

Though the government had been anxious to promote the issue of securities it was slow to consider the problems of maintaining a market in them.[1] Given the lack of regulations and the unreliability of the bonds and shares, it was hardly surprising that when a market formed itself those associated with it were not the most respectable members of the community. Pawnbrokers, second-hand furniture dealers and money changers entered the new business, often as an extension of their services to the impoverished ex-samurai, who were being paid in government bonds. In 1878, partly on the initiative of Shibusawa, the Tokyo Stock Exchange was established, many of the informal bond dealers becoming members. Even Shibusawa's patronage, however, could not rescue the Exchange from its ignominious origins, nor make good the absence of protective legislation for stockholders. The Exchange more resembled a gambling den than a serious capital market. Companies issued shares to be paid for by instalments, while investors borrowed bank money to purchase the shares, pledging them to the banks as security. The vast majority of transactions were in futures, and a huge proportion of them involved the shares of the Stock Exchange itself.[2]

While the Stock Exchange concentrated largely on speculation, the banks were able to usurp what should have been the prime function of the Exchange: that of responsible intermediary between industry and the investing public. At first the banks merely lent money to prospective investors, but later on they were themselves to become underwriters, buying and distributing shares and debentures. They were thus able to use their depositors' money to finance the share issues of their associated companies; while companies that did not have, or did not want, close relations with particular banks were not easily able to appeal directly to the public for funds, and so keep or gain their independence of a financial oligarchy. We shall see this early history reflected in the great

[1] T. F. M. Adams (1964: 24–5).
[2] For details see Masaki Hisashi* (1973: 10).

power of the banks in Japan today, and in the relations between industry and society.

THE RECRUITMENT OF GRADUATES AND MANAGEMENT 'FAMILISM'

I now propose to move forward a few decades and consider two developments in what would today be called the personnel policy of companies. The period I have in mind begins in about 1886, when the Matsukata deflation ended, and a great increase took place in industrial production and in the number of companies, and when, also, the Japanese intelligentsia began to have second thoughts about Westernization and to find new joy in old and 'beautiful customs'. The period ends in the early 1920s, with Japan a major power, its Empire achieved by impressive victories over China and Russia, and its industries strong and successful; at the same time the Japanese intellectual world was as tumultuous and as alive to ideas, especially foreign ones, as it had been just after the Restoration. The personnel policies concern managers on the one hand and labour on the other: the enlisting of graduates in the service of the large Japanese company, and the adoption of the new, yet atavistic ethos of 'familism' as a means of controlling labour.

It was hardly surprising that the Meiji industrialists and entrepreneurs valued education highly. Confucian regard for learning had been inculcated in Japanese society for three centuries of Tokugawa rule. The early business leaders were themselves the better educated members of a well-schooled nation.[1] The predisposition to value learning for its own sake was complemented by a general awareness that knowledge was a means to the development of Japan, and that the first step towards catching up with the West was to learn how things were done. The government gave high priority to education. A Ministry of Education was established in 1871, and in 1872 work began on the organization of a complete education system in which the curricula would take account of commercial and industrial needs. There were also important private initiatives. Keiō Gijuku, the forerunner of the present Keiō University, which is still closely associated with business, had been established by the educator Fukuzawa Yukichi as early as 1858. Businessmen combined Confucian ideals with self-interest by setting up institutes for higher vocational training, Commercial Schools, Merchant Marine Schools, and technical colleges to teach practical arts like dyeing and spinning.[2]

From the very first, industrialists were anxious to fill their senior

[1] Hiroshi Mannari (1974: 162–70 and 260–3).
[2] Japanese National Commission for Unesco (1959: 100–13, 146–7).

management posts with the best educated men. The difficulty was that universities were few. Keiō Gijuku and certain other private colleges, the University of Tokyo, and the Institute of Commerce (later Hitotsubashi University) were the only major centres of higher learning throughout the 1880s and most of the 1890s. The demand for their graduates from government was so great that few of them entered industry. A survey of 354 industrial managers active in 1900 reveals that only eight per cent. had higher education.[1] In the first two decades of the twentieth century, however, the older universities expanded, and those that did not already have them set up departments of law, economics, and commerce. New institutions were also established both by private groups and the state— the Imperial Universities of Kyoto (1897), Tōhoku (1907) and Hokkaido (1918) dating from about this time. Beneath the universities in the educational hierarchy there was an increase in the numbers of students at technical and commercial higher vocational colleges.[2] The flow of university graduates into management during these years was so rapid that a sample of 198 business leaders of 1920 shows that no fewer than forty-six per cent. were university educated, and a further seventeen per cent. had been to 'specialist schools' including the higher vocational colleges.[3] A slightly later, larger sample of 500 directors in 153 companies in 1928 reveals that fifty-five per cent. were university graduates,[4] a proportion comparable with that in European industry today.

It is unlikely that all these graduate managers owed their positions at the top of industry to their degrees. Some, doubtless, were senior managers less because they were graduates than because they were the sons of rich merchants or influential ex-samurai; they had merely attended university as a matter of course before taking up appropriate appointments in industry. Yet whatever secondary interpretations there are for the rise of the graduate manager,[5] the fact is that by the 1920s higher education, particularly at certain great state and private universities, most especially the University of Tokyo, was coming to be seen as the most natural qualification for the management of major companies. It has remained so to this day.

[1] Japanese National Commission for Unesco (1966: 296).
[2] Japanese National Commission for Unesco (1966: 150).
[3] Hiroshi Mannari (1974: 172–4).
[4] Japanese National Commission for Unesco (1966: 288–96).
[5] Another possibility is that it is not so much that large firms had made graduates directors, as that young graduates taken into firms of modest size in the 1900s and 1910s had, by the 1920s, made their firms sufficiently large and important that they themselves could be classed as leaders of industry.

A large proportion of the graduates among the business leaders of the 1920s were lawyers or economists.[1] There were various reasons for this, not the least being that perhaps forty per cent. of university students and graduates in the first years of the century were lawyers,[2] a law degree being thought of as the best preparation for government service. It is also probable, however, that lawyers, economists and graduates in commercial studies were specifically chosen by industrialists. If so, their choice implied a perception that management was something to be learned or at least prepared for; and that the best preparation was the study of relations between people and between institutions, of human organization. The emphasis on such studies argued (and, of course, promoted) a view of management as a bureaucratic and co-operative venture: the government of a company rather than the imposition of an entrepreneurial will on a market place and a work force by superior skill, courage or judgement.

There is an interesting comparison to be made between management ideologies in Japan and America in these years. In Japan, from the very beginning of industrial growth, Confucianism and nationalism made management a collective and ostensibly altruistic activity. The individualistic, profit-motivated entrepreneur had existed in the early Meiji period, probably existed in the 1920s, (and certainly exists today), but he did not have the full approval of the community. In the United States, too, by the 1920s managers were coming to see themselves as harmonious movers of men. But in America the co-operative management ideology was new, and represented a major change from the previous notions of the businessman agonistes, the inventor-entrepreneur, and the self-evidently superior victor against the commercial odds, which had held sway in the 1890s and 1900s.[3] Though in America the individual entrepreneur was by 1920 ceasing to dominate business in practice, his robust ideals lived on to reprove timid and temporizing corporate officials. In Japan there could be unqualified approval for the hard-working, stable, gregarious, sociologically self-conscious fledgling manager, fresh from his law or commerce course. In America even today memories of pristine individualism unsettle the collective ideal.[4]

[1] In Mannari's sample 31 per cent. of 133 graduates had studied economics or commerce and 23 per cent. law and government. Only 26 per cent. had studied any branch of science. Hiroshi Mannari (1974: 175: Table 23).

[2] My estimate, based on figures given in Japan National Commission for Unesco (1966: 83, 296).

[3] Reinhard Bendix (1963: 287–308).

[4] Reinhard Bendix (1963: 333 ff).

A similar ethic of harmony and co-operation, though of a more factitious kind, pervades the story of the second important development of company personnel policies during this period, the establishment of 'familism'. There have now been a number of accounts[1] of the rise of 'familism', many of them designed to refute the suggestion by James C. Abegglen that paternalistic labour practices in modern Japanese companies are a continuation of traditional employment methods.[2] It will only be necessary, therefore, to tell the tale briefly here.

Between 1868 and 1890, Japan was essentially an agricultural country with one major manufacturing industry: textiles. Cotton spinning and silk reeling, though vital in their contribution to the exports that financed the purchase of foreign machinery and payment for foreign technical advice, constituted only a small part of the national product, and employed a tiny fraction of the labour force. A great deal of the production in these industries took place in family workshops. Those establishments big enough and sufficiently well organized to be called factories rarely employed more than thirty or forty workers; so that it was nearly always the case that employees and employers knew each other personally. An overwhelming proportion of the textile workers were women, usually young women brought in from country areas, lured by the prospect of making a little money for themselves or their families before they returned to their villages to marry. Frequently recruitment took place by agreement between the factory's representatives or agents and family heads and village elders. In these circumstances, where industry was a minority pursuit, where the units of organization were small, where continuity existed between the society of the factory and the village, and where the authority of the managers, older, male and urban, over the workers, young, female and rural, was so thoroughly in keeping with dispositions in society at large, there was no pressing need for industrialists to justify their prerogatives, or plan systematic employment policies.

A number of events occurred between 1890 and 1920 to alter this state of affairs, and force employers to develop ideas and practices to support their positions and justify their authority. By the turn of the century factories were troubled by labour shortages and increases in labour mobility. New industries which employed men rather than subservient young girls came to the fore. The first steps towards the formation of labour unions began to be taken. And throughout the period there

---

[1] Johannes Hirschmeier and Tsunehiko Yūi (1975: 200–12); R. P. Dore (1973: 385–403); Byron K. Marshall (1967: 62–73); Kōji Taira (1970: 119–27); M. Y. Yoshino (1968: 65–84).
[2] James C. Abegglen (1958: especially 99–100).

continued a campaign for the enactment and then enforcement of labour legislation.

The labour shortage in the textile factories resulted largely from a growing awareness among the peasantry of the often hideous conditions which existed in them, and a reluctance to go to factories or to stay in them. Some employers tried to solve the problem by agreeing to restrict competition for workers, but the only sure solution was to make employment conditions more satisfactory. Since so many of the employees were young farm girls it was quite natural for employers to offer them benefits such as housing, food, and classes in Japanese accomplishments, so reconstituting in an industrial setting the kind of paternalism that the girls might have experienced if they had been engaged for domestic service by a village landlord.

In the metal working and engineering industries, which grew in importance from about 1900, the employees were men, and were therefore rather more difficult to control. Skilled workers, who were always in short supply, would frequently move from firm to firm, causing the disruption of work schedules in every factory they left. Employers in these industries were forced to abandon daily wages and to offer their workers the prospects of a career, with better jobs and higher pay after an appropriate length of service, and welfare schemes and profit-related bonuses as further inducements to stay.

If the exigencies of the labour market forced firms to behave in a paternalistic manner, the appearance of labour unions and the controversy over labour legislation challenged managers to produce a coherent defence of their place in industrial society. Spasmodic labour unrest had occurred from the very beginning of the Meiji period, there having been riots at the notorious mine at Takashima, and strikes in textile factories.[1] The frequently appalling conditions in Japanese factories offered every incentive for the development of unions, but they did not come into being until after the Sino-Japanese War of 1894. The government was unsympathetic to them. The Peace Preservation Law of 1900 placed unions in a legal limbo. They were not specifically proscribed, but they were rendered unable to act legally. In 1912 Suzuki Bunji, a Christian with socialist leanings, founded the Yūaikai, or Friendly Society, an organization roughly modelled on the early British workmen's groups of that name.[2] Its policies, which were at first determined almost entirely by Suzuki, were moderate and conciliatory, arguing for better labour

[1] Kazuo Ōkochi (1958: 20-1).
[2] Stephen S. Large (1972).

legislation, while at the same time asserting the common interests of, and ideal harmony between, labour and capital. Gradually, however, as the Japanese economy suffered first from monetary inflation and then, at the end of the First World War, from unemployment, the Yūaikai became more militant, eventually establishing itself as a union federation in 1919.

The campaign for factory legislation reached its peak at about the time when the first labour unions were forming and being subjected to government harassment. In the story of the factory laws, however, the government and the bureaucracy appear more as heroes than villains. Indeed, the bureaucrats were almost the sole proponents of the laws, the infant labour movement doing surprisingly little to further their establishment.[1] The motives of the bureaucrats were various, but one of them was to improve Japan's standing in the world, for from as early as 1878 the Japanese government had been aware that firms in the West showed care and solicitude for the well-being of their workers.[2] Draft factory legislation was begun in 1882. Its stipulations were made more rigorous after public revelations about the conditions in the Mitsubishi mine at Takashima in the magazine *Nihonjin* in 1888. Though the new draft was welcomed at first, its proposals provoked intense opposition, and it was not until 1911 that a very attenuated Factory Act was passed.

Both the rise of the union movement and the imminence of labour legislation evoked a range of similar reactions among industrialists. A few gave more or less limited approval to the new developments. Others professed to welcome them in principle, but argued that it was too early to allow them full practical expression; usually because having unions and labour laws would cost industry too much money and make Japanese business uncompetitive. But a common reaction was to assert that the unique circumstances of Japan made Western imports like unions and labour laws unnecessary. In Japan the relations between managers and employers and between capital and labour were essentially harmonious. Employees loved their masters, just as they had always done, and masters preserved their traditionally benevolent attitudes towards those who worked for them. Industry was pervaded by a spirit (to which unions and laws would surely prove inimical) of mutual understanding, peace and solicitude; so much so that it was possible to assimilate the factory to the family.

The idea of 'familism', the epitome of Japanese uniqueness, arose with

[1] R. P. Dore (1969).
[2] Eugene Soviak (1971: 22).

apparent naturalness out of the circumstances of the time, and was for that reason a powerfully persuasive doctrine. The metaphor of the family, besides harking back to Tokugawa tradition, was perfectly adapted to interpret employment practices forced on employers by the labour market. The notion of firm-as-family was also consistent with one of the central political concepts of the Meiji period, a concept widely supposed to have remote historical antecedents, but one which was in fact a new garment of old threads: that the Japanese nation itself was a gigantic family with the Emperor at its head. Such a well-connected and plausible doctrine as familism, therefore, was able to assert itself over the brash and contentious theories that might have proceeded from some obvious facts: that there were enormous differences in the way managers and workers were treated, that industrial relations were sometimes very bad, or that fraud and speculation were endemic on the stock exchanges. In Japanese industry today one hears rather less of the particular analogy with the family, largely because the Japanese family itself has changed and no longer constitutes a simple pattern for conduct. There remains, however, an influential ideal of harmony and co-operation in relations among employees and between employees and their firms.

I should end this section by remarking that the two employment policies discussed in it not only took place at the same time but were also, perhaps, related to each other. It was the first generation of bureaucratic managers recruited straight from universities who actually adopted the ideal of familism. The best trained men, and those who might have been expected to be the most receptive towards Western ideas of individualism, preferred instead a traditional-looking thesis which served their interests better. It is even possible that the graduate managers were indispensable to the general acceptance of familism. For it may be that familism would have foundered if in the 1910s and 1920s companies had still been led by owner-entrepreneurs of the school of Iwasaki and Yasuda, wolves too fierce to masquerade as leaders of the flock; whereas the new generation of business leaders could justly present themselves as company servants, more privileged, certainly, than their subordinates, but part of the same community of endeavour.

THE 'ZAIBATSU', 'DUALISM' AND 'LIFETIME EMPLOYMENT'

The thirty-five years between 1920 and 1955 were perhaps the most eventful in Japanese history. Natural disaster was followed by economic depression, war, defeat, foreign occupation and imposed changes, and finally resurgence. Remarkable developments took place in many aspects of Japanese life. The population increased vastly. Cities grew, were destroyed, and grew again. Farmers saw their position deteriorate and then improve beyond all precedent. The economy was transformed. Political ideas established themselves and were exploded. Constitutions and laws were re-written. The behaviour and attitudes of ordinary men (and, even more, women) altered considerably. My interest, however, is not with the obvious changes that occurred during this turbulent era, but with three features of Japanese industrial organization which appeared at, or even before, the beginning of the period and which persisted in one form or another throughout it.

The first of these three features was the domination of industry by large companies belonging to combines known as *zaibatsu*. The concentration of modern industry in the hands of a small number of entrepreneurs was, of course, initiated by the policies of the Meiji government. Businessmen like Yasuda, Iwasaki of Mitsubishi, and Minomura of Mitsui had been offered subsidies, and even the materials to start new enterprises, and then were left to compound their successes, free from taxation. Many of the early entrepreneurs founded a number of companies in different industries, and it was these companies, linked by common origins and common ownership, supplied with money by the same bank, and trading preferentially with each other, that comprised the core of the *zaibatsu*. Groups like Mitsubishi, Yasuda, Sumitomo or Mitsui, having started advantageously, continued to benefit from government influence in, for example, the allocation of import licences for technology. They also gained immeasurably from their privileged access to capital. Each *zaibatsu* had a bank, which acted as a money pump. Deposits from the public were channelled towards the other member companies of the group, by loans or by the underwriting of share and debenture issues. The ability to raise capital easily allowed the *zaibatsu* to take the lead in the development of heavy, capital-intensive industries like engineering and chemicals between the two World Wars.

By then much of the Japanese industrial economy was dominated by the four major *zaibatsu* and a number of minor ones.[1] Each *zaibatsu* had at its centre a holding company, controlled by the founder family. This would own a large proportion of each of the dozen or so core companies, including the bank, the trading company, the trust company, and the insurance company. Each of the core companies would own a further percentage of the equity of many of the others, so that the *zaibatsu* as

[1] One of a number of good accounts of the pre-war *zaibatsu* is G. C. Allen (1940).

a group controlled 40–100 per cent. of the capital of each of the major members.[1] Each core company might have one or two associates, affiliates or subsidiaries, so that the whole *zaibatsu* appeared as a vast agglomeration of related companies extending over a range of different industries. There was a great measure of central management co-ordination, with the officers of the holding company holding presidencies and directorships in the core companies. The member firms did business together, making particular use of the group trading companies as agents and to some extent initiators of new business. So great was their collective power and so wide were their interests that the *zaibatsu* had some pretension to economic self-sufficiency.

With the rise of militarism the political influence of the *zaibatsu* was reduced, for the army was antipathetic to big business. Economically, however, the *zaibatsu* were indispensable. Even though the army did its best to further the interests of its own client combines, the Big Four *zaibatsu* benefited disproportionately from wartime circumstances, and were able by 1941 to claim control of thirty-two per cent. of the national investment in heavy industry, and almost fifty per cent. of Japan's banking resources.[2]

After the Second World War the Occupation authorities instigated legislation designed to dismantle the *zaibatsu* and prevent them reforming.[3] Holding companies, cartels, and restrictive selling arrangements were proscribed. Controls were placed on reciprocal shareholding by companies and on interlocking directorships. The measures were to be executed and interpreted by a new quasi-judicial body, the Fair Trade Commission. Within a few years the old *zaibatsu* with their family holding companies and interlocking shareholdings and directorships had gone, and a number of the bigger trading companies and industrial firms had been broken into separate pieces. But during the execution of the new laws American opinion on their advisability changed, and as a result they were not put into effect with the thoroughness which had originally been intended. Few financial institutions, for example, were broken up. After the Allies left Japan, many of the large firms that had been split into separate entities reconstituted themselves; and the core companies of the former *zaibatsu* began to enter into arrangements with each other. Even today, therefore,

---

[1] According to figures referring to 1945 given by Eleanor M. Hadley (1970: 62–7). The *zaibatsu* were forced by public opinion to sell shares to outsiders during the 1930s, so that the proportion of shares held by *zaibatsu* members was probably even higher earlier on.

[2] Eleanor M. Hadley (1970: 45–57).

[3] This account is based on Eleanor M. Hadley (1970: 107–201). Other studies of the same subject include T. A. Bisson (1954).

there are constellations of companies with a common name—Sumitomo Metal, Sumitomo Chemical, Sumitomo Real Estate, and so on—each constellation including a bank and a trading company. Within each, also, companies trade together and co-operate, and there are cross-holdings of shares and common directorships. Yet even though these constellations are commonly called *zaibatsu*, and even though their constituent companies are usually descended from the prewar *zaibatsu*, they are very much more loosely co-ordinated than were their defunct progenitors. I shall discuss them in the next chapter.

A second consistent feature of industrial organization throughout the period was evidently associated with the domination of the economy by the *zaibatsu*. This second feature has been given a number of names, including 'industrial dualism' and 'dual economy'. These refer to the coexistence within the Japanese economy of large firms, engaged in capital-intensive modern industries, achieving high productivity and paying high wages; and small firms, sometimes in traditional industries, using less capital, achieving lower productivity, and paying lower wages. The origin and even the nature of 'dualism' have been the subject of extensive discussion, with dozens of contributions in English alone.[1] The controversy has risen over a number of problems: whether small firms are or were inferior in every respect to large ones, for small firms show higher returns on capital employed;[2] and how far the persistence of 'dualism' over such a long period depends on employment practices, sub-contracting, differences of technical level, access to capital, union activities and government policies. The discussion has been made very complicated by the variations in production and wage differences between larger and smaller firms at different stages of the business cycle, and by the changes in the extent of 'dualism' in particular industries over the years.

It seems likely that 'industrial dualism' is not a unitary phenomenon. The differences in various aspects—value added, profit, wages—of large and small firms may not be due to a single set of causes at any one time; and the causes may not be the same in every period. It can be said, however, that differences in wages and productivity between larger and smaller firms became clearly apparent towards the end of the First World War and have remained so until today. It is probable that these differences came into being partly as a result of the government policy of aiding large *zaibatsu* firms. One reason for their persistence was the advantage

---

[1] See Yasukichi Yasuba (1976); Miyohei Shinohara (1970: 23–5, 303–64) and Seymour Broadbridge (1966).
[2] Yasukichi Yasuba (1976: 249–98).

larger firms had in acquiring and applying new technology. Another was that in certain industries at least the practice of sub-contracting became prevalent, and small sub-contractors were placed at a disadvantage to large principals. The rise of labour unions in bigger companies after the Second World War must also have had some effect on the differences between firms. To all these historical influences must be added the advantages that bigger firms have over smaller ones everywhere: economy of scale and power over the market place.

The third consistent feature of industrial organization can also be seen as an element of difference between larger and smaller firms. This is 'lifetime employment', the ideal—which is partly honoured in practice—that an employee should join his firm from school and stay with it until retirement.[1] With this is associated a second ideal, that rewards should be linked to age and length of service. Clearly both 'lifetime employment' and 'pay by age' had antique precursors, especially in the practices of the Japanese merchant 'houses'; but both appeared in modern industry only in the twentieth century. 'Lifetime employment' was, like management 'familism', primarily a response to labour mobility. Indeed, the two were very closely associated. Employers began to recruit workers from school in order to train them within the company. Then, to induce them to stay, pay and promotion systems were devised which, while being meritocratic, offered workers phased increases in pay in the course of their careers.

Statistical evidence suggests that 'lifetime employment' was not firmly established between the two World Wars,[2] and one might have supposed that the practice would have faded away after the Second War. In fact, however, after the war both 'lifetime employment' and 'pay by age' became sufficiently common to be popularly thought of as normal and traditional forms. The reason for this was paradoxical. The labour union movement, weak enough before the Second World War, had almost ceased to exist by 1945, when the Occupation authorities decided to encourage the formation of workers' associations as part of the effort to build a democratic nation. With the country devastated and communications bad, it was difficult to gather together workers in the same industry

---

[1] Much of what has been written on 'lifetime employment' has taken the form of criticism of the assertion that 'lifetime employment' is a traditional practice and that it involves moral loyalty which transcends material advantage; see James C. Abegglen (1958: 17, 130–1). Among the rejoinders are Ken'ichi Tominaga (1962), Robert E. Cole (1972), Robert M. Marsh and Hiroshi Mannari (1971), (1972), and (1976: 225–53); and Kōji Taira (1970: 97–127).

[2] Kōji Taira (1970: 153–60).

from different regions. Instead workers organized their new unions round the enterprise or plant in which they were working.[1] Within a few years enterprise unions had proliferated and union membership grew with considerable rapidity. There was at the time an enormous surplus of labour. The damage sustained by Japanese industry during the war had reduced the number of jobs available just when demobilization and the repatriation of people from the expropriated colonies had increased the number of people looking for work. Under these conditions the new enterprise unions were naturally most concerned to preserve the jobs of their members and to prevent dismissals; for a worker who lost his job might not find another. 'Lifetime employment', which before the war had been the expedient of management, was now the conscious objective of labour unions.

Union activities also contributed to the postwar prevalence of the pay by age system.[2] The enterprise unions iterated the slogan of 'equal pay for equal work', but they were constitutionally ill-suited to pursue the goal; for within a single enterprise union there would be a number of workers doing different jobs. A more natural aim for an enterprise union was to keep the average wage levels of its members comparable with those paid to the members of similar enterprise unions in other companies. Pay would therefore be related to company membership rather than individual function. Moreover, in the early postwar years wages were extremely low, and it was imperative to arrange that those workers who had the greatest family responsibilities should have the most money. In 1946 an important precedent was established by an agreement won by the electric power workers. Wages were to be paid according to age and number of dependants, as well as skill and experience. As in the case of 'lifetime employment', prewar management thinking and postwar necessity combined to common effect.

'Lifetime employment' and 'pay by age' were and are more characteristic of large firms than small ones. A company which offers security of tenure and a promise of automatic salary increases to its employees is undertaking a considerable commitment for a very long period. Smaller companies are rarely sound enough to do this. But 'lifetime employment' is not merely a symptom of 'dualism', a distinction between larger and smaller firms. It is also a cause. Large companies which offer 'lifetime

[1] It has been suggested that the Communist World Federation of Trade Unions encouraged the formation of enterprise unions because they, more than trade unions, would lead to the creation of management-worker committees and worker control. Paul Timothy Chan (1969: 210).

[2] Eitarō Kishimoto (1968).

employment' to their employees forfeit an important means of adjusting to business depressions: they cannot cut back their work forces. One way in which large companies can retain some degree of flexibility is by employing numbers of 'temporary' workers. These may stay with their firms for some time, but lack security of tenure and are liable to be dismissed when times are hard. Before the Second World War the proportion of 'temporary' workers in some firms was very large. A second way in which a large firm can adjust is by curtailing orders to the small firms which act as sub-contractors to it. These small firms have no alternative but to lay off or dismiss their workers. The dualistic effect is therefore its own cause: big firms are stable and their workers enjoy security partly because small firms are weak and their workers' positions unsafe.

CONCLUSION

The purpose of this historical prologue has been to give origin and context to the particularities of the Japanese company. Frequently the origins have been obscure and the context confusing, for like most histories, that of the company in Japan has its share of incompatible influences and paradoxical developments. The paternalistic merchant 'house' and the uncharitable nineteenth-century cotton mill are both among the company's ante-cedents. In 1860 the prevalent metaphor for the firm is the family, and business is a despised avocation. In 1880 entrepreneurs are triumphant and the company has been recognized as an instrument of public service and a means to prosperity. By 1910 the family is back in fashion as a figure of business speech, and the products of a modern education system can appeal to traditional paternalism to excuse their opposition to labour laws urging the most elementary decencies.

The history of the company also contains a large measure of chance, and invites speculation on a number of might-have-beens. How would Japanese industry have developed if the Meiji Restoration had taken place a few decades later, in 1900, when electric power had become available; or even in 1917, when the world was full of wholly different ideas from those fashionable in 1868? Would the incidence of industrial 'dualism' have been less marked if the Stock Exchange had enabled small companies to raise money; and would that have been possible if the Exchange had not been manned by disreputable people? What would have become of the company if Iwasaki had lived longer and Shibusawa had not lived at all?

Clearly a story so full of paradoxes and contingencies does not allow us to think of the Japanese company as a simple compound of traditional and modern elements. Traditions have lapsed and been reconstituted. Changes have occurred so fast, but nevertheless at different speeds in different institutions, that old and new jostle and displace each other. Nor is it always easy to distinguish the Japanese influence and the Western. Western imports are soon used for Japanese purposes, and indigenous means applied to ends defined in Western terms. Ideas both from home and abroad are chosen eclectically to fit each other and the times. Parallel developments occur in Japan and the West with slightly different causes and implications.

Though it is of little use to look for discrete particles of Japanese-ness and Western-ness in the Japanese company it is apparent that, taken as a whole, the history of the company in Japan is very different from its history in any Western country. I must now examine the present results of this unique history. I shall begin by showing how even such a feature of the company as its role as a unit of industrial organization, that one might have assumed to be the same everywhere, is in fact anomalous in Japan.

CHAPTER III

The Industrial Context

The organization of industry in Japan is in one respect very similar to that in the United States, Germany or the United Kingdom. It revolves around the same institutions. There are banks, companies, labour unions, bills of exchange, employment contracts and markets. Forms and practices are sufficiently similar to those of the West that a European or an American can establish and run a successful enterprise in Japan without more difficulty than can be resolved by good lawyers and helpful handbooks. Yet there are differences. As a result of the historical influences already discussed, these familiar institutions often work in mildly anomalous ways, or exhibit tendencies which may be present but with less emphasis in the West. The cumulative result is a pattern of industrial organization peculiar to Japan. This chapter will be concerned with four tendencies in the Japanese industrial company which together constitute, perhaps, the greater part of that peculiarity.

The first of these characteristic tendencies is for the company in Japan to be an elementary unit, a clearly defined cell of industrial or commercial activity, rather than merely one of a number of industrial organizations whose memberships overlap. The second is for the company to be narrowly specialized, engaged in one line of business or perhaps a few closely allied ventures. The third is for companies to be graded, to be arranged in a hierarchy, in which the bigger they are the better their standing. This tendency is obviously associated with the 'industrial dualism' mentioned earlier. The last tendency is for the company to be associated with other companies in some form of group. Here, of course, the historical reference is to the *zaibatsu*.

When I have explained these tendencies and examined how they are associated with each other, I shall show how they are manifested in a particular Japanese company, and how they affect the conduct of its business and its relations with other companies.

With this example I hope to illustrate the central argument of this chapter, which is that because the Japanese company is the elementary unit of Japanese industry, and because it is specialized, hierarchically ordered, and commonly associated with other companies, it is possible to talk of a society of industry. In the society of industry a company takes its place according to what it does, whether it is dominant in its particular line of business, how it is attached to prestigious companies or groups of companies and so on. An analogy useful to Anglo-Saxons would be the society of education in Britain or America, in which universities, colleges and polytechnics are assessed (and assess each other) partly by the number of Nobel prizewinners associated with each institution, partly by the eminence of their alumni, and partly also by whether they exchange visiting examiners with the best and most famous universities, or play with them at games. I shall end by trying to show how the society of industry in Japan influences the inner workings of the Japanese company and the effect the company has on the wider community, as a preliminary to discussing these matters in later chapters.

THE COMPANY AS AN ELEMENTARY UNIT

We distinguish three sets of institutions in Western industry. The first set consists of companies, the units of management, ownership, and finance. The second set are industries and markets, informal institutions defined by reference to certain products, technologies, systems of distribution, legislative arrangements, and so on. The third set are trade unions and other associations of people in industry. The three sets of institutions are all obviously related, but the connections between them are complicated, because each institution is only partially associated with the others. A large firm, like Unilever, will be engaged in a number of different industries and will deal with dozens of different types of worker and many separate unions. An industry, such as the soft drink industry, will involve not only several companies but also a number of divisions of companies, including Unilever, whose involvement in that particular industry represents only part of a range of activities; and the people who work in the industry belong not only to those companies but also to various unions and associations. Finally, a union may be represented in dozens of companies and parts of companies, and its members may be engaged in a similarly large variety of industries. These industrial institutions are superimposed on the map of industry without regularity, just as in an old city the boundaries of postal districts, local authorities, and electricity supply areas are all out of alignment.

In Japan, however, the institutions of industry are rather more likely to be coextensive. The company, the unit of management and ownership, is very frequently the unit of an industry, and also the unit within which labour associations are confined. It is as if the political, postal, and electrical districts of the city coincide; not so much, however, because of far-sighted city planning, as because the lie of the land has imposed this regularity as the city has grown.

There are many examples of how the company fits within the boundaries of industries and markets. Table III.1 shows how in each of several different industries, the largest share of production and sales is held by companies which are dedicated to that industry:

Table III.1. The company as member of an industry in selected industries, 1975–6

	Turnover,* Fiscal 1975 '000 m yen	A† The given industry %	B† Related industries %	C‡ Unrelated industries %
		Percentage of turnover in		
The Paint Industry				
Dai Nippon Tōryō	49.9	78	12	10
Nippon Paint	55.4	90		10
Kansai Paint	60.4	84		14
Shintō Paint	22.6	84		16
Tōa Paint	16.7	89		11
Chūgoku Marine Paint	21.1	82		18
Rock Paint	16.3	75		25
Nippon Oils and Fats	59.6	30		70
The Cable and Wire Industry				
Furukawa Electric	204.0	56	34	11
Sumitomo Electric Industries	211.8	73	8	19
Fujikura Cable Works	78.3	90		10
Dainichi-Nippon Cables	67.3	90		10
Shōwa Electric Wire & Cable	75.6	67	13	20
Hitachi Cable	105.2	76	18	6
The Construction Machinery Industry				
Komatsu	360.9	70	12	18
Caterpillar Mitsubishi§	158.9	n.a.		
Katō Works	49.5	32	59	9
Tadano	27.7	92		8
Yutani Heavy Industries	17.7	94		6
Sakai Heavy Industries	11.6	28	67	5

[*continued overleaf*]

Table III.1 (continued)

| | | Percentage of turnover in | | |
	Turnover,* Fiscal 1975 'ooo m yen	A† The given industry %	B† Related industries %	C‡ Unrelated industries %
The Camera Industry‖				
Nippon Kōgaku	57.9	67	23	10
Canon	75.0	54	27	19
Asahi Optical	27.7	94		6
Minolta Camera	48.0	75		25
Olympus Optical	45.9	48	42	10
The Beer Industry				
Kirin Beer	528.6	90	10	
Sapporo Breweries	191.8	90	10	
Asahi Beer	145.7	75	25	
Suntory	352.1	13	85	2

Source: Japan Economic Yearbook, 1976–7: 296–327.

* Companies have different year ends so that turnover figures are not strictly comparable.

† I have arbitrarily assigned products to categories A and B as follows: Paint Industry: A, paint of any kind, thinner, and lacquer; B, lead chemicals, fluorescent products. Cable and Wire Industry: A, cables and wires; B, rolled copper products, powdered alloys, coils. Construction Machinery Industry: A, construction machinery, cranes; B, industrial vehicles and machinery. Camera Industry: A, cameras, accessories, lenses; B, spectacle lenses, microscopes, optical instruments, medical instruments. Beer Industry: A, beer; B, soft drinks, Western liquor.

‡ All other products are assigned to category C. Since some firms count such components of turnover as installation charges and spare parts as 'other products', the effect of this classification is to understate the extent to which Japanese companies confine themselves to their industry.

§ An analysis of the turnover of Caterpillar Mitsubishi was not obtainable, but it can safely be presumed to be largely in categories A and B.

‖ The two big manufacturers of photographic film, Fuji Photo and Konishiroku, also make cameras. But cameras constitute only a small part of their business, and their share of total camera production is not great.

It is difficult, in asserting that companies fall neatly into industries, to avoid all trace of tautology. No industry can be exactly defined, and different definitions may make an industry appear more or less heterogeneous, and argue the inclusion or exclusion of certain firms. If, for example, the manufacturers of inks on the one hand and chemical precursors of paint on the other were both to be allocated to the paint industry, then clearly the picture presented in Table III.1, of the paint industry as the preserve of specialized paint companies, would be inaccurate. Yet the fact is that the Japanese themselves tend to think of industries as homogeneous, and of companies as belonging to an industry or even to part of an industry. Newspaper articles frequently refer to the 'Big Two' of the printing industry, or the 'Big Four' of ball bearings. Managers measure the progress of their company by comparing it with 'other firms in the same industry' (dōgyō tasha). Workers relate their wages to those their counterparts in the leader of the industry are getting. Whatever the actual degree of specialization—and I shall return to the argument that companies are indeed specialized—firms are certainly thought of as units of an industry. Conversely, to mention an industry is to bring to mind a particular set of firms.

If the company can be seen as the component of an industry, it is also the unit for the division of the labour force. There has been some mis-understanding about the nature of the 'lifetime employment system', the origins of which I described in the last chapter. Not the least of the diffi-culty is that the phrase itself is misleading. Nevertheless, it is a fact that a large number, if not a majority, of male employees join bigger companies straight from school or college, or with at the most two or three years of industrial experience, and stay with those companies until the age of fifty-five. For these employees the company they work in is more than a temporary affiliation. It is an institution in which they have long-term membership. Moreover, that membership is, for most of them, the prime attribute defining their position in the world of work. They are not car workers: they are employees of Toyota, and Toyota is a company in the car industry.

The nature of Japanese labour unions contributes to the importance of the company as the unit of labour. Japanese unions tend to be enterprise unions, uniting the members of one plant or company, rather than trade unions, associating people in different companies doing similar jobs. Most of the national union organizations are confederations of enterprise unions, and their members are not individual workers but unions. Thus where an employee of General Motors is at the same time a member of the United Auto Workers, a quite separate organization, our Toyota worker is a member of the Toyota Union, a body which is constitution-ally dependent on Toyota itself. His links with any national federation are indirect and contingent on his enterprise union's affiliation with that body. There are, to be sure, trade unions of the Western kind in Japan. The best known examples are the Japan Seamen's Union and the Japan Teachers' Union—the activities of this latter being, of course, outside commerce. But though the economic influence of the seamen and the political importance of the teachers are considerable, the workers belong-ing to trade unions constitute only a tiny proportion of the working population.[1] There are also professional associations like that of the Certified Public Accountants, whose members are found in different companies. The associates of these professional bodies may meet each other on occasion; but their separate companies continue to be their prime affiliations. Both they themselves and others are likely to view their associateships merely as incidental qualifications.

In general, then, the institutions of Japanese industry are aligned, rather than loosely superimposed as in American or British industry. Industrial organization has a pattern to it, and the common and recurring element of it is the company, which therefore has a significance in Japan it lacks in the West.

There is proof of this significance in the extent to which ordinary Japanese are well informed about companies. Company handbooks equivalent to *Moody's* in the United States, and very much more detailed than *The Times' Thousand* in Britain, are issued quarterly in very large numbers and at low prices. Details of the size, quality of management, or affiliation of companies, which would be known only to specialists in the West, are almost common knowledge in Japan. There are even popular weekly magazines devoted largely to gossip and scandals concerning companies: the imminent bankruptcy of shipping lines, the land speculations of trading companies, and the unpleasant habits of company presidents. This interest in companies is, of course, inseparable from a general preoccupation with industry, business, and economics. It is also true that companies work hard to advertise themselves. Even firms which do not sell their products directly to the public, such as diesel manufacturers or shipbuilders, will sponsor popular programmes on television in order to explain their achievements to the world. But companies are known because they are central to many activities concerned with industry; and the fact that they are known naturally makes them even more significant.

I should mention one great advantage that derives from the tidiness of Japanese industrial organization and the pre-eminence of the company among industrial institutions. This is that people with different interests in industry find it easier to have a common frame of discourse. It is possible to find in Japan, as elsewhere, the manager who knows nothing of how unions work, the economist innocent of the methods and problems of management, or the unionist with a blurred understanding of economic

---

[1] There are a few federations of unions which combine the enterprise unions of major manufacturing companies and those of their subsidiaries and affiliates. The most notable of these is the Car Workers' Federation, which unites the unions of Nissan Motor and its suppliers; see Alice H. Cook (1966: 73-5). The member unions of such a federation obviously have very different interests at times. cf R. P. Dore (1973: 123).

principles. Yet such dangerous ignorance is, perhaps, rarer in Japan than in the West, because people with different points of view are all likely to have a knowledge of the company in common, and to see each others' activities at least partly in terms of their effects on the company. The simple device, to return to an earlier metaphor, of co-ordinating the districts of the city may reduce contention and increase understanding between the city functionaries.

THE SPECIALIZATION OF THE COMPANY

It is hard to find satisfactory quantitative evidence for the specialization of Japanese companies, and the extent to which—at least compared with Western firms—they stick to a particular last. One reason for this is a difficulty we have already encountered. There is no easy way of defining an industry, to which a company may or may not restrict its activities. The differences between the industrial classifications used in different countries make international comparisons particularly imprecise. There have, moreover, been very few studies of specialization in Europe and America,[1] and I have not been able to find any at all which refer to Japan. Even so, to anyone with experience of both Western and Japanese industry the idea that the Japanese company tends to have a narrower range of interests would be a commonplace. He would be able to bring to mind dozens of corroborative examples of the kind provided in Table III.1. Toyota and Nissan make cars and little else; compare their parsimony of interests with the activities of Ford or General Motors. General Electric of America builds jet engines and operates coal mines, while its British namesake is in the furniture business. Neither Hitachi nor Tōshiba, both of them diversified companies by Japanese standards, spreads its net so wide. In the food industry there is no Japanese company as multifarious as Nestlé, General Foods or Cavenhams. Instead there are meat companies, instant food manufacturers, makers of dairy products, or fishing companies. No Japanese steel company goes so far as to sell chemicals,

---

[1] The most influential contribution to the subject appears to be that of Charles H. Berry (1971), who proposed an index of diversification and applied it to large American firms. Diversification in the average large American firm in 1965 appears to have been between 0.379 and 0.645 on Berry's index, according to the preciseness of industrial classification used. The first of these figures represents a firm with roughly 80 per cent. of its output in one industry and 10 per cent. in each of two others; the second a firm with 50 per cent. of its output in one industry, 20 per cent. in two more, and 10 per cent. in a fourth. Alexis P. Jacquemin and Henry de Jong (1977: 105–9) offer a more refined formula for an index and provide a brief discussion of diversification in European industry.

3

like United States Steel—though Nippon Kōkan has an important ship-building division. The Japanese paper industry is characterized by large firms making only a limited range of products: Honshū makes paper-board, Ōji paper for newspapers, and Kanzaki coated papers. There could be no greater contrast with the 'forest product' concerns of North America and Europe.

There are, to be fair, Japanese companies with a wide range of interests. The most notable is Mitsubishi Heavy Industries, which makes cars, ships, aircraft, industrial equipment and a multitude of other products. There are several other firms of substantial size which are engaged in as many different industries as any of their Western counterparts. Kubota makes agricultural equipment—but also pipes and prefabricated houses. Dainippon Ink produces resins, plastics and building materials as well as ink. Nevertheless, the general rule holds. Japanese companies do tend to be specialized.

There are two aspects to this specialization. One is the apparent reluctance of firms to diversify either by merging with companies in different industries or else by starting new lines of business on their own account. Instead they tend to diversify by creating separate, specialized, and more or less independent subsidiaries. The other aspect is the way in which Japanese firms confine their activities not simply to a particular industry but to a mere part of the process of manufacture or distribution necessary to the industry, and sub-contract the other parts of the process to specialized firms.

Let us begin with the question of diversification. One obstacle to this is the nature of the labour market. Because of the tendency of the employees of large firms to stay with their employers it is difficult—though not impossible—for a company which wants to diversify to acquire skilled labour and managers with appropriate experience. If a firm does take in experienced outsiders, either by merging with another firm or else by recruiting in the labour market, then it may have trouble fitting them into its existing organization, in which positions are filled by people who have been with the company for a long time. To avoid problems, firms tend to train their existing employees for any new venture, a procedure which takes time and makes continuous and rapid diversification impracticable.

But the labour market is only one reason for the specialization of the Japanese company. A far more important one is the Japanese view of management and business. There is, as I have mentioned, a common assumption that a firm should belong to an industry and make its contribution to the economy through its efforts in that industry. There is an obvious parallel here between these ideas of the modern company and the governing principles of the merchant house, which concentrated on one type of business as a member of the guild which regulated that business. Today, of course, there is no legal barrier to diversification in most industries, and few modern managers would accept the suggestion that their firm had no call or licence to move into a new field. Yet managers will often show an impressive allegiance to their industry, even an industry in decline. They will observe that their troubles have arisen because 'that's the sort of business we are in'; but someone has to make cloth or build ships for the community, even if there is not much money to be made in either of those trades.

Such attitudes are derived in part from the way managers are trained. Training methods, too, are in some ways reminiscent of those of the merchant house. There are institutes and academies of a universally applicable art of management, but within the firm the emphasis is on thoroughly learning a business, preparatory to managing a company engaged in that business. Future administrators, most of whom have general degrees in law, commerce and economics, go through a short induction course and then begin work on the shop floor.[1] Thereafter they spend some time in different parts of the firm before joining the department to which they are assigned. Trainees thereby gain a general understanding of how the firm works and what the business involves. At the end of such a training their views of industry and company are likely to be rather different from those of Western marketing men or accountants, who think of their skills as serviceable in many industries, and of their firms merely as particular contexts in which their skills may be used.

The Japanese mode of thought has a profound influence not only on the extent to which companies diversify but also on the way in which they do. One of the quickest ways by which a company can diversify is to merge with a company in a different industry. In the United States firms with all manner of different interests, like ITT or Litton Industries, have been built by acquisitions, often after stock exchange takeover bids, of enterprises in unrelated industries. In Europe, too, conglomerates have formed in the same way. In Japan, however, the holding companies which bind conglomerates together are forbidden by law. In addition,

---

[1] This sort of training programme was used, for example, in Hitachi: R. P. Dore (1973: 53–4). But there, as in the company I studied, the pressure of work was forcing a curtailment of the training programme.

certain articles of the Commercial Code, by giving considerable powers to shareholders controlling a mere third of a company's shares, make it difficult for a firm to take over another without prior agreement. On the few occasions when forcible takeovers have been attempted the government has acted to prevent the acquisition.[1] Yet agreed mergers have been common enough. Dai-Ichi Kangyō Bank, Yamashita-Shinnihon Steamship, Mitsui Tōatsu Chemical and Nippon Steel were all created by mergers. Big firms like Nissan Motor and Kobe Steel have acquired smaller rivals. In the supermarket industry many companies, but particularly Jusco, have made a policy of expanding by merger. But all of these examples, and indeed most mergers in Japan, are between firms in the same industry. The merging of firms in widely different industries is comparatively rare.

Table III.2, which is derived from a study by the Japanese Fair Trade Commission of mergers which took place in 1970, shows how firms choose their partners. The majority of mergers, involving nearly eighty per cent. of all the assets transferred, take place within an industry. Of those mergers which took place between companies in different industries most involved the takeover of trading firms or land and real estate companies. Although the Fair Trade Commission makes no comment on these types of merger, it can be presumed that manufacturing firms which bought trading or retail companies were doing so not so much to diversify as to ensure better distribution for their products. The biggest acquisitions of real estate companies by firms outside that industry were made, understandably enough, by mining and construction companies and firms engaged in transport and warehousing. Other types of company may have merged with real estate companies as a means of acquiring land. Only fourteen per cent. of all mergers, representing merely 4.1 per cent. of gross assets transferred by merger in 1970, took place between firms in apparently unrelated industries. We cannot, however, be entirely sure that the rather general industrial classifications used do not give a false impression of a reluctance to diversify by merger.[2]

[1] As when Sankō Steamship tried to take over Japan Line between 1971-3. Some details are given in *Nihon Keizai Shinbun* (evening edition), 2 May 1973, p. 2, 'Sankō-Jirain: temochi-shiki no ayashimi' (Sankō-Japan Line: doubt about the holding formula).

[2] Richard E. Caves and Masu Uekusa (1976: 28-30), using the same Fair Trade Commission report as their source, give a rather different picture of mergers in Japan. The report indicates an increase between 1967-70 in the number of mergers between firms in different industries *(kongō gappei)*—including, however, mergers between manufacturing firms and trading and real estate companies. Caves and Uekusa render this as an increase in 'conglomerate' mergers. The report does not provide the information from which tables analogous to Table III.2 could be compiled for the years before 1970; so that it is difficult to say

Table III.2. Company mergers within and between industries, 1970

Industry of active merger partner	No. of mergers	Gross assets acquired (m yen)	Of which percentage acquired by mergers (and no. of mergers):			
			within the industry %	with wholesale and retail companies %	with land and estate companies %	of all other types %
Agriculture, forestry, fishing	13	603	32.2 (5)	35.3 (4)	— (—)	32.5 (4)
Mining	9	10,430	0.8 (2)	29.5 (2)	46.2 (1)	23.5 (4)
Construction	63	5,055	48.6 (39)	1.8 (6)	39.6 (5)	10.0 (13)
Manufacturing industry:						
Food	55	30,437	95.8 (40)	1.9 (5)	1.8 (7)	0.5 (3)
Textiles	54	8,915	74.4 (45)	6.8 (3)	1.3 (3)	17.5 (3)
Wood, wood products	30	1,465	78.2 (24)	20.6 (2)	0.8 (1)	0.4 (3)
Paper, pulp	13	14,936	98.2 (7)	— (—)	1.6 (4)	0.2 (2)
Printing, publishing	23	766	85.4 (15)	— (—)	5.2 (3)	9.4 (5)
Chemicals	38	44,932	98.1 (26)	1.3 (4)	0.3 (4)	0.3 (4)
Rubber, leather	6	1,057	85.7 (2)	6.6 (1)	4.4 (1)	3.3 (2)
Ceramics, pottery	32	9,108	83.1 (16)	12.6 (9)	1.6 (3)	2.7 (4)
Iron, steel	19	41,175	99.0 (14)	0.7 (3)	0.3 (2)	— (—)
Non-ferrous metals	6	21,517	98.9 (5)	— (—)	— (—)	1.1 (1)
Metal products	41	8,451	90.7 (33)	0.2 (1)	0.9 (4)	8.2 (3)
General engineering	27	40,147	3.5 (14)	96.3 (4)	0.2 (5)	0.0 (4)
Electrical engineering	29	3,267	41.9 (18)	57.5 (8)	0.5 (1)	0.1 (2)
Transport equipment	9	35,247	99.0 (7)	0.9 (1)	0.0 (1)	— (—)
Precision engineering	10	441	72.1 (5)	7.7 (2)	6.1 (1)	14.1 (2)
Other manufacturing	3	443	100.0 (3)	— (—)	— (—)	— (—)
Retail, wholesale	479	121,590	81.1 (368)	5.6 (12)	14.0 (44)	4.9 (67)
Land, real estate	117	21,380	67.9 (73)	0.8 (3)	26.6 (3)	26.5 (32)
Transport, warehousing	120	22,853	69.8 (100)	1.9 (9)	11.9 (17)	2.8 (14)
Services	93	15,120	83.0 (59)	1.9 (9)	— (—)	3.2 (8)
Finance	14	13,944	99.5 (12)	— (—)	— (—)	0.5 (2)
Electricity, gas	—	—	— (—)	— (—)	— (—)	— (—)
TOTAL/AVERAGE	1,303	473,329	78.4 (932)	10.5 (79)	7.0 (110)	4.1 (182)

Source: calculated from *Kōsei Torihiki Iinkai*, 1971: 80–1, 84–5: Reference Tables 8, 10.

It is difficult enough to provide reliable quantitative evidence relating to diversification by mergers; but it is even harder to find objective proof that Japanese firms do not diversify simply by starting new lines of products. The inescapable impression, however, is that to the extent that Japanese firms do diversify they do so in a different way. When a large firm decides to enter a new market it frequently does so by setting up a subsidiary company to undertake the business. Or, if the large firm does begin to make a new product or offer a new service on its own account, it commonly separates off the divisions and departments involved at an early opportunity. One of the best of countless examples of this practice is the creation, in 1972, of Fujitsū Fanuc, a specialized manufacturer of numerically controlled machine tools, out of the machine tool division of Fujitsū, the biggest Japanese computer manufacturer. Dozens of similar subsidiaries are formed by large companies every year. Tōshiba, a major electrical company, has subsidiaries and associates making machinery and ceramic products. Construction firms like Taisei have established subsidiaries to make prefabricated housing. Security companies such as Nomura have created real estate and property firms. Banks have affiliated leasing companies, department stores have supermarket subsidiaries, and supermarkets have ventured into the restaurant trade by similarly indirect means.

At first glance this sort of behaviour would seem to be very like that of American or British companies, for these, too, will establish a subsidiary in order to engage in a new industry. To the extent that the parent company has committed capital to the venture and allocated managers and workers to it, and to the extent that the subsidiary may be consolidated with the parent company in financial accounts, then the setting up of such a subsidiary is tantamount to the diversification of the company.

In Japan, however, the subsidiaries of a big company are not necessarily closely tied to it. Until 1977, Japanese companies did not have to prepare consolidated accounts. Once a company had established a subsidiary, therefore, the sales and profits of the subsidiary could be treated quite separately from those of the parent company. Because the performance of the subsidiary did not necessarily reflect on the performance of the parent, it was possible for the managers of the parent to allow the managers

---

how many more genuinely diversified companies were formed in that year than in previous ones. Many of the important mergers which took place in the 1960s are catalogued in the report (*Kōsei Torihiki Iinkai*: 1971; 53–9), and most of them appear to have been between firms not merely in the same industry but in the same parts of an industry.

of the subsidiary considerable freedom to run their own business. In spite of recent changes in accounting procedure, which I will deal with in a later chapter, subsidiaries will probably continue to be managed independently. Apart from this, Japanese subsidiary companies usually belong to different industrial associations from their parents, enjoy separate relations with other companies and banks, recruit different types of people, maintain their own labour unions, and establish their own personnel policies.

Most important of all, a Japanese subsidiary is normally expected to achieve still greater independence of its parent company as it succeeds in the business for which it was established. As the subsidiary grows, its management becomes ever less subservient to the management of the parent. It borrows money and enters into contracts with other firms without guarantees or letters of acknowledgement from the parent. It can even issue its shares to third parties and so reduce the parent company's shareholding. By contrast, a Western subsidiary which grew particularly well would probably be subjected to ever tighter control from the parent as it came to comprise a larger proportion of the business of the whole group.

Perhaps the most spectacular example of a subsidiary's gaining independence of its parent company is that of Toyota Motor. This firm was formed from a division of Toyoda Automatic Loom in 1937. By 1943 the parent company's shareholding had been reduced to just over one-third of Toyota Motor's equity. Today, of course, Toyota Motor is much larger and more famous than its progenitor. Toyoda Loom holds only a few per cent. of Toyota Motor's shares, and is not even the largest shareholder. There are many other instances of a subsidiary's gaining fuller and in some cases complete autonomy. Komatsu Forklift, hived off from the construction equipment firm Komatsu in 1948, is now no longer a subsidiary. Hitachi Kōki, a leading maker of power tools, was established by Hitachi in the same year and is now legally independent. Kawashō, a specialized trading company descended from Kawasaki Steel, and Asahi Organic Chemical, previously a subsidiary of Asahi Chemical, provide two further examples. In the Japanese case, therefore, the establishment of subsidiaries is a process which leads not to the formation of a single diversified company but to the growth of a relatively loosely organized industrial group, of a kind I shall be describing in detail further on. Although the origin of the group lies in the diversification of a large company, each member company of the group tends to be separate and specialized.

Indeed, the existence of such industrial groups in Japan is itself one of the reasons why Japanese companies are specialized. If a company is established in order to represent a group in a particular industry, then its management is expected to keep the company active in that industry and not to attempt to diversify, particularly if diversification would mean trespassing on the territory of another group member. Perhaps the most impressive example of the specialization of companies within groups is to be found in the chemical industry. Where in the West giant firms like ICI, BASF and Dow make a huge range of chemicals, each of the big Japanese industrial groups has separate companies making a limited number of products. Thus the Mitsubishi group contains, among others, Mitsubishi Chemical (petrochemicals, fibre precursors, carbon products), Mitsubishi Gas Chemical (xylene, methanol), Mitsubishi Petrochemical, Mitsubishi Plastics, Nippon Synthetic Chemical (vinyl monomer, polyvinyl alcohol), and Mitsubishi Rayon.

It would be wrong to say that all diversification in Japan takes place through the creation of subsidiaries. Firms do enter new fields. Usually their new activities are extensions of their old ones. The motor cycle manufacturer Honda has established itself in the car industry with impressive success. The textile company Kanebō now makes cosmetics; the new business has in common with the old a concern with chemicals and with fashion. Certain shipbuilders have turned to terrestrial engineering.[1] There are also firms which have struck out into areas which must have been almost entirely unknown to them. The camera manufacturer Olympus has in recent years begun making miniature tape recorders; while a company called Amano, which originally specialized in timing devices, has entered the market for dust collection equipment. But most diversification does seem to take place through the setting up of independent subsidiaries. As a result Japan's is a paradoxical economy. Though new industries spring up and flourish in energetic profusion, yet firms stay specialized and do not change their businesses.

The second aspect of the functional specialization of the Japanese company is the way in which a firm will farm out what in the West would be considered essential parts of its business to other companies. A great number of Japanese firms, and especially smaller ones, sell through trading companies and wholesalers, and rely on hauliers to carry their goods to their customers. The companies thereby leave themselves free to concentrate on manufacture. Yet they do not even undertake the complete process of manufacture, but rely instead on sub-contractors. Thus the activities

[1] Cf. Tuvia Blumenthal (1976: 147–8).

that are carried out by a large Western company, activities ranging from gathering raw materials, refining them, turning them into parts, assembling components, marketing the product and carrying it to the customer, may in Japan all be undertaken by separate companies, specialized in a particular task. The paradigmatic contrast is between an American and a Japanese steel works. In the former a single steel company may do everything from digging the ore and the coal to delivering the finished bars and coils. A visit to a Japanese steel plant reveals that even some of the processes intrinsic to steel making, such as moving the molten metal the hundred yards from the furnace to the mill, may be carried out by subcontractors.[1]

How does the specialization of the Japanese company affect its organization and its place in industry? One important corollary of specialization is the homogeneity of Japanese work forces. A company confining its activities to one industry, and involved only in certain stages of the manufacturing process within that industry, is unlikely to need employees with very different skills. Those who work for it are more likely to have common views, common knowledge and common backgrounds than—to make the contrast extreme—a Western conglomerate selling cars, writing insurance, and making chemicals. It is rather easier for the specialized company to create a team spirit and even a sense of community. There is less danger that different categories of people within the firm will misunderstand each other or espouse different causes.

Another consequence of functional specialization is to lessen the emphasis on financial management within the firm. The language of management in a diversified company necessarily has to be finance, for its separate divisions have nothing in common besides their contribution to the company's financial results. Targets have to be set and achievements measured in financial terms: each department will be allotted a certain proportion of the firm's working capital, and will be required to provide an appropriate return. Such a method of management helps to ensure the efficient use of the company's—and by extension the community's—resources. The disadvantage, however, is that while money unites different parts of the organization, it divides different groups and categories of people associated with the company. The more profit is used as a goal of management, the more prominent becomes the question of the distribution of

---

[1] Japanese companies are, however, unwilling to farm out management functions to outsiders. There is less reliance than in the West on marketing and management consultancies and even on legal firms, Japanese companies preferring to employ their own legal specialists.

3*

profit between employees and shareholders, or managers and workers. The specialized Japanese company can avoid too much reliance on financial measurements, with their disturbing ambivalence. Instead it can express its aims in uninvidious units: tons of steel, numbers of cars, and percentage share of the beer market. This does not mean to say, of course, that the Japanese company is uninterested in profit, any more than the Western conglomerate can afford to ignore market shares. But the Japanese firm does not have to make profit so critical a test of its success.

Lastly, the specialization of the company entails a great measure of interdependence between companies. The fact that each company undertakes only part of a whole process of manufacture and distribution, means that the fortune of each company is closely linked with that of other firms involved in the process. Small enterprises depend for orders on the large companies to which they sell components. Large companies rely extensively on sub-contractors. The number of these sub-contractors is all the greater because of the way in which companies stick to a narrow range of activities. At risk of being glib it could be said that production in America or Britain is a matter of organizing people within companies; in Japan it is a matter of organizing companies. Relations between relatively specialized companies, the passage of goods and services and the extension of credit between one company and another, are of enormous importance in the Japanese industrial system.

INDUSTRIAL GRADATION

The third significant tendency to be observed in the Japanese company is a correlation between the size of a company and its productivity, the level of wages it pays, the number of university graduates it employs, the stability of its labour force, the rate of interest charged on its loans, and a number of other measures of the firm's quality. The bigger a company the better its quality, and the smaller the worse. I propose to call this tendency 'industrial gradation'.

I have chosen this term rather than 'industrial dualism' for two main reasons. The first is that there is rarely the stark contrast or obvious disjunction between large and small firms that the word 'dualism' should imply. Instead there is continuous variation. So in Table III.3 value added per head in each of a number of industries appears on the whole to increase in step with the number of employees in a firm—except in the textile industry in which many large firms are constantly in difficulty. In only one of the six industries referred to in the table, precision machinery, is there evidence of disjunction; for in that industry firms of less than 1,000 workers are all similarly inferior in value added per head to firms of over 1,000 workers.

Table III.3. Indices of value added per head by size of establishment in selected industries, 1971

In each industry value added* per head in establishments of 1,000+ workers = 100

	Food	Textiles	Printing/ Publishing	Chemicals	Electrical machinery	Precision machinery
Number of establishments	88,106	110,083	30,020	5,952	24,143	9,322
Size of establishment (no. of workers)						
20– 29	39.2	114.3	33.9	52.7	41.2	64.2
30– 99	51.6	110.7	37.6	60.4	42.8	71.1
100–499	72.5	117.1	57.3	88.3	52.7	70.8
500–999	88.2	120.5	76.3	105.3	72.5	68.9
1,000+	100.0	100.0	100.0	100.0	100.0	100.0

Source: calculated from *Japan Statistical Yearbook, 1975*: 178–9: Table 130.

* Value added = value of production — cost of materials used — domestic excise tax — depreciation.

Table III.3 does not of itself settle the question of whether disjunctive dualism really exists, because it is difficult and perhaps impossible to prove that the continuity which appears in an analysis of differences between firms or factories of different size is not a statistical artefact. It could be, for example, that continuous variation arises simply because two different industries have been lumped together. Suppose that there were two paper companies, one paying wages of 50 units and the other of 25; and two pulp companies, one paying wages of 80 units and the other of 40. Within each industry one firm pays twice as much as the other, good evidence for disjunctive dualism. But combining the figures to produce statistics for the pulp and paper industry suggests a continuum of wage rates. Even so, a finer analysis of a relatively homogeneous industry, retailing, shown in Table III.4 below, reveals gradation rather than duality. Table III.4 provides evidence, incidentally, that industrial gradation is not confined to manufacturing industry.

Table III.4. *Sales per employee and sales per square metre in retail stores of different size, 1970*

No. of people per store	No. of stores	Percentage which are corporations* %	Persons engaged	Sales/ Employee ('ooo yen)	Index: stores of 100+ employees = 100	Sales/m² ('ooo yen)	Index: stores of 100+ employees = 100
1– 2	940,808	3.9	1,480,584	2,278	(24.5)	163	(23.0)
3– 4	330,616	21.2	1,105,074	3,728	(40.0)	280	(39.5)
5– 9	141,672	59.2	881,749	5,240	(56.3)	302	(42.6)
10–19	39,105	79.2	508,215	5,545	(59.5)	400	(56.4)
20–29	9,223	80.8	217,912	5,446	(58.5)	495	(69.8)
30–49	5,707	81.0	212,341	5,808	(62.4)	589	(83.1)
50–99	2,826	88.3	189,202	7,080	(76.0)	661	(93.2)
100+	1,344	96.7	330,927	9,315	(100.0)	709	(100.0)

Source: calculated from *Japan Statistical Yearbook*, 1975: 278: Table 203.

* By 'corporations' are meant not only joint-stock companies (*kabushiki kaisha*) but 'limited companies' (*yūgen kaisha*) roughly equivalent to limited partnerships.

Apart from the statistical evidence of continuous variation, there is the point that small firms can grow into big ones, and with considerable speed. In doing so they change in organization and in efficiency in such a way as to become more like other large companies. The rise to prominence of great numbers of companies, and the vigorous flux of Japanese industry, are powerful arguments against the idea that there are two discrete or nearly discrete categories of large and small companies, with nothing between them.

The second reason for preferring to talk of 'gradation' rather than 'dualism' is that the former term is a more accurate representation of how the Japanese themselves view companies. As Chie Nakane has pointed out,[1] Japanese class companies (as well as many other important institutions) as *ichi-ryū* 'of the first water', *ni-ryū*, 'of the second water', and so on. A company of the first water would be large and well known, and would enjoy a significant share of the market for its product. It would probably be one of the 'Big Three' or 'Big Five' of its industry. Secure itself, it would offer security and high wages to its employees, together with a range of benefits—housing as a matter of course, but also, perhaps, clinics or holiday lodges. Since so many people would want to work for such a company, it would be able to choose graduates from the best universities for its management ranks, and most of its workers would

[1] Chie Nakane (1970: 91–2).

have at least high school education. A company of the second water would be rather less well known. It would have a smaller, but still significant market share. Part of its business might be dependent on a larger company. Its wages would be lower, its benefits less alluring. A rather lower proportion of its managers would be graduates of famous universities. Companies of the lower orders would be still smaller, less firmly established, and less able to offer their employees a good life, or attract men and women of quality to its service. Thus industrial strength, munificence of employment practices, and the merit of employees are all associated in the public estimation and are all indications of a company's standing.

Why is gradation so conspicuous a feature of industry in Japan that the general public can see things in this way? There are, perhaps, two principal causes of industrial gradation which can be observed in any economy. The first has to do with 'economy of scale'. Big firms tend to have a larger production capacity in relation to their inescapable overheads. A big steel company, for instance, will have more and bigger blast furnaces for the same number of supervisory staff, salesmen, researchers, and so on than a small steel company. Other things being equal, the big company can translate economy of scale into greater wealth, better conditions for its employees, and so on. The second cause is the superiority of big firms over small ones in their dealings with markets, both the markets for their products and those for their raw materials, capital and labour. Bigger firms are better able to set the prices for their products at a level convenient to themselves. They can also acquire the materials they need for production at lower prices because they can offer their suppliers large orders in return for discounts.

Industrial gradation is therefore detectable in many national economies, but it is probably more marked in Japan than elsewhere. Few countries, however, produce comparably detailed statistics, so that it is hard to know how great the margin of difference is.[1] One obvious reason for the Japanese gradation is historical: the concentration, in the last century and the early part of this, of economic power in the hands of relatively few people, and the advantages given by the government and the banking system to large scale enterprise. The postwar organization of labour unions by enterprises must also have contributed to gradation. In Japan, as in other countries, large firms are more likely to have unions than small ones. But Japanese unions, instead of trying to establish equal wages and benefits in firms of all sizes, are dedicated to getting their own particular

---

[1] A point made by K. Bieda (1970: 196). For details of industrial gradation in different countries see Seymour Broadbridge (1966: 51-2) or P. Sargant Florence (1972: 78-88).

firms to pay wages appropriate to their size, and certainly better wages than smaller firms offer.

The extent to which large firms rely on sub-contracting is another cause of gradation, at least, in some industries. In a car firm like Nissan, seventy per cent. of the cost of goods and services used in the production of a small car is represented by orders to sub-contractors.[1] Nissan is essentially an assembler of bought-in parts. Conversely, more than sixty per cent. of small and medium enterprises in a range of industries from clothing to non-ferrous metals—but particularly engineering and electrical engineering—are engaged in sub-contracting.[2] When business is bad the large principal firm cuts down on its orders to sub-contractors and pays them lower prices. They in turn must impose harsher conditions on their sub-contractors. The smaller a firm is, therefore, the more unstable it is. In even mild recessions dozens of small sub-contractors will go bankrupt.

The way in which sub-contracting allows larger firms to benefit at the expense of smaller ones is exemplified in Table III.5, which shows how Nissan exacts more credit from a subsidiary and supplier, Nihon Radiator, as Nissan's profitability declines. Nihon Radiator in turn exacts more credit from its own suppliers. The correlation between the business difficulties of Nissan and the tendency of both Nissan and Nihon Radiator to delay paying their suppliers is very far from perfect. But the table does show how a minor sub-contractor to Nihon Radiator might have been forced to wait for payment for three or four months in the September business term of 1974, when car sales were bad.[3]

The example of Nissan and its subsidiary brings us naturally to another reason why industrial gradation bears such an emphasis: the dependence of Japanese companies on credit. As always, there are exceptions and some firms are entirely debt-free; but most rely extensively on short term finance, either in the form of trade credit or else of bank loans.

Credit from suppliers is particularly important for smaller firms. A survey in 1973 of more than 20,000 companies with between 50–300

---

[1] The proportion rises to 90 per cent. for textile machinery. *Ōkurashō Insatsukyoku: Yūka Shōken Hōkokusho Sōran, Nissan Jidōsha Kabushiki Kaisha* (March 1977: 16).

[2] Richard E. Caves and Masu Uekusa (1976: 112–5).

[3] I owe to Mr Patrick Gifford the observation that in boom times the principal company may find its gross profit margins lowered, because the sub-contractors raise their prices for parts which are in particularly short supply. Note that in Table III.5 the supplier's profitability can exceed that of the company it supplies. The balance of advantage remains, however, with the large principal firm. It is better to forgo an element of profit in good times than risk bankruptcy in bad.

Table III.5. *Variation in the profitability and terms of trade credit of a principal and a sub-contracting company*

	Business term ending								
	March 1971	September 1971	March 1972 (before the oil crisis)	September 1972 (before the oil crisis)	March 1973	September 1973	March 1974	September 1974 (after the oil crisis)	March 1975
Nissan Motor									
Profit before non-recurring items as percentage of turnover	7.1%	6.4%	7.9%	7.3%	7.2%	6.2%	3.7%	1.5%	2.4%
Average number of days before suppliers paid for goods	60 days	52 days	55 days	50 days	54 days	58 days	63 days	60 days	59 days
Nihon Radiator									
Profit before non-recurring items as percentage of turnover	7.3%	7.1%	8.2%	7.1%	6.7%	5.2%	2.6%	1.2%	2.7%
Average number of days before payment received for goods	40 days	44 days	41 days	40 days	46 days	56 days	60 days	60 days	56 days
Average number of days before suppliers paid for goods	68 days	70 days	68 days	70 days	73 days	78 days	83 days	74 days	81 days

Source: Daiwa Securities Co., *Analysts Guide*, 1975.

Notes: *Ōkurashō Insatsukyoku: Yūka Shōken Hōkokusho Sōran, Nihon Radiata Kabushiki Kaisha.*
In March 1975 Nissan Motor held 55·54 per cent. of the shares of Nihon Radiator. Seventy-six per cent. of Nihon Radiator's orders on tha tdate were from Nissan.
Profit is non-consolidated profit for both companies.

Calculation of terms of trade credit: $\dfrac{\text{Accounts} + \text{Notes receivable}}{\text{Sales in previous six months}} \times 180 \text{ days};$ $\dfrac{\text{Accounts} + \text{Notes payable}}{\text{Cost of Sales' in previous six months}} \times 180 \text{ days}.$

employees showed that fifty-four per cent. of the current assets of the average company had been financed by promissory notes and bills.[1] For every hundred yen of cash and stocks held by the company or money due to it from customers for goods sold, the company owed fifty-four yen to its suppliers. The average period between the company's receiving goods and paying for them was 114 days. At the same time as it was receiving credit for the goods it bought from suppliers, a company would have to offer credit to its customers by agreeing to accept their promissory notes instead of cash for goods delivered. The average company had to wait 67 days to receive final payment for its sales.

Both customers and suppliers are frequently trading companies, which play a very important part in Japanese commerce. They range in size from vast international firms like Mitsubishi Corporation to small regional wholesalers of a limited range of products, but in most cases their function is similar: to move goods between companies and to finance their movement. A large trading company might provide the raw materials to a manufacturer, accepting promissory notes in payment, while another might act as a general wholesaler for the manufacturer's finished product, paying the manufacturer with short-dated promissory notes, or even cash. The goods may then be sold on, again in exchange for promissory notes, to regional wholesalers and even district wholesalers before finally reaching retailers. In certain industries,[2] however, the trading companies do not physically handle the goods. The manufacturer sends the goods to the shops in his own vans, while at the same time the greater and lesser wholesalers exchange invoices and promissory notes in order to finance the sale.

The extensive reliance on trading credit, which is by no means confined to small companies, emphasizes two aspects of business which are familiar, though less conspicuous, in the West. First, every sale or purchase requires companies to assess each other's credit, and forces managements to be conscious of where their companies and their companies' trading partners stand in a commercial hierarchy, one which is made more or less formal by the fact that trading companies, bill brokers and banks grade the promissory notes issued by different companies according to the issuer's

[1] *Japan Statistical Yearbook 1975:* 318–19: Table 233. The credit periods given are arrived at by dividing the sum of bills and accounts receivable by sales and multiplying by 365, and dividing the sum of bills and accounts payable by cost of sales and multiplying by 365.

[2] In, for example, the power tools industry among numerous others. See the *Placing Circular, Makita Electric Works Ltd. (Issue of 3.3 m shares of Common Stock evidenced by Continental Depositary Receipts),* 10 March 1976, p. 9. For a general discussion of the distribution system M. Y. Yoshino (1971) can be recommended.

standing. Secondly, the reliance on credit helps to ensure what would be true in any case, that nothing succeeds like success, and nothing makes a company grow like being big. For bigger and stronger companies get better credit terms from their trading partners than smaller and weaker ones and thus acquire competitive advantage. The use of promissory notes therefore makes companies aware of gradation and helps to maintain it.

The Japanese banking system, which is the alternative supplier of short term money to industry and commerce, consists of a number of types of bank which can easily be placed on a scale of power and prestige. At the pinnacle of the banking system are the long term credit banks, especially the Industrial Bank of Japan, and the 'city banks', based on the great metropolises but active all over the country. Beneath these come the 'trust banks', whose business is concerned with long term lending and a miscellany of financial services. These, too, have national networks of branches. Next in order come the regional banks, active mostly within one or two prefectures. Still lower are the mutual banks (which are not in fact mutual). These make their sphere of operations the town or city region. Perhaps the lowest form of bank (though inferior orders of financial life do exist) are the credit associations *(shinyō kinkō)*, operating within two or three boroughs of a large city, or a country district.

The effect of this hierarchy of banks on the gradation of industry is to reinforce a universal tendency of banks to favour big borrowers over small ones—other things being equal. The larger, national banks borrow money cheaply and lend it cheaply to large companies. The smaller banks pay more for their deposits and borrowings, and charge more to the small companies to which they lend.[1] Even more important, the smaller the bank the less able it is to provide large loans to individual small customers; so that small enterprises have difficulty in raising money to buy new and expensive capital equipment in order to become big and more efficient.

Another set of institutions which contribute to industrial gradation in the same way as banks, by imposing on the mass of companies their own hierarchical tendencies, are the universities, of which there are about four

[1] This remark is a gross simplification. City, regional and mutual banks are differently affected by money market conditions, and have different average lengths of loans and deposits as well, of course, as different qualities of borrower. Straightforward comparison of interest rates can therefore be misleading. In any case loan interest rate figures are rendered nearly meaningless by the habit of taking 'compensating balances' in return for loans. For unqualified statistics see *Japan Statistical Yearbook 1977*: 359: Table 260E, and for an introduction to the banking system L. S. Pressnell (1973).

hundred.[1] Just as bigger banks lend cheaply to bigger companies, 'better' universities send their graduates to 'better', and therefore usually bigger, companies. The Japanese education system is dominated by a handful of major universities, particularly the great state universities of Tokyo, Kyoto, Osaka, and Hokkaido. Entrance to these is by competitive examination, and is aspired to by large numbers of high school leavers. High schools which are notably successful at getting their pupils into these universities in turn attract many applicants from middle schools. Thus children are selected for and channelled towards the 'best' universities from an early age. It follows from this that a big firm, which is able to recruit from the University of Tokyo, is likely to get graduate entrants of a higher intellectual quality than a small firm which can only recruit from a little-known local university. Academic ability may not, of course, accord perfectly with the managerial talents that companies need, and local universities may well produce some promising graduates, who have somehow failed to be selected for more prestigious institutions; but the differences between the graduates of the best and worst universities are very marked, and the difficulty small firms have in recruiting graduates of the highest quality puts them at a great disadvantage.

Though it is clear that banks and universities help cause industrial gradation, the reverse is equally true. Banks are placed in order by their ability to lend to big companies, and especially to be 'main banks' to them. Universities are accorded prestige because they provide easy passage to jobs in government and big business. Each system of ranking reinforces the others, but all of them represent and encourage a predisposition on the part of the Japanese to place things in hierarchical order. Whatever material reasons there are for industrial gradation, whatever principles of economy of scale and market mechanism are at work, there is an important sense in which gradation exists in the mind. It does not occur to British or American people that because a company is small, then it and therefore its employees are *necessarily* in an inferior position; and if its employees are in an inferior position then they must be of poor quality, because otherwise they would have achieved greater things. And the result of the thought not having occurred is that the inferiority is not apparent, and may not even exist. But in Japan small companies, economic instability, poor pay, and inferior human material are all commonly associated, and the result is that they do indeed go together for all but a minority of outstanding small companies that direct attention to the

[1] For an extended discussion of the relations between companies and universities see Koya Azumi (1969).

general rule by overcoming it. What bank would lend cheaply to a smaller company, and what customer would order from one in preference to a much larger rival, when all the world knows that small companies are unstable, and poorly managed by uninspiring people? What graduate of the University of Tokyo would apply to a small trading company in preference to Mitsubishi, in spite of common knowledge and common sense? Industrial gradation has, in short, both material and ideological causes, and the latter are quite as important in maintaining it as the former.

INDUSTRIAL GROUPS

The last of the four distinctive tendencies of the company is that of companies to be linked together in industrial groups. There are three main types of industrial group.[1] The first, most familiar to Westerners, is the descendant of the prewar *zaibatsu*. The second is the bank group, consisting of companies dependent for funds on a major bank. The third type is the industrial family, comprising a major manufacturer and its related subsidiaries: Nihon Radiator, for example, would be a member of the Nissan family, along with a dozen other companies.

In the last chapter I described the prewar *zaibatsu*, the four biggest of which, Mitsui, Mitsubishi, Sumitomo and Yasuda, were groups of companies in which each company was partly owned and entirely controlled by a family holding company which stood at the centre of the whole *zaibatsu*. Each *zaibatsu* contained a bank, a trust company and an insurance company to provide funds and financial services, and a trading company to buy and sell goods on behalf of the member firms. These latter, operating in a number of different industries, were bound not only to the central holding company but to each other by interlocking shareholdings, directorships held in common, and preferential business arrangements. The *zaibatsu* were broken up by the Occupation authorities, and the family firms abolished. But after the Allied troops left and Japan regained her independence, some of the companies of the prewar *zaibatsu* began to knit themselves together. They exchanged shares with other firms which bore the common *zaibatsu* name, deliberately relied on the group banks, trust banks, and insurance companies, and did business with each other through the trading companies. They also exchanged directors and set up clubs where the presidents of companies could meet. In this way there

---

[1] Eleanor M. Hadley (1970: 301–15) notes a fourth, the *kombinato*, a group of firms in industries like oil or chemicals which depend on each other for raw materials or precursors.

took place between 1952-65 a revival of the prewar *zaibatsu*, and the word is commonly used for the collections of companies with the names of Mitsubishi, Mitsui or Sumitomo, which were all once divisions of giant combines.

By comparison with their progenitors, however, the postwar *zaibatsu* are loose alliances, in which member companies co-operate only to a limited extent and there is scarcely an attempt at central direction. Let us take the example of the Mitsubishi *zaibatsu* before and after the war. Before the war, each major company in the Mitsubishi combine had several directors who also sat on the boards of other Mitsubishi companies. Mitsubishi Heavy Industries and Mitsubishi Electric had eleven and twelve such directors respectively.[1] Most of the interlocking directorships were held by the directors of the holding company: in 1937 the seventeen holding company directors held between them ninety-six directorships in nineteen major core companies. In 1976, however, no Mitsubishi company appeared to share directors with more than four other companies, most companies shared only one or two directors, and one important company, N.Y.K., seemed to have no interlocking directorships at all.[2] The most common arrangement seemed to be that the presidents of two companies would sit as junior directors on each others' boards. The density of the connections was consistent with the interpretation that Mitsubishi companies were keeping abreast of each others' activities, but no more.

Instead of the prewar arrangement of shareholdings, in which the family holding company alone controlled a majority or near-majority of the shares of most of the companies of a *zaibatsu*, today, when holding companies are illegal, *zaibatsu* members do not hold more than a few per cent. each of each others' shares. As Table III.6 shows, even the total group holding in any one group member falls short of a majority of the capital.

It is also likely that the modern *zaibatsu* differ from the prewar versions in the extent to which member companies take in each others' business.

---

[1] Eleanor M. Hadley (1970: 477-8).

[2] Judging by standard company handbooks and the *Yūka Shōken Hōkokusho Sōran* of selected Mitsubishi companies for business terms ending in 1976. The interlocking directorships referred to are those linking quoted Mitsubishi companies. In March 1976, for example, the president of Tokyo Marine and Fire Insurance held more than twenty directorships, mostly of minor companies, often joint ventures with other Mitsubishi firms. He therefore presumably met the directors of other Mitsubishi companies on a regular basis. But there were only three important Mitsubishi companies, the Bank, Mitsubishi Corporation, and Meiji Life, with representatives on Tokyo Marine's board. N.Y.K. had no interlocking directorships in the strict sense, but two members of the N.Y.K. board had come from Mitsubishi Corporation and one from Mitsubishi Bank.

Table III.6. Cross-shareholdings among selected major companies of the Mitsubishi group, 1974

Percentage of issuer's equity held by:

Issuer	M. Bank	M. Trust Bank	Tokyo Marine	Meiji Life	M. Heavy Industries	M. Corporation	M. Electric	Asahi Glass	Kirin Beer	M. Chemical	N.Y.K.	TOTAL Top 20 Mitsubishi companies
	%	%	%	%	%	%	%	%	%	%	%	%
M. Bank		1.3	4.7	5.9	3.3	2.0	1.4	2.0	0.8	1.1	1.1	26.9
M. Trust Bank	2.2		1.7	7.7	3.1	3.7	1.7	2.2	1.0	0.8	1.4	32.3
Tokyo Marine	5.8	2.9		3.9	2.0	0.7	0.1	1.8	0.5	—	1.1	21.7
Meiji Life*	—	—	—		—	—	—	—	—	—	—	—
M. Heavy Industries	5.8	2.7	3.2	3.6		2.5	1.4	1.0	0.3	—	0.9	23.2
M. Corporation	7.9	4.1	7.8	4.8	5.9		2.0	1.6	0.5	—	2.7	42.2
M. Electric	3.4	1.0	1.6	4.5	2.6	1.7		0.2	0.1	—	0.0	16.3
Asahi Glass	7.7	4.1	6.1	4.3	1.6	1.7	0.3		1.0	—	0.3	29.3
Kirin Beer	3.0	1.5	0.7	3.7	0.7	0.9	0.2	1.0		—	0.2	12.7
M. Chemical	5.7	2.2	3.8	8.0	—	—	0.3	0.7	—		0.2	24.5
N.Y.K.	4.4	3.6	6.7	2.5	7.2	1.7	—	0.3	0.3	—		27.5

Source: Okumura Hiroshi, 1975: 180–1.

* Meiji Life is a mutual life assurance company.

Intra-group trade in the prewar zaibatsu was substantial, though firms did not buy from each other if they could get better terms from outsiders.[1] Today zaibatsu companies will still deal with each other for preference. A shipper through Mitsubishi Corporation will perhaps pay less if he uses N.Y.K. ships and insures with Tokyo Marine. Yet even a casual observer of the Japanese industrial scene will notice occasions when group companies go outside the group for goods and services. Mitsubishi companies may employ trading companies from other zaibatsu. Buildings owned by Mitsubishi Real Estate do not necessarily have fitments made by Mitsubishi Electric.

Frequently the way people think and the principles upon which organizations are run become more clearly apparent when something goes wrong. In December 1974 an incident occurred which revealed a great deal about the cohesion of a present-day zaibatsu. An oil leak took place from the storage tanks of the Mizushima Refinery of Mitsubishi Oil. Oil poured into the Inland Sea, desecrating one of the most beautiful regions of Japan, and destroying marine life in the area. It quickly became

[1] G. C. Allen (1940: 637).

obvious that the costs of restitution and repair would be far too large for
the company alone to bear—the eventual cost was about 50,000 million
yen,[1] or twice the net assets of Mitsubishi Oil as shown on the balance
sheet at the time. Now Mitsubishi Oil, like most other Japanese oil companies, was partly owned by the foreign oil company which supplied it
with oil. 48.7 per cent. of its shares were held by Getty Oil, and only a few
per cent. by other Mitsubishi companies. It was, in fact, Mitsubishi in
name but not in nature. As the huge extent of the damage became known,
the Mitsubishi group was notably reluctant to come to the aid of what
was described as an 'outside lord' of the group—the reference being to
those feudal lords in the Tokugawa period who were not of the Tokugawa family or its associates. In a newspaper article[2] two months after
the incident, the president of the Mitsubishi Bank is reported to have
remarked that Mitsubishi Oil was Getty's company rather than Mitsubishi's; and the president of the Mitsubishi Mining & Cement rejected
the idea that his firm should pay a higher price for oil from the Oil Company to help the latter overcome its problems. Mr Fujino, the representative of the association of presidents of the Mitsubishi Group, said, 'If
this were the time of the *zaibatsu* of the old days, then management would
have been from a common kitty, and there would have been joint responsibility. But now, even though companies are members of the group,
they are mutually independent companies and their shareholders are
separate.' And yet, as the leaders of the group admitted, Mitsubishi had
its name both on the company and, by extension, the episode. Eventually,
as the losses piled up at Mitsubishi Oil, and in the absence of any offers of
help from Getty,[3] the Mitsubishi group did decide to rally round, and
arrange a substantial loan to re-establish the stricken company.[4]

The Mitsubishi Oil episode may be worth a full-scale study when the
materials become available to make that possible, for it shows clearly the
lack of cohesion of the modern *zaibatsu*, in which no holding company

[1] The company gave this figure for the costs in the course of a statement announcing its
intention to sue the makers of the tanks, one of them a Mitsubishi company. *Nihon Keizai
Shinbun*, 19 December 1975, p. 23, 'Mizushima jiko: keiji sekinin o tsuikyū e' (The Mizushima accident: towards a charge of criminal responsibility).

[2] *Nihon Keizai Shinbun*, 1 February 1975, p. 8, 'Mitsubishi Sekiyū e no shien: bimyō na
gruupu kakusha' (Help for Mitsubishi Oil: members of the group in a delicate position).
It is very possible that the impression given by the Mitsubishi leaders that Mitsubishi Oil
would not be helped was part of a campaign to induce Getty to come to the rescue.

[3] Getty Oil formally 'discontinued recognition of its share of Mitsubishi Oil's operations'
and so disclaimed, as it was indeed entitled to do in law, any responsibility for the losses of
its Japanese affiliate. *Getty Oil Company 47th Annual Report, 1975*, p. 48.

[4] *Nihon Keizai Shinbun*, 27 September 1975, p. 7, 'Mitsubishi Sekiyū ni kyōchō yūshi'
(Joint financing for Mitsubishi Oil.)

exists to bind the separate companies together indissolubly. It shows, also, the significance of a mere name in keeping a group together, by placing the reputation of each member company in the care of others.

The second type of industrial group is that centred on a bank, in much the same way as the German Deutsche Bank or Dresdner Bank groups.[1] Sanwa, to take the best known example, is a major 'city' bank. Its group consists of a dozen or so major companies, to which the bank lends money and in which it owns shares. Among these companies are Teijin, a large manufacturer of artificial fibres, and Takashimaya, one of the biggest department stores. A bank group such as Sanwa's is substantially less cohesive than a modern *zaibatsu*, for two reasons. The first is that the various companies that belong to it, though all indebted to the group bank, need not be particularly closely associated with each other. There is no sense of common history, no illustrious name to bring them together. It is not surprising, therefore, that the industrial companies in the Sanwa group do not feel the need to hold each others' shares.

There is also a tendency for large companies to become independent of any particular bank, and this, too, explains the comparative looseness of bank groups. The power of the banks in Japan has been and is very great, because for most of Japan's modern history capital has been in short supply, and the banks, which have traditionally acted as money-pumps, collecting funds from small depositors and pushing them into large industrial firms, have been able to influence industrial decision-making. Even so, the preponderance of the banks has, perhaps, been over-rated. The availability of other sources of finance has enabled a number of companies, like Makita Electric Works, Maruichi Steel Tube, or Brother Industries, to do without bank borrowing altogether; while many more companies have very little debt. Matsushita Electric Industrial, Nippon Musical (the makers of Yamaha musical instruments), Shiseidō, the largest cosmetic company in Japan, and Taishō Pharmaceutical are all leading companies in their fields with little or no reliance on bank finance. Moreover, although most Japanese companies appear to be heavily in debt, they are not always as inextricably engaged to banks as might appear from their balance sheets.[2] This is because in Japan the law does not require that land and other assets should be periodically revalued. To make the reasoning clearer, let us take the example of a company that

---

[1] For a brief account of these refer to Frank Vogl (1973: 43–8).

[2] The average ratio of debt: net worth (=shareholders' capital) of 725 companies in manufacturing industry listed on the First Section of the Tokyo Stock Exchange was 5.51: 1 in the second half of 1974–5. Daiwa Securities Company Ltd., *Analysts' Guide, 1975*.

borrows 900 yen from a bank, adds it to 100 yen of its own capital, and buys as its sole asset a piece of land worth 1,000 yen. At the moment of purchase the company's debt:capital ratio is 9:1, so that it is financially unstable. Over the years the land doubles in value. The total assets of the company now being 2,000 yen, and the debt remaining at 900 yen, the net assets, which are attributable to the shareholders and count as capital, can be assessed at 1,100 yen. The debt:capital ratio is now 9:11, and the company is financially very much more stable. When it first borrowed 900 yen, the company was utterly in its bankers' power. Now, however, it could conceivably sell its land, pay its debts, and still have 1,100 yen to offer its shareholders; and its relations with its bankers may be rather different. Yet only if the true current value of the land appears on the balance sheet can outsiders appreciate the change in the company's position. There are a number of Japanese companies which appear to be over-borrowed, but which would seem to have very little debt compared with their assets, if only their balance sheets were revalued. Their relations with their bankers are not, therefore, quite as subservient as inspection of their balance sheets might lead one to suppose.

If banks as a whole are not as powerful as they are sometimes thought to be, the influence of any one bank, even over companies which belong to its group, is moderated by the intense competition that exists between banks. For Japan is a grossly over-banked country. There are now more than fifty commercial banks with deposits in excess of 500,000 million yen, besides numbers of foreign banks, insurance companies, and governmental banks, all capable of large-scale lending. Add to these the myriads of smaller banks, quasi-banks, and co-operatives, and it will be apparent that the treasurer of a big company can easily choose whom to borrow from. Now, as a company in a bank group gets bigger two things happen. The group bank becomes less able and less willing, for reasons of financial prudence, to provide the growing company with most of its funds. At the same time, the company becomes attractive as a potential borrower to a number of outside banks. As the company borrows more from these outside banks its relations with the group bank are attenuated. Table III.7 shows how Kobe Steel has, over a period of fifteen years, moved from Dai-Ichi (later Dai-Ichi Kangyō) Bank towards Sanwa Bank. By 1966 the president of Kobe Steel was attending the Sanwa Bank group president's club.[1] Yet at the same time the company kept in touch with Dai-Ichi

---

[1] Eleanor M. Hadley (1970: 265), who gives further examples of changes in allegiance to banks in the subsequent discussion. Kobe's relations with banks were almost certainly affected by its merger with Amagasaki Steel in 1965.

Table III.7. Changes in the relations between Kobe Steel and its major banks 1960–75

	Fiscal year								
	1960 %	1962 %	1964 %	1966 %	1968 %	1970 %	1972 %	1974 %	1975 %
Percentage of Kobe's short-term debt provided by:									
Sanwa Bank	19.2	18.1	18.6	27.4	27.9	25.3	21.7	17.6	17.1
Dai-Ichi Kangyō Bank*	20.8	32.0	35.2	27.4	27.9	25.3	21.7	17.6	17.1
Taiyō Kobe Bank†								13.7	11.7
Percentage of Kobe's long-term debt provided by:									
Sanwa Bank	0.5	0.7	0.2	0.6	0.6	0.3	1.6	2.1	2.2
Industrial Bank of Japan	15.7	12.1	15.0	12.6	12.6	10.6	9.8	8.6	9.5
Long-Term Credit Bank of Japan	11.4	9.7	11.9	11.7	10.2	8.6	7.9	6.3	5.9
Yasuda Trust	n.a.	n.a.	n.a.	13.6	12.4	11.8	10.2	8.3	8.4
Percentage of Kobe's issued share capital held by:									
Sanwa Bank	1.20	1.25	1.25	3.97	3.97	4.10	4.44	4.44	4.44
Dai-Ichi Kangyō Bank	1.75	1.78	1.80	3.93	3.93	4.07	4.42	4.42	4.41
Taiyō Kobe Bank								3.11	3.11
Industrial Bank of Japan	n.a.	n.a.	n.a.	1.46	1.71	1.84	2.17	2.04	2.28
Yasuda Trust	n.a.	n.a.	n.a.	1.61	1.68	1.89	1.85	1.78	1.85

Source: Ōkurashō Insatsukyoku: Yūka Shōken Hōkokusho Sōran, Kabushiki Kaisha Kōbe Seikōsho.

* Figures for years up to 1971 refer to Dai-Ichi Bank only. Nippon Kangyō Bank, which merged with Dai-Ichi in that year, had little business with Kobe Steel.
† Taiyō Kobe Bank was formed by merger in 1973.

Kangyō, and the inference is that it may have been playing off the two rival banks against each other. Note also the correlation between shareholdings and loans.

Bank groups suffer, therefore, from an inherent defect, that the more successful their member companies are, the less likely they are to remain largely under the control of the central bank. Bank groups are also liable to be affected adversely by the government's recent policy of requiring banks to keep their loans to any one company to below a certain proportion of the bank's capital.[1] Since the capital of Japanese banks is small in relation to their loans, some banks will have to reduce their loans to favoured customers and so risk losing influence over them. In the longer run the coherence of bank groups is further threatened by the prospect that capital will no longer be in short supply, and that other sources of capital than the domestic banks, notably the stock exchange at home and banks and underwriters from abroad, will become relatively more important.

The last type of industrial group is formed round a large manufacturing company such as Hitachi, Nissan, or Toyota, and consists of a constellation of subsidiaries, affiliates and sub-contractors. Table III.8 shows details of some of the more important companies of the Matsushita Electric Industrial group.

Around the major company and each of the important affiliates and associates in a group like Matsushita there will be dozens, perhaps even hundreds, of smaller suppliers and sales companies, in which one or other of the Matsushita companies may have a shareholding. The group as a whole will present a clear example both of specialization and of industrial gradation. Nearly every company will be engaged in a narrow range of activities, so that each will be dependent on the rest. At the same time every company will have its place in a hierarchy, with the large, powerful and stable leaders of the group at the top, and companies of decreasing size, stability and efficiency arranged beneath them. The order will be maintained in the way already explained, by sub-contracting and the extension of credit.

Groups like this are formed by a combination of two processes. One is the conscription into the group of small companies which come to depend on large group members for their custom or their credit. The other is the hiving off of specialized divisions from the large companies at the centre

---

[1] The banks still have a period of grace before they have to comply. *Nihon Keizai Shinbun*, 26 December 1974, p. 3, 'Ōguchi yūshi kisei no jisshi yōryō o tsūtatsu' (Communication of the main points of the administration of the large-scale financing regulations).

Table III.8. Selected companies belonging to the Matsushita group, 1976

	Percentage of equity owned by M.E.I. in 1976* %	Annual Sales ('000 m yen)	Business (% of sales)
Leaders			
Matsushita Electric Industrial	—	1,066	Radio equipment (46%), household electrical goods (36%)
Matsushita Electric Works	27.1	266	Lighting, electrical installation (57%), building materials (23%)
Subsidiaries			
Matsushita Electric Trading	52.2	372	Export-import (100%)
Victor Company of Japan	51.1	110	Stereo, etc. (48%), TV (29%)
Matsushita Reiki	53.0	98	Refrigerators (68%), freezing equipment, air conditioners (17%)
Matsushita Communication	73.5	72	Communications equipment (21%), electronic equipment (21%), audio-visual (27%), automobile equipment (31%)
Matsushita-Kotobuki	66.6	53	Electrical goods, especially heaters (75%)
Matsushita Seikō	52.5	45	Air conditioners and coolers (82%)
Kyūshū Matsushita Electric	61.8	34	Radio equipment (55%), electrical engineering (25%)
Associates			
National House†	33.3	35	Housing materials (69%), houses (15%), land (16%)
Fukuoka Paper	40.3	24	Corrugated board (83%)
Miyata Industries	45.0 (13 mths.)	17	Bicycles (71%), fire extinguishers (21%)
Asahi National Lighting†	22.1	10	Domestic lighting (87%)

Source: *Tōyō Keizai Shinpōsha: Kaisha Shikihō*, 1977 (1st quarter).

* Group companies have different year ends so that sales and shareholding figures are not strictly comparable.

† Matsushita Electric Works had as many shares as Matsushita Electric Industrial in these companies.

of the group. I have already given a brief account of this second process, but I should perhaps say something more about why it takes place. It is easy enough to see why Japanese firms establish subsidiaries. If the main firm is trying to diversify into a new business, then the creation of a subsidiary, a distinct and separate corporation in law, can have legal and administrative advantages. The establishment of a subsidiary may also be good for morale. It is easier to give loyalty to a separate small company, even if it is owned by another firm, than to the Fine Chemicals Division of a huge organization; and more satisfactory to be a director of the former than assistant chief manager of the latter. These arguments apply in the West as much as Japan, but in Japan there is the additional reason that people think it natural that a company should belong to one industry, and desirable that it should have the homogeneous work force that specialization permits.

But why is a Japanese subsidiary given so much more latitude than a Western one, so that subsidiaries and parents form relatively loose industrial groups rather than centralized conglomerates? One important advantage is that the arrangement allows the parent company to be very flexible in its dealings with outside firms. Each ostensibly independent subsidiary or associate in a group can have a different set of relations with rival suppliers or trading partners, in a way that mere divisions of a large company cannot. The group as a whole can therefore distribute its patronage widely. The Matsushita companies, for example, rely on—or rather use, for the degree of dependence is low—a number of banks. Most call Sumitomo their main bank, but Reiki associates itself with Daiwa and Nippon Victor with the Industrial Bank of Japan. In this way certain group companies can develop relations with the major rivals of Sumitomo, but without endangering the group's general commitment to that bank.

A second reason why parent companies give their subsidiaries, and particularly their successful subsidiaries, a considerable degree of freedom is in order to enable the subsidiaries to be listed on stock exchanges. Once a subsidiary is listed, the large number of its shares which are held by the parent company become much more freely negotiable. The parent company can sell some, and so reap the benefits of its diversification; but without necessarily relinquishing ultimate control over the subsidiary. I said earlier that in the West successful subsidiaries tend to be given less, rather than more independence, in proportion to their importance to the parent company. There are, however, a few examples of semi-independent subsidiaries. Until recently the relations between Studebaker-

Worthington and Masoneilan in the United States, and between ICI and Imperial Metal Industries in Britain, were comparable with those between Japanese parent and subsidiary companies; though in both cases circumstances have changed and the comparison can no longer be made.

There is another reason why confederations consisting of parent and semi-independent subsidiary companies are so common in Japan. It is, however, a reason that applies less to the Matsushita group,[1] which is outstandingly powerful and well-managed, than to certain others. This is that such confederations allow the managements of the large companies at their centres scope for smoothing over difficulties and concealing problems from the public. Because until 1977 there was no need for Japanese companies to prepare consolidated accounts, a parent company could use its influence over a subsidiary to represent its own accounts in a favourable way. The parent could, for example, sell its goods to a sales subsidiary and accept the subsidiary's notes in payment. The parent company's sales would appear to be growing—at least to anyone who did not consider whether the sales subsidiary really had sold the goods to the general public. The more subsidiaries a parent company had, and the more independent their management seemed to be, the more difficult it became to determine the true state of the parent.[2] Since 1977, Japanese companies have been required to consolidate companies in which they own more than fifty per cent. of the shares, but the methods of 'window-dressing' accounts can easily be applied in much the same way in cases where the main company owns less than a majority shareholding in its associate. The main company may still be able to induce the lesser one to help it conceal business problems, not only because of its large shareholding, but also because it dominates the business of the smaller company, guarantees its loans, or buys its raw materials.

What do the industrial groups of various types have in common? One feature shared by all is a sense of community. In the case of the new *zaibatsu* the sense of community, the idea that certain companies with

---

[1] Matsushita, which is listed on several stock exchanges outside Japan, has prepared Western-style consolidated accounts for many years.

[2] As a result frauds have been easy to perpetrate. One of the biggest was the affair of Nihon Netsugaku, a domestic air conditioning company which collapsed in 1974. Netsugaku used an unquoted manufacturing subsidiary as a means of creating fictitious business. The parent company and subsidiary were also said to have borrowed large sums from different sets of banks. See *Nihon Keizai Shinbun*, 11 August 1974, p. 11, 'Nichi Netsugaku: fukuzatsu na funshoku no teguchi' (Nihon Netsugaku: complicated techniques of window dressing).

common origins ought still to be associated with each other, is the principal reason why there is a community at all. Even where the group hangs together for material reasons, the members of the group recognize that they are connected with each other and that the informed public is aware of the connection. A second feature of all the industrial groups is that they are hierarchically organized, and that industrial gradation is evident in all of them. The new *zaibatsu* are led by vast firms like Mitsubishi Heavy Industries, financial institutions like Mitsubishi Bank, and trading companies; these exert their influence on lesser group members, and these in turn on numerous affiliates, subsidiaries, and sub-contractors. In the bank groups, by definition, the bank leads the group. In the Matsushita-type federations the large companies at the centre provide not only business but also financial help for the smaller suppliers or sales agencies.

A third common feature is the degree to which member companies of groups are specialized. In the new *zaibatsu* and the industrial families, especially, each company will operate in its own field of business, partly so as not to compete and partly in order to do business with other group members. In the bank groups, it is true, the division of labour is less marked. In the Sanwa bank group there are two major trading companies, Nisshō-Iwai and Nichimen. Even so, their strengths lie in different areas, the former in metal trading and engineering and the latter in textiles and foodstuffs.

The corollary of the idea that every company in an industrial grouping belongs to a particular industry is that belonging to the same industry is a common attribute of a number of rival companies from different industrial groupings. The managers of Japanese companies pay great attention to what is happening in the 'other firms in the same industry' and company enterprise unions take conditions in them as their main points of reference. There may well be institutional ties between the firms of an industry. Companies may belong to an industrial association, and even engage in price-fixing, or enter into a cartel under its auspices. The company unions may have corresponding institutional associations with their opposite numbers in rival companies; they may well belong to the same union federation. Thus the managers and workers in a company like Mitsubishi Electric will keep an eye on what is going on in Tōshiba, the equivalent company in the Mitsui group. The management will read about Tōshiba's new extension to a factory in the specialist journals and perhaps hear gossip about it at the Japan Electrical Manufacturers' Association; and the Mitsubishi Electric Union people will know through their union federation about the demands being made at Tōshiba for extra overtime payments. The same division of labour, then, that provides a *raison d'être* for the industrial groupings in which companies find themselves, also gives scope for contacts and the exchange of information between companies of the various groups.

The fourth feature of industrial groups of all sorts is the way in which group members buy shares in each other as an expression of corporate relations. The constitutional and legal view of shareholders and shareholdings in Japan, as in the West, is that shareholders are the residual owners and ultimate controllers of a company through the board of directors whom they elect. It is a commonplace that in Western industry power has passed from the shareholder to the management of companies, but it is a commonplace with an element of confusion. We can perhaps distinguish two separate historical phases, at least in the United States. Between about 1900 and 1930 individual entrepreneurs were replaced by large management organizations,[1] whose intricate workings could not easily be understood by outsiders. During this period, also, shares came to be widely distributed among individual shareholders who were too numerous, too scattered, and too ill-informed to exert their legal rights of control.[2] By 1930 the managements of certain large corporations were probably effectively free of the control of the shareholders.[3] Since before the Second World War, however, there has been rapid growth in the size and number of institutional investors: insurance companies, pension funds, and investment trusts.[4] These commonly hold large blocks of shares in individual companies, and can from time to time exert influence over their administration. This influence is not, however, exerted directly by the investing public, the beneficiaries of insurance and pension funds. Instead it is exercised by professional managers. In one sense the shareholders of individual companies have regained an element of control; but the important relations between shareholders and managers are really relations between different sets of managers. Power over industry as a whole has passed to a category of professional managers and away from the individual private investor, who either buys a few hundred shares directly, or, more commonly, leaves his shares to be managed professionally.

In Japan, Professor Mito and his collaborators have suggested,[5] the

---

[1] Reinhard Bendix (1963: 226–44).

[2] Adolf A. Berle and Gardiner C. Means (1967: Chapter V and 327–8).

[3] Caution is needed because though Berle and Means' conclusions may be valid their argument is weak. See C. S. Beed (1966).

[4] Richard J. Barber (1970: 54–7). See also R. W. Goldsmith (1958).

[5] Mito Kō et al.* (1973: 197–201).

rise of professional management teams and of institutional shareholders took place at the same time. After the Second World War family holding companies were abolished, so that managers became independent; but companies began to buy each others' shares.[1] They did so, and still do so, for many reasons. One is to prevent foreign take-over bids, though the regulations hindering the inflow of foreign capital are so effective that there has never been a genuine need for mutual shareholding as a second line of defence. A more significant reason is, perhaps, that buying shares enables companies to provide for a rainy day. Shares once bought do not have to be revalued on the balance sheet, so that if they rise in real value over fifteen or twenty years they come to constitute a 'hidden asset'. Such hidden assets can be pledged, and by mortgaging property with only a small book value a company can secure a large loan. In harsh times they can be sold, and an apparently trivial disposal of book value assets will produce large revenues.[2] Another reason for mutual shareholdings is that in Japan, unlike in Britain or the United States, shareholdings are widely publicized in, for example, company handbooks and popular magazines. Buying a company's shares is therefore a public affirmation of a relationship. Yet another reason is that by buying each others' shares companies can insulate each other from the stock exchange, which has still not shaken off its historical association with unhealthy speculation. At any event the typical large Japanese company today will have ten or twenty important institutional shareholders, in which it in turn will hold shares. Unlike Western institutional shareholders, which invest largely for dividends and capital appreciation, Japanese institutional shareholders tend to be the company's business partners and associates; shareholding is the mere expression of their relationship, not the relationship itself. It is certainly an advantage of this arrangement that Japanese managements do not need to be afraid of the influence of shareholders interested only in short-term financial gains. But a major disadvantage is that company managements are, even more effectively than their Western counterparts, protected from having to deal with anyone outside a coterie of government officials and industrial and financial managers very like themselves.

A final point to be made about the three types of industrial groups is that the relations between companies within them frequently change. Bank groups are the most obviously susceptible to internal rearrangements, but in industrial families and *zaibatsu*, too, there are continual adjustments. Some companies find themselves doing more and more business outside

[1] Mito Kō et al.* (1973: 166–74).
[2] For an account of 'hidden assets' see *Wakō Shōken Chōsabu** (1972).

the group, and so gradually weaken their constitutional and sentimental attachments to it. Other companies may fall into difficulties and have to be rescued by powerful group members. Such companies lose much of their independence and may become mere subordinates of the group leaders. Among the smaller companies attached to any group there will be a great deal of movement, as new firms are recruited, while old ones edge towards other groups, or go bankrupt. It is this mutability of the relations between companies, the formation of and disengagement from alliances, and the gain and loss of independence, that most conspicuously differentiates any of these groups from the centralized conglomerate.

Marumaru: A Case Study

It would be wrong to give an impression of the industrial setting of the Japanese company entirely by the negative method of describing how that setting differed from its Western equivalent. Ideally I would want to describe how the typical Japanese company fitted into its industrial context. But the typical Japanese company does not exist, and for want of it I shall describe instead a company I shall call Marumaru, a medium-sized producer of corrugated board and boxes.

Marumaru was first formed in 1949 by the merger of three small timber and woodwork companies in the prefecture of N———. One of the three companies was the subsidiary of a large monopoly corporation, and this corporation became the largest shareholder in Marumaru. Shortly afterwards, however, the corporation was forcibly dissolved by the Occupation authorities. The factories of the corporation in N——— and adjacent prefectures were separated off to form a new company, Mumei. Marumaru was now in the curious position of being able to choose its own parent company. It could continue as a subsidiary of the original corporation, now much reduced in size; or it could associate itself with Mumei. The latter course proved most convenient, and Marumaru entered Mumei's orbit.

The first few years of Marumaru's existence were very difficult. As a result of the merger which had brought the firm into existence the company was over-manned, and there was a shortage of orders. Within the first year there were labour problems, notably a bitter strike, said to have been instigated by communist extremists, which lasted for three months. Factories were damaged first by fire and next by a typhoon—though a second typhoon did the company a service by destroying houses in the area, and so increasing the demand for wood for rebuilding. Because of all these problems, Marumaru made small losses in its first two years of

4

existence, and only exiguous profits in the next two. Nevertheless there were signs that the company was under able and determined direction. Like most Japanese companies, Marumaru had older men as president and vice-president, and most of the directors were in their late middle years. But beneath them was a general manager *(shihainin)* who, I was told, really ran the company. This man was only twenty-nine years old. Ten years after Marumaru's inception the founder president retired and the general manager took his place. He was still president of Marumaru when I joined the company, twenty or more years after its foundation. None of the senior managers had any doubts that he had always been, and still was, responsible for the success of Marumaru. They themselves were thought of by others and probably considered themselves his mere lieutenants. The president looked and behaved like the leader he had been for twenty years. Still young, by Japanese standards, for the president of a company, he gave an impression of intelligence and energy, combined with polish and a charm which had endeared him to a large number of employees.

In the third year of Marumaru's existence, plans were drawn up to begin production of corrugated board. The very idea seemed foolishly presumptuous. Marumaru was a minor provincial wood company with a hundred or so employees and the slenderest of profits. It was proposing to enter a modern industry of which none of its members had any experience, and in which large quantities of capital would have to be employed. Nevertheless, the president (then general manager) whose idea it was, persuaded the parent company, Mumei, to support the venture, and he also induced certain banks to lend the company money. In its fifth year of business Marumaru began to produce corrugated board and boxes in a small warehouse lent by Mumei. It was characteristic of Marumaru that though the premises were unprepossessing, the machines installed were the best and newest then available in Japan.

No sooner had the factory in N——— prefecture begun to pay its way than Marumaru set about establishing itself in the Tokyo area. Once again, a presumptuous plan had to be defended to banks and to the parent company; but work soon began on what was to be Japan's largest corrugated board factory on a site near Yokohama. (It was in this factory and the Tokyo head office of the company that I conducted most of my research.) Thereafter, a new plant was built every two or three years, so that by the time I joined Marumaru the company was competing in most of the important regional markets. While corrugated board production was expanding, the wood and timber division contracted. In 1959 sales of corrugated board exceeded those of wood in value for the first time. By

1966 more than ninety per cent. of turnover was in paperboard; and in 1970 the last of the wood factories was closed down.

I would not want to give the impression that Marumaru's success was achieved easily. The management's strategy was to borrow as much as possible and invest it in new factories and equipment, and then, even before that investment had begun to yield rewards, to borrow more and invest more. Though the risks were always taken carefully, there was no doubt of the enormous strain imposed on the employees by this plan for expansion. Each new factory was bigger and more expensive than the last, and too great a delay in reaching the profit and production targets might have meant the bankruptcy of the whole company. Production and sales staff drove themselves to the utmost, working late into the night six days a week, and even on Sundays.

By 1970, when I joined the company, Marumaru had grown by these efforts into a concern of substantial size. Its turnover was in the region of 15,000 million yen a year, and it employed eight hundred and fifty regular employees. By the time I left, fourteen months later, there were one thousand two hundred company members, and Marumaru had become a large company according to the official definition of the term. Indeed, though Marumaru was still a subsidiary of Mumei, and only one of a number of companies in the Mumei group, it had become three times as large as its parent; and was rapidly superseding Mumei as the centre of the group.

The Mumei group, of which a (slightly falsified) diagram appears in Fig. III.a, was an association of the Matsushita type, though on an infinitely smaller scale, with forest products and packaging, rather than electrical goods, as its sphere of interest. Mumei, the only company in the group quoted on a stock exchange, was engaged in the packaging industry. It owned three or four subsidiaries apart from Marumaru, but none of them was important. Marumaru had also created subsidiaries of its own. Some of these were hived-off service departments, which had originally had Marumaru as their only customer, but were now taking orders from outside the group. Marumaru owned, for example, the greater part of the shares of a road haulage firm, Maru Transport, which had begun by operating the forklift trucks inside Marumaru's factories and the lorries that delivered Marumaru's corrugated cases, but which now hired out its vehicles and undertook outside work. Other subsidiaries were not extensions of Marumaru's activities but ventures into new industries—industries which were usually connected, however, with those of Mumei and Marumaru. Thus, as a natural diversification for a company which had previously been in the wood business, there was a land development company, which was constructing a new suburb and a golf course. There was also a small bottling company, whose bottles were packed in Marumaru's cases. Apart from these subsidiaries, in which Marumaru had a controlling interest, there were a number of affiliates, in which Marumaru's shareholding was less than fifty per cent. The largest affiliate was a small corrugated board company in a rather remote region, Chihō Corrugated, which Marumaru had decided to buy into rather than compete with. Most of the other affiliates were much smaller concerns, whose business was ancilliary to Marumaru's.

The companies of the Mumei-Marumaru group naturally co-operated in business as far as possible, none of them entering on a new venture without the agreement of the others. Central direction of the group was made possible by cross-directorships. The president of Marumaru was at the same time vice-president of Mumei, and several Mumei directors sat on the Marumaru board. The smaller subsidiaries were used to some extent as retirement paddocks for old warhorses from the larger companies, a senior manager from Marumaru being made a director of a subsidiary on leaving Marumaru at the age of fifty-five. This practice was very much to the advantage of the parent companies, which were able to rid themselves of men who were highly paid because of their long service, but not necessarily very good at their jobs; and the newly appointed directors, too, had reason to be satisfied. The practice was not, however, good for the subsidiaries, because of the possibility of strains between native middle managements and the directors and top managers imposed upon them, and the risk, also, of the direction of the subsidiaries becoming lethargic and conservative. It was significant that Marumaru, though technically a subsidiary of Mumei, had never taken superfluous managers from its parent.

Though the senior managers and directors of the group companies kept the group's interests in mind, and though there were common emblems and occasional group ceremonies to help bring the people in the various companies together, for most of the employees in any company of the group the other companies were distant, though potentially friendly worlds. The Mumei and Marumaru head offices were two minutes' walk from each other up a flight of stairs in the same building, yet I spent six months in the Marumaru head office without meeting more than two or three Mumei employees, and those I did meet had come to Marumaru on business. Again, at the Yokohama factory of Marumaru, few Marumaru employees outside the despatch sub-section knew the officials of Maru Transport, whose offices were on the factory premises. The Maru Trans-

Fig. III. a. Shareholdings in the Mumei-Marumaru group, 1971

Note: $\underline{A \quad X\% \quad} B$ represents the fact that A holds $X\%$ of B's issued capital

The sizes of boxes representing companies is in rough proportion to turnover

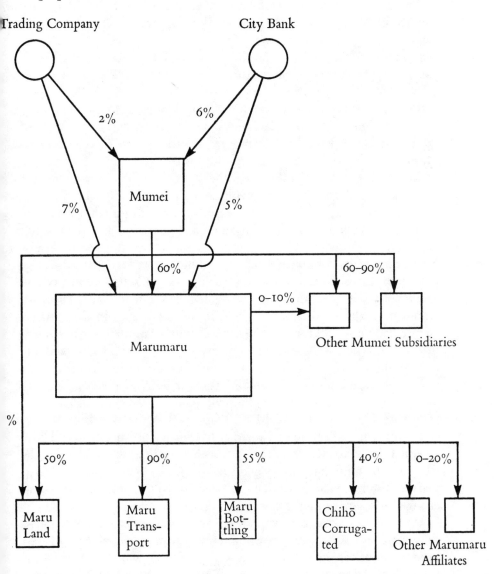

Trading Company

City Bank

2%

6%

Mumei

7%

5%

60%

60–90%

0–10%

Marumaru

Other Mumei Subsidiaries

%

50%

90%

55%

40%

0–20%

Maru Land

Maru Transport

Maru Bottling

Chihō Corrugated

Other Marumaru Affiliates

port drivers did, however, play ball games in the lunch break with the Marumaru employees they worked with.

Its work brought Marumaru into contact with literally thousands of other companies. They were associated with Marumaru in one—and sometimes more than one—of four capacities: allies, rivals, suppliers, and customers.

The allies comprised not only the other companies of the Marumaru and Mumei groups but, on the one hand, a city bank and a trading company, which each held five to ten per cent. of the issued shares of both Marumaru and Mumei; and on the other hand a number of small companies that depended on Marumaru to supply them with raw materials or work.

Relations between Marumaru and the bank and the trading company were close, but in a commercial rather than a social sense. The bank (one of those that had lent Marumaru money to buy its first corrugator) was Marumaru's largest creditor, and the terms of its loans were said to be slightly more generous than those of other banks. One of the superannuated managers of the bank had been made an auditor in Marumaru, with the job of maintaining the flow of funds from the bank through his personal connections within it. The trading company, which was a member of one of the *zaibatsu*, obtained paperboard and other supplies for Marumaru, earning its commissions by extending credit; for Marumaru, like most Japanese companies, paid for its supplies by sixty- or ninety-day promissory notes, so that the corrugated boxes made by Marumaru would normally be delivered before the materials used in their manufacture had been paid for. During my stay with Marumaru it was evident that the influence of the trading company was increasing. Its capital stake in Marumaru grew from less than two per cent. to more than seven per cent. of Marumaru's equity; and Marumaru began a policy of buying goods made by firms of the trading company's *zaibatsu*, from the company cars and the lorries of Maru Transport, to the soft drinks in the company canteen. Yet no one at either Marumaru or Mumei would have accepted the contention that their companies were now members of the *zaibatsu*. The trading company and even the bank, so important in Marumaru's history, were essentially business partners, and if conditions changed Marumaru might have to find different ones.

The small allies, some of which were among the affiliates of Marumaru shown in Fig. III.a, were very numerous. Nearly half of Marumaru's production of corrugated sheet was sold to independent small firms to be turned into boxes to fulfil orders too trivial to be worth Marumaru's while. Certain labour-intensive processes, such as the making of internal fitments or linings for Marumaru boxes were carried out by small sub-contractors. The work was done on antiquated machines, sometimes bought from Marumaru at reduced prices, in conditions which were often hazardous. Again, the waste scraps of board from each Marumaru factory were collected and sold by one of four or five tiny scrap companies associated with Marumaru. All these small companies, though legally and socially independent, relied utterly on Marumaru for orders, for raw materials, for markets and for guarantees of credit for their bank borrowings.

In one sense rival companies appeared from Marumaru as remote institutions. No Marumaru employee had ever worked for another major board producer, and few, if any, had seen the factories of, say, Rengō, the largest of all Marumaru's competitors and the dominant company in the industry. (By contrast, Marumaru men had been visiting the same European and American factories for more than a decade, and their detailed reports were circulated throughout the company; in some ways middle management knew more of American practice than of the doings of the local competition.) Conversely, when I visited one of Marumaru's chief rivals, I was impressed by the ignorance there of Marumaru. There were, of course, occasions when representatives of corrugated board companies had to meet and discuss matters, and I attended such a meeting. Though all the participants had met several times before, the atmosphere was formal and everyone addressed everyone else not by name but by company—Marumaru-san, or Rengō-san. I only met two sets of people in Marumaru who had made acquaintances of their counterparts in other companies. These were the young salesmen, who used to meet the salesmen of rivals when visiting customers, and sometimes stopped to chat; and certain of the directors, who knew the senior men of other companies because the monopoly corporation of which Mumei had once been part had sired corrugated board producers in other parts of the country.

Yet Marumaru people were very conscious of the existence of rivals. Competition in the corrugated board industry was extremely fierce. Rengō had only about twelve per cent. of the market, and there were perhaps ten firms of roughly the same size as Marumaru, each with between two and six per cent. of it. These market shares were a matter of common knowledge to Marumaru employees, and they were undoubtedly considered the most important indication of Marumaru's success. Most employees (we shall consider the exceptions later) were aware that their own welfare depended on that success, and would have been almost as alarmed as the senior management if the market share had fallen. Besides this general attention to market shares, managers and workers alike took careful note of news about 'other companies in the same industry' that came to Marumaru with a tantalizing indirectness from trade journals, from customers, from the manufacturers of corrugated board machinery, and from the relevant section of the Ministry of International Trade and Industry. Company X was putting in a 24-inch corrugator at its Nagoya factory. Company Y was likely to lose part of its business with a big electrical manufacturer. Company Z, perhaps because of that disastrous strike last year, had made a slightly higher wage offer than Marumaru. These and other similar snippets of news about companies that so few people had actually seen greatly affected the morale of the employees. For it was just as important that Marumaru should keep up with the competition in the introduction of new machinery, or in wages and welfare benefits, as in sales.

Suppliers and customers were naturally in a reciprocal relationship. Those companies which supplied Marumaru with goods behaved towards it as Marumaru itself treated the firms which bought its boxes. Both suppliers and customers were very heterogeneous. The suppliers varied from the vast engineering companies that sold Marumaru machines, to the coffee shops on the corner which brought drinks round when guests came to the office; the customers from large electrical machinery or soft drink companies placing orders for tens or hundreds of thousands of complicated boxes, to small agricultural co-operatives which came to Marumaru for a few hundred low-grade cases. The general principle that governed relations between suppliers and customers of all shapes and sizes was that the customer was always right. Competition in nearly every field was so fierce that suppliers almost inevitably took up the post of supplicants for the customer's precious business. Not only, for example, did Marumaru have to accept two- or three-month promissory notes in exchange for its boxes, particularly if the customer was big or if trading conditions were poor; Marumaru also had to hold boxes in its warehouse until the customer required them, at considerable cost in space and insurance charges.

Another obvious indication of the privileged position of the customer was the practice of gift-giving. In the summer and at the New Year, teams of three or four salesmen from ink companies or starch producers would call at the Marumaru factories and present their compliments to foremen and section heads, as well as higher officials, and offer them calendars, towels or boxes of beer. In its turn Marumaru sent gifts and regards to its own customers. Each factory would spend the equivalent of thousands of dollars on whisky, shirts, soap, beer and handkerchiefs for the managers and even ordinary employees in customer companies, and the salesmen would spend a week or two taking them around. The ingratiation was not confined to the gift-giving seasons but continued all the year. Salesmen and factory managers called on customers, played golf with them, took them to meals, and found little services to perform for them. The customer was at all times given the gratitude and deference due to someone who had been kind and condescending enough to buy Marumaru's products. Even the switchboard girls, as they put a customer's call through, would thank their opposite numbers for all the occasions on which they had helped Marumaru.

So on its own small scale Marumaru exhibited the tendencies earlier illustrated by reference to more illustrious concerns. The company was specialized, functionally dependent on subsidiaries and affiliates, placed in a hierarchy of other companies, and attached to a group. Yet the history of the company showed how over the years diversification could take place, hierarchical relations be altered, and the associations with other companies be made firmer or less firm.

THE SOCIETY OF INDUSTRY

If there is a sum of all the differences of tendency between the Japanese and Western industrial context, it is that there exists in Japan a society of industry. Industry consists of a vast collection of companies, and these can be placed in order according to simple criteria: the business they are in, their size and market share, their affiliations with bigger companies and banks, the level of wages they pay, their methods of recruitment, their customers and suppliers, and their shareholders. This order is not a hidden regularity which can only be deduced or detected by the outside observer. On the contrary, what makes the use of the phrase 'society of industry' appropriate, is that the order is obvious to those involved in industry, and indeed is partly the creation of their explicit rules. Companies should be specialized, large companies are better, safer and more profitable than small ones, business partners should exchange shares. The result is that specialization, industrial gradation, and industrial groups are made more prominent. Principle becomes practice, and practice in turn upholds principle.

No discussion of the Japanese company can disregard this context. The
4*

society of industry circumscribes, for example, the organization and administration of the company. Companies, as we shall see, have to have certain plans of management, and have to recruit new people in certain ways, because they have a position to uphold. Managers have to borrow money merely to buy the shares of other companies, or to build hostels for employees, because such investments are expected of firms of their size and influence. Even those business decisions which appear reducible to the simplest managerial mathematics – whether to borrow more money or less, whether to install a second machine in a factory – can only be taken after considering how the society of industry might be affected. Would borrowing the money suggest an increase in dependence on the lending bank; and if so, should rival banks be invited to lend it? Would the new machine displace sub-contractors and affiliates to which the company has a moral debt, or on which it could lean for support during a recession?

The influence of the society of industry is evident not merely in the way companies are organized and managers take decisions, but in far more fundamental attributes of the firm. It conditions the way people think of work, and the way discipline is imposed upon them. I have already mentioned that the aims of the Japanese company can usually be expressed in terms other than financial, in units of production; and production is something that everyone can agree to increase without reservation. But production need not be an end in itself. The more a company makes of a thing the bigger the company becomes, and the bigger it becomes the better respected not only the company but also its employees will be. The production of soap is itself a good thing, but the employees of a soap company are also working to make their company one of the Big Three of soap, so that people will have heard of the firm they work for; and also, of course, so that they can reasonably demand the same standards of pay and conditions that the other firms who make up the Big Three are offering. As for discipline and authority, it is clear that much of the discipline that would have to be imposed administratively in a more self-sufficient Western company is imposed through the market in Japan. The employees of a small sub-contractor know that the big principal company can reject the parts their company produces if delivery is late or quality poor; and rejection may mean decline for the company and poor bonuses for themselves, or even bankruptcy and unemployment. The constraints the society of industry places on the company constrain them in their turn.

The existence of a society of industry also affects the relation between industry and the community. There is in R. P. Dore's *British Factory—*

Japanese Factory[1] the illuminating observation that English Electric accepted 'without question its duty to employ its legal quota of physically handicapped'. By contrast, English Electric's Japanese counterpart, Hitachi, sought to 'ensure that its permanent employees constitute a quasi-élite force, recruited only from the upper ranges of the intelligence distribution. The menial jobs which can be done by those of lesser ability—packing, cleaning, fetching and carrying – are carried out by temporary workers, or by the workers of on-site contractors'. The British firm acknowledges its responsibilities as part of a wider society which includes industry. The Japanese firm is jealously aware of its high position within the society of industry, and is prepared to reject the claims society at large may make on it. English Electric provides jobs and so distributes its wealth to all sections of the community. Hitachi, itself a privileged organization, prefers to make its most direct contribution to privileged individuals. Generalize from this example and it is possible to see how the society of industry influences the distribution of power and wealth in society as a whole.

These effects of the society of industry will become clearer in later chapters. I want to end this one with a warning: that the existence of the society of industry in Japan makes it difficult fairly to compare Western and Japanese companies which are ostensibly in the same line of business. Toyota and General Motors are both vast companies in the motor industry, but no comparison between the two should be made without the realization that Toyota is the leading company of a complex of associated but legally independent companies, and that a great part of its production depends on co-ordinating their activities; that Toyota, as befits its high status in the motor industry and among Japanese companies of all types, has to pay high wages to its employees and offer them security of tenure, so that it can choose the finest recruits from the most esteemed schools; and that to do this Toyota has to maintain high productivity, partly by making use of the talents of its employees, and partly by exploiting, on occasion, the subordinate companies in its own group. Once these facts are realized it becomes evidently inappropriate to make a simple comparison of productivity, or financial arrangements, or personnel policies, or methods of management between the Japanese and American firms. It is by no means easy to find the like with which like must be compared.

[1] R. P. Dore (1973: 70).

CHAPTER IV

The Organization and Management of the Company

THE COMPANY IN LAW AND PRACTICE

To explain how a company is organized and how it works one has to begin with the law, because without appropriate laws companies could not exist, and because the law constrains the behaviour of companies. Yet there is everywhere a great difference between the lawyer's conception of the company and the layman's. When a Japanese speaks of Toyota, or an American of General Motors, he has in mind a vast team of people gathered together to make cars. The company consists of these people, managers and workers, together with the buildings they work in, the machines they use, and so on. The law, both in Japan and in the United States or Britain, has a very different view. In law the company is a corporation, a legal personality quite distinct from the individuals connected with it. They may be its employees, or its directors, or its shareholders, but they do not constitute the company.

Japanese law recognizes four types of company (Article 53 of the Commercial Code; *Yūgenkaishahō*). The most important for our purposes is the *kabushiki kaisha* or joint-stock company, which corresponds to the American corporation or the British limited liability company, and it is this that I shall be referring to when I talk of a 'company' from now on. A company must have articles of association (Art. 166.I)[1] stipulating its name, purpose, details of its shares, the names and addresses of its promoters, and certain other information required by law, together with whatever rules for the conduct of the company's business the promoters may agree upon, provided that the rules comply with the law.

The Japanese Commercial Code adopts a similar view to Anglo-Saxon commercial law on the control and administration of the company. Ultimate control lies with the shareholders, who exercise their power through the general meeting. This must be held at least once a year, or at

[1] This and all subsequent references are to Articles and Clauses of the Commercial Code of Japan.

the end of each fiscal period, if that is less than one year (Art. 234). The responsibility for the management and conduct of the business of the company is assigned by the shareholders to the board of directors, each director having to be elected by the general meeting (Art. 254.I). There is no legal provision for different ranks of directors, the normal rule being that the board may be bound by the votes of the majority of directors present at a meeting (Art. 260.2). Japanese law differs from Anglo-Saxon, however, in requiring companies to have one or more 'representative directors', chosen by the board, and empowered, as their name implies, to sign documents on the company's behalf (Art. 261.I).

In some respects Japanese law provides the shareholders of a company with even more substantial powers over it than they are accorded in many countries in the West. Shareholders controlling at least three per cent. of the capital of a company may request a court to force the resignation of an errant director (Art. 257). A majority of more than two-thirds of the shareholders represented at a general meeting is required to approve various important decisions affecting the company, such as changing the articles of association (Art. 343), altering or disposing of the company's business or an important part of it, or adopting the business of another company (Art. 245), or merging with another company (Art. 408.IV). These provisions mean that shareholders controlling only one-third of the shares of a company (or even less in practice) have significant powers of veto over the actions of the board. Moreover, the interests of the shareholders in the business are supposed to be protected not merely by the directors but also by a class of officers with no counterpart in Anglo-Saxon countries: the statutory auditors. Each company must have at least one statutory auditor, elected by the general meeting. His duties, which were made uniformly onerous for companies of all sizes by a revision of the Commercial Code in 1974, include monitoring the activities of the directors (Art. 274.I), forestalling any derelictions of duty by them (Art. 275.2), and checking that the documents submitted by them to the shareholders at the general meeting are in order (Art. 275).

In spite of these legal provisions, however, the ordinary individual Japanese shareholder who buys a few thousand, or even a few tens of thousands of shares in a company, but otherwise has no relations with it, has very little influence over its affairs. On the one hand the directors whom he and other shareholders are supposed to have elected are rarely concerned with his rather limited interest in the company. On the other hand he and other smaller shareholders are overshadowed by big shareholders, usually banks and trading partners of the company, whose interest in the company is not principally that of shareholders but of business associates.

The interests of the shareholders in the firm are legally represented in two main ways, by the board of directors and the general meeting. Now the directors of most Japanese companies come from the ranks of the employees, after having worked their way up through management over twenty or thirty years. Indeed, it would be more accurate to say that the majority of directors still are managers, because they still run departments or divisions of the company. There are three or four ranks of director. The lowest is that of the ordinary director (*torishimariyaku*), who might be a department head or the second in command of a division. The next rank is that of managing director (*jōmu torishimariyaku*), who is usually responsible for two or three departments or a small division. Above him are the senior managing directors (*senmu torishimariyaku*) and the vice presidents (*fukushachō*), in charge of larger units of the company, with the president (*shachō*) at the top. After their long years of service as employees, such directors are more likely to prefer the interests of the employees, with whom they have worked for decades, to the interests of the share-holders, especially the ever-changing, unknown, small shareholders. Collectively, also, the board has much more the look of a senior manage-ment meeting than of the convocation of the representatives of the shareholders. Most of the directors have responsibility for running part of the company, and are not in an ideal position objectively to review the performance of a management which includes themselves and their senior and junior colleagues. The ranking of the directors is also a barrier to critical discussion. It would be a remarkable ordinary director who passed adverse comment on some general principle of the firm's policy in the presence of so many of his seniors in management.

The boards of many Japanese companies do include a small minority of outside directors, perhaps two or three out of a total of thirty or more. These outside directors will usually be the representatives of the firm's allies in the society of industry. There may be retired bank managers from the company's main banks, or the senior director of a sister company in the same industrial group. Some directors may have been elected to the board because of their contacts and connections. Notable among these are retired civil servants who have 'come down from heaven' from Ministries concerned with the company's business. Some outside directors may possibly be slightly more inclined than the directors promoted from within the firm to give weight to the shareholder's interests. If, for example, a firm becomes unprofitable, the director who used to work in the big bank which lends to the company, and owns five per cent. of the company's shares, may well express a dissatisfaction which coincides with that of the small shareholders. In normal circumstances, however, the outside directors will share the point of view of their colleagues in the firm's management, partly because their backgrounds will be similar, and partly also because most of them will have been doing full-time jobs in the company since their appointments to the board.

The duties of the statutory auditors also include protecting the shareholders. Until 1974, when the Commercial Code was changed to increase their responsibility, the statutory auditors of most large companies were ex-employees who had just failed to make the ranks of the directors, or else retired people from banks or associated firms. Such men were most unlikely to be able to restrain the conduct of the directors. Since the law was changed some large companies are said to have gone to considerable trouble to find statutory auditors of the quality required to discharge their now onerous duties; and it is just possible that in time a breed of statutory auditors will assert a new influence as censors and tribunes in Japanese industry. For the time being, however, the auditors are likely to be the same sort of people, with the same attitudes, and no great willingness, in spite of their legal rights and duties, to upset directors' decisions.

The other institution that is supposed to protect shareholders' interests is the general meeting; but in Japan even more than in the West, the general meeting has ceased to serve its function, at least as far as minor shareholders are concerned. Japanese shareholders tend to be divided into two types, each with quite different motives for holding shares. There are big institutions which own perhaps sixty per cent.[1] of the average company; and there are individual investors. Now in Britain or America, also, institutional shareholders control a large proportion of the shares of many public companies. They are, however, institutional shareholders of rather a different nature from those so important in Japan. In Britain and America it is pension funds, unit trusts, and insurance companies that own the most shares.[2] These have bought their holdings for the same reason as smaller

---

[1] The ratio of shares of all stock exchange companies held by corporations (excluding investment trusts) has risen from 23.66 per cent. in 1950 to 61.4 per cent. in 1973. For details of the changes see Okumura Hiroshi* (1975: 44 f).

[2] A rough comparison between share distributions in Japan and Britain appears below. Note that categories are not strictly comparable: Japanese pension funds, which are relatively small, are included in bank and insurance company accounts.

	U.K. (1975) %	Japan (1973) %
Percentage of issued shares held by:		
Persons	38.3	32.7

[continued overleaf]

individual investors, in order to receive dividends and capital gains. Not only are the interests of the large and small shareholders similar, but it could also be said that the large shareholders guard and support the smaller ones, by using their knowledge and their great influence on financial markets to ensure that company managements give all shareholders a fair deal. In Japan, by contrast, the institutional shareholders are usually the banks and trading partners of a company whose shares they own. They have bought their shares not so much for dividends as to ensure the co-operation of the company as a borrower or customer or supplier. It is true that there are pension funds and investment trusts, but the money entrusted to these is frequently used less to increase the fund or trust than to further the interests of the organization managing it. A trust bank may use its pension trust to buy shares in a company which will borrow from the banking division. A securities company may make the investment trust it controls the instrument of its underwriting department; the investment trust will buy the newly issued shares or bonds of the under-writing department's customers. In general, therefore, Japanese institutional shareholders invest as a means to doing business with companies. Provided that the management of a company gives them the business they want, they are little disposed to endorse the demands of smaller shareholders for increased dividends, or indeed support any share-holders' movements which conflict with the directors' policies for the company.

The disadvantages of the smaller shareholder are aggravated by the attitudes of most companies to the general meetings they are required by law to hold. The directors of companies do as little as possible within the law to enable individual shareholders to ask them questions about their handling of the company's business. A survey made in 1977 of the general meetings of 763 quoted companies showed that the meetings of 710

	U.K. (1975)	Japan (1973)
Percentage of issued shares held by:	%	%
Banks	0.7	16.2
Insurance companies	15.5	15.7
Investment and unit trusts	11.0	1.2
Pension funds	16.3	—
Non-financial corporations	4.1	27.5
Public sector	3.6	0.2
Overseas sector	5.9	2.9
Other	4.6	3.6
	100.0	100.0

Sources: *Trade and Industry*, 5 August 1977, p. 256 and Okumura Hiroshi* (1975: 81).

(93 %) lasted less than half an hour.[1] To help prevent shareholders being importunate, directors make use of gangsters known as *sōkaiya*—general-meeting-mongers—who will discourage the too inquisitive among those few shareholders who do attend general meetings, for a suitable fee. *Sōkaiya* have a complementary source of income from blackmailing managements with something to hide from shareholders or the public.

In practice, therefore, and despite the law's provisions, the directors and upper managements of Japanese companies have enormous freedom of action, provided that they keep the approval of the large allied companies and banks which own their company's shares; and these allied companies are controlled by directors and senior managers like themselves. The directors, having themselves been employees, are likely to feel sympathy for their own subordinates, but they do not have a statutory obligation to consider their employees' views, much less report to those below them. Minor shareholders have little or no influence on management.

Now in some ways it is entirely right that minor shareholders should have less say in a company's affairs than, for example, employees. Those who work in a company give their lives to it, especially in Japan, where the degree of employees' commitment is often very great. Shareholders may have only transitory connections with a company, especially, again, in Japan, where the traditions of the bucket-shop stock exchanges of the last century still persist. It would be quite wrong that a speculator who bought a few hundred shares in a company should be more influential than a man who had given twenty years service to it. Moreover, it has to be said that shareholders in very many Japanese companies have no reason to be dissatisfied with their investments. The growth of sales, profits and dividends of Japanese companies has not been inferior to that of companies elsewhere. Yet the disfranchisement of the small shareholder does have bad consequences. The right of anyone, employee or outsider, to buy one share in a company, attend a general meeting, and question its president, is a curious one. No doubt if company law were to be re-invented today someone would devise a more straightforward way of ensuring the public accountability of companies. Nevertheless, the general meeting is the

---

[1] *Daiwa Shōken Chōsabu** (1977: 59–61). For a discussion in English of an earlier survey with similar results, and an account of the *sōkaiya*, see Ichirō Kawamoto and Ittoku Monma (1976). General meetings in the West, too, are often short; and they have on occasion been foreshortened to the inconvenience of shareholders. Certain shop stewards of Tube Investments Ltd sent a list of questions to the directors before a general meeting. The meeting closed after only twelve minutes without any discussion of the questions because, according to the chairman, the stewards had not actually asked them at the meeting. *The Times*, 24 May 1977, p. 19, 'Stewards foiled at TI annual meeting'.

only set occasion on which it is possible for an ordinary member of the public—or, indeed, a junior employee—to ask the director of a company how and why he is following certain policies. Conversely, the general meeting is the only occasion on which an industrial manager, responsible for the direction of a great company, addresses himself to the interested public. The absence in Japanese companies of directors representing interests entirely separate from the business, and the effective suppression of the shareholders' general meeting, do not simply have the effect of placing the small shareholder at a disadvantage. They also dissociate companies from other institutions and from the community in general, and contribute to the autonomy of the society of industry.

THE STANDARD RANKS

Though the Commercial Code of Japan, like the equivalent laws in Western countries, devotes a great deal of attention to the general meeting and the board of directors, as the supreme organs of control of the company, it has little to say about the organization of the huge team of people who, to the layman at least, really constitute the company. As far as the Commercial Code is concerned companies can employ people as they wish, and place them in whatever positions of authority and subordination are considered appropriate—though there are, of course, Labour Laws to prevent firms mistreating their employees. In the absence of legal guidance one might expect that there would be a great variety of different company organizations. In fact, however, a large number of Japanese companies are organized in the same way. People are allocated to functional divisions, such as sales sections, buying departments, engineering support units or work shifts. The nature and relations of these functional divisions obviously vary with the business of the company. At the same time, people are also assigned their places in a series of ranks. These ranks are so similar in companies of all sorts and sizes that I shall call them 'standard ranks'.

The system of standard ranks as it appeared at Marumaru is set out in Table IV.1. Some Japanese companies lack 'deputy heads' (jichō), and in some the ranks are systematically elaborated by the addition of the words 'assistant' (fuku or hosa) or 'deputy' (dairi) to a rank name; but the system of standard ranks at Marumaru was merely a simple variation of a universal scheme, and the rank names themselves are part of the common Japanese language.

It appears from the literal meanings of the names of some of the standard

Table IV.1. The standard ranks at Marumaru

Rank	Direct translation	English equivalent*	Legal status
Shachō	Company head	President	Director (representative)
Fukushachō	Deputy company head	Vice-president	Director
Senmu torishimariyaku	Special duty executive director	Senior managing director	Director
Jōmu torishimariyaku	Ordinary duty executive director	Managing director	Director
Torishimariyaku	Executive director	Director	Director
Buchō	Department head	Department head	Employee†
Jichō	Deputy head	Deputy department head	Employee
Kachō	Section head	Section head	Employee
Kakarichō	Sub-section head	Sub-section head	Employee
Hanchō	Team head	Foreman	Employee
Hira-shain	Ordinary company member	Worker, executive	Employee

* The English equivalent is what Japanese of each rank customarily put on their English name-cards.
† See text (p. 108).

ranks that those in them are heads (*chō*) of a unit of organization, and one would expect that the importance of the rank would be proportional to the size of the unit. In fact, as Fig. IV.a. shows, at Marumaru many section heads had no specific section to be head of. The same was true, though to a lesser extent, of sub-section heads. Many deputy heads were, however, in charge of important but unnamed management units. There are similar instances in a great many other Japanese companies. It is best to think of the standard ranks as being like ranks in an army—and that of 'brigadier' would be a good example, for not all brigadiers command brigades—in that they denote status relative to other ranks, but not necessarily function or scope of authority. The words 'sales section head' (*eigyō kachō*) on a man's name card may mean that he is head of a section that undertakes all a firm's sales activities, or the head of a section within a larger unit devoted to sales, or, again, that he is merely a senior man in a sales unit, but without specific responsibilities. All that is certain is that he is of a given station and that he is concerned with sales.

As with army ranks, also, standard ranks are used in addressing people and in reference to them. A section head at Marumaru would be called '*kachō*', and he would be spoken of as '*Yamamoto kachō*'. This use of the standard rank names gives the ranks immense social significance. Neither a rank holder nor those he deals with can easily forget his status relative to theirs.

Moreover, because the ranks are standard throughout so much of Japanese industry, a man's rank within a company retains its meaning when he goes outside it. A department head at Marumaru would be addressed by his rank when he visited a customer or a bank, and he would expect to be received by someone with a rank appropriate to his own in the other organization. The appropriate rank would not necessarily be that of department head. If he were visiting a big client, a Marumaru department head would see a section head; for a section head in, say, Hitachi, might be responsible for more people than there were at Marumaru, and Hitachi could hardly be expected to produce a department head every time someone of that rank from a mere supplier came to call. On the other hand, if the Marumaru department head were visiting a supplier or a small sub-contractor, he would expect to see at least a department head, and possibly a director or managing director, according to the size of the other firm and its relations with Marumaru. The position of his company in the society of industry therefore qualifies the rank of a Japanese employee or director in his dealings with the outside world. Those who work in fast-growing (or rapidly declining) companies are

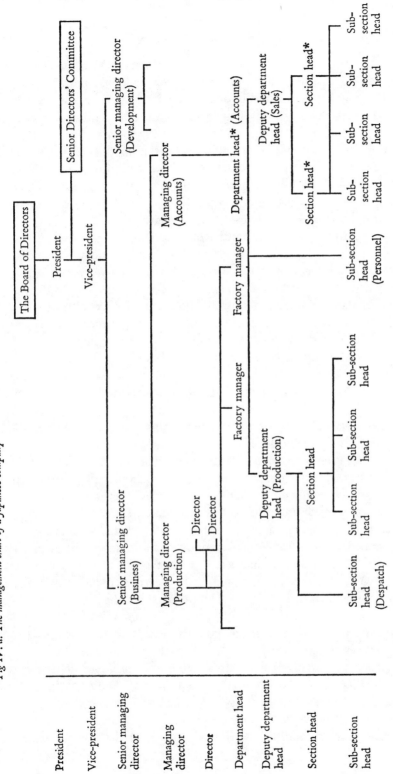

Fig IV. a. *The management chart of a Japanese company*

Note: In this chart, which is based on that of Marumaru, positions marked with an asterisk represent nominal headships, there being no unit for the holder of the position to head.

likely to be most aware of this. The senior managers at Marumaru could not, fifteen years earlier, have gone to see even a deputy head of a big firm without an appointment, but once Marumaru had achieved a certain size it had become permissible for them to ring up a department head and suggest a game of golf. As Marumaru had become more important, their own status had improved. This continuity in the ranking of companies and of people, made easy by the standard ranks, constitutes an incentive for anyone who works in a company to help make his company large and famous. For he may gain almost as much if it improves its position in the society of industry as if he moves up the standard ranks.

Within a company the most significant feature of the standard ranks is, quite simply, that everyone in the company is placed on them. This means that senior and junior, superordinate and subordinate workers in a company can see themselves as being on the same ladder, rather than as being in separate categories or classes. The standard ranks also supply a common frame of reference for people in different departments or sections doing different kinds of job. A worker on the shop floor can look forward to becoming first a sub-section head and then a section head, with exactly the same privileges as sub-section heads and section heads in the sales department or the accounts section, who might be university graduates.

The unifying influence of the standard ranks was very evident at Marumaru. There, as in all Japanese companies, there was a statutory distinction between directors and employees. The directors were ostensibly there to look after the interests of the shareholders, and were not employed by the company nor subject to its rules. Neither directors nor employees paid much attention to this distinction. Instead they thought of directors simply as the occupants of the highest standard ranks, who for the most part had worked their way up from the lowest ones. In the course of that progress they had risen to the rank of department head. Then, when they had been appointed to the board, they had resigned as employees and taken their retirement allowances; but they had continued to do the same jobs as before, and to hold the same rank of department head concurrently with that of director. Eventually the director department heads would continue up the standard ranks, becoming managing directors or senior managing directors; while the employee department heads would stay in that rank, until they were either promoted to directorships or else until they retired at fifty-five. (Directors, who had, of course, already retired, stayed on the board indefinitely.) Becoming a director, therefore, was a precondition of future progress in the standard ranks, rather than the acquisition of a new role, entirely different from that of an employee.

A second classificatory distinction, that between managers and workers, was in some ways of even less consequence than that between directors and employees. The definition of a manager at Marumaru—and no Japanese word corresponded precisely with the English[1]—would have been someone in the standard ranks who was not a member of the company union. The line between being and not being a union member was set, more or less arbitrarily, between the standard ranks of team head and sub-section head. Ordinary company members and team heads were required to be members of the union;[2] sub-section heads and higher ranks were excluded from membership, and could therefore be counted as managers. The passage from union membership to management was much easier than that from employee to director. Once a man had become a team leader he was almost certain to pass up the standard ranks and become a sub-section head within two or three years of his appointment. The transition was made almost imperceptible because the duties of sub-section heads were usually very similar to those of team leaders, and because the fact that they were managers, far from making the sub-section heads better off usually made them poorer. They were no longer eligible for overtime payments and were liable to have their bonuses reduced or paid in arrears if the company was in difficulty.

The organization of Marumaru as a unified, classless hierarchy was evident from the way in which people in the different standard ranks were treated. As a man passed up the standard ranks he naturally received better pay and bigger allowances. The size of his desk and the capacity of his clothes locker increased. He was able, when travelling on company business, to spend more money on hotels. But for the most part the variations in privilege were continuous. There were remarkably few

[1] Several Japanese words can be used to translate 'manager'. The word 'keieisha' literally means 'manager', but is used largely to refer to directors, usually in the context of management-union relations. 'Kanrishokusha' is the formal phrase denoting those employees (i.e. not directors) excluded from the union on grounds of seniority. I scarcely ever heard this phrase at Marumaru, though cognates of the word 'kanri' (supervision, administration, management, control) were used by sub-section heads, who were themselves technically managers, when complaining about the incompetence of those immediately above them. 'Tantōsha' means 'person responsible'. Many Japanese companies are coming to use this word and, indeed, the English word 'manager' itself, to designate functional responsibility, as in 'sales manager'. 'Jōshi', strictly speaking, means 'superior', but it is often used to denote those in the management ranks above the speaker. None of these words, however, expresses the idea of a category of rulers as opposed to a category of those who are ruled.

[2] Except if they worked in certain strategically important sections, such as the research department, the personnel department, or on the telephone switchboards.

privileges available only to those above a certain station. There were no special dining rooms for managers or directors, for everyone ate together. Nor were there any separate lavatories. Everyone wore the same work clothes, except that different standard ranks had caps with different coloured bands.

These arrangements were reflected in informal behaviour. Everyone was acutely aware of relative rank. Before a committee meeting, for example, two or three minutes would be spent seating the participants in the correct order. When a set of employees went out together for an evening on the town the senior members would automatically assume the roles of hosts, choosing the bars they should go to and, of course, paying for most of the drinks. The less senior members would pay for drinks at the cheaper bars, and the juniors in the party would probably not pay at all. But despite the consciousness of rank, people rarely saw themselves as members of one group ranged in opposition to another, as workers against managers, seniors against juniors, or administrative staff against production workers—though there were occasionally times when such perceptions were possible.

Not all Japanese companies present quite such a simple and harmonious picture of unified hierarchy as Marumaru. Marumaru was a relatively small company, where most people knew at least a third or half of all the other company members. It was also a rapidly growing firm, with plenty of opportunities for promotion from worker to manager or manager to director. In some large Japanese companies workers above and below certain standard ranks are categorized as staff (*shokuin*) and workers (*kōin*) —though Dore's Hitachi was apparently very like Marumaru.[1] Even in smaller companies, slower growth or an unhappy history of labour relations can bring about a sharp division between management and workers, as in the Tokyo diecast factory studied by Robert Cole.[2] It is also very possible that in family firms, where directors, unlike the directors of most Japanese companies, are also large shareholders, there may be a distinction between board and management which did not exist at Marumaru. Nevertheless it is still true that the system of standard ranks contributes to a sense of a united community, and helps preclude conceptions of 'them' and 'us'.

If the standard ranks can unify a company by putting different types of people on comparable terms, they can also cause a number of organizational problems. One is that there may be a need for a larger or smaller

[1] R. P. Dore (1973: 224–7).
[2] Robert E. Cole (1971: 62–6, 213–24).

number of sets of superiors and subordinates within one part of a company than the standard ranks provide. A common solution to this problem is to establish subsidiary ranks, such as 'deputy section head', and to set up a system of grades, so that section heads of higher and lower grades can be distinguished. A second problem is that common rank names make possible invidious comparisons between unrelated units of the company. A unit will have prestige in proportion to the rank of its leader. If the leader is of low rank, morale may be poor, partly because the unit's interests will not be well represented against the interests of units with higher ranking leaders, and partly because opportunities for promotion within the unit will be fewer.

Another difficulty caused by the standard ranks is that since they are marks of status rather than commissions of authority, and since men are called by their ranks, a man comes to feel that his rank attaches to his person and not to his office. If he is transferred, therefore, he expects to keep his rank. A section head must either move to the headship of another section or, if there is no section for him to head, he must be put between a deputy head and a sub-section head.

One common method of dealing with such awkward issues is by some form of manipulation of the management chart. At Marumaru, for example, the company was at one stage divided into two divisions, the development division and the executive division, each headed by a vice-president. The vice-president of the development division was sent to help establish a new subsidiary, leaving a problematical gap in the ranks. If the place at the head of that division were to have been taken by a senior managing director, the new incumbent would have had to be made vice-president, to put him on equal terms with the head of the executive division. Apart from the difficulty of choosing the right senior managing director for promotion, there was the question of what would happen when the new subsidiary was established and the original vice-president returned to Marumaru. An elaborate reorganization of divisions and departments took place and was presented to the company as a grand attempt to increase the efficiency of the factories. In point of fact, of course, the reorganization had little or nothing to do with the factories, and was merely a means of redistributing responsibilities at the top of the company so that no one's standard rank need be altered. Similar apparently fundamental changes in organization had occurred at least annually in Marumaru's past, no doubt for the same sort of reason.[1]

When a similar problem arose as a result of transfers or movements of

[1] They also occurred at the provincial bank studied by Thomas P. Rohlen (1974: 31).

middle managers a different tactic had to be adopted, because it would have been impracticable to reorganize an entire factory for every transfer. Consider the case of a man newly promoted to section head, and put in charge of a unit usually headed by a deputy manager. Because the man had only just become a section head, it would have caused resentment among other section heads and deputy heads if he were to be made a deputy manager on taking up the post. Yet it would have been equally unacceptable to decree that the unit would from now on be the province of a section head, for that would have upset morale within the unit, as well as the unit's relations with other parts of the organization. The solution would be to give the section head effective charge of the unit, but subordinate him to an absent deputy manager. This device was employed so often that the official organization charts of middle management seemed full of gaps. In three of the biggest factories there were supposed to be 109 people in the ranks from team head to department head (=factory manager), but there were only 66 incumbents. Fig. IV.b. shows the organization of the Yokohama factory and how posts were filled or left vacant.

Various attempts were made from time to time to modify the standard ranks or even to abolish them, in order to obviate these problems. While I was with Marumaru the rank names were replaced by 'English' ones: 'chief' for 'team head', 'cap' (short for 'captain') for 'section head', and so on. The new names did not denote headship of a unit, so that had they been successfully adopted they might have made it easier to arrange transfers and promotions. But they were universally unpopular, because they made it impossible for outsiders to tell a man's rank, and caused embarrassment when employees visited other companies. For similar reasons an effort to replace the standard ranks in one factory by functional titles, such as 'Materials supervisor' (*shizai tantōsha*) seemed likely to fail, because those working in that factory inevitably compared themselves with section heads and sub-section heads at other plants.

AGE AND ABILITY IN PROMOTION

So far we have been looking at the properties of the standard ranks as a static system; but Japanese companies have, of course, to assign people to these ranks and promote them from one rank to another. We must now consider how they do so, and, conversely, how those in companies pass up the standard ranks in the course of their careers.

The Japanese company, like any other efficient administrative apparatus,

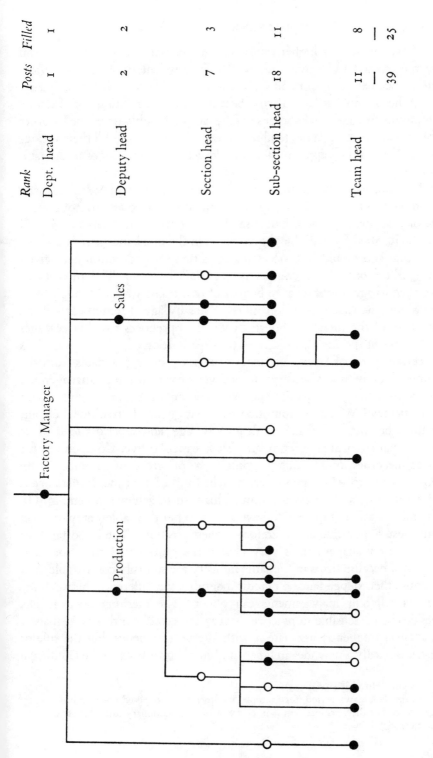

Rank	Posts	Filled
Dept. head	1	1
Deputy head	2	2
Section head	7	3
Sub-section head	18	11
Team head	11	8
	39	25

● Posts with holders

○ Posts without holders

has fewer people in higher ranks than lower ones. Its organization can be represented by a pyramid, with one president, two or three vice-presidents, between four and six managing directors, twenty-five department heads, and so on. Partly because of the 'tradition' of 'lifetime employment', and partly because of the lack of a highly developed market for executives, companies tend not to take in outsiders to fill their various ranks. Instead they appoint those in a lower rank to positions in the rank above.

The choice of who should move from a lower to a higher rank is made by reference to two criteria: age and ability. The two are not, of course, wholly compatible, though the use of each offers practical advantages and can be justified by plausible arguments. On the one hand there is a vague idea that age should be a necessary condition for promotion and, given the right standards of competence, a sufficient one. The importance attached to age might seem to be part of traditional ways of thought. It is certainly true that promotion more or less by age is reminiscent of the practices of the merchant house, in which apprentices rose by set stages to responsible positions; and also of the organization of villages by age-sets in certain parts of Japan. Yet before the war young graduates from the Imperial Universities were promoted very early to senior management positions in big companies, just as they might be in a government bureaucracy.[1] Whether promotion by age is genuinely traditional or not, it must be admitted that if rank goes by age, and superiors tend to be older than subordinates, company life is easier to live. Competition for place becomes more muted—something of great importance in an organization to which people are attached for a long time. Experience is given its due, and everyone allowed his turn to achieve something. On the other hand, companies do have a need to put their ablest employees in the most responsible and therefore highest positions. The importance of quality of management is very clearly recognized in Japan, not least, perhaps, because firms in the same industry are so easily comparable; and because their dependence on credit magnifies the differences between the results different managements can obtain. The meritocratic principle, besides being sensible in practice, is very respectable in theory.[2] Japanese managers frequently associate it with Western influence, but the rule of merit is hardly a new idea in Japan, and surely goes back to the Confucian

[1] Hazama Hiroshi* (1963: 155).

[2] In the Tokugawa period, for example, meritocracy, as opposed not to promotion by age but to heredity, assumed great importance as a revolutionary ideal. See Thomas C. Smith (1967).

dictum that 'the administration of government lies in getting proper men'.[1]

The allocation of ranks in Japanese companies depends, therefore, on a compromise between age-seniority and meritocracy. The nature of the compromise naturally differs with circumstances. In small, fast-growing firms the emphasis may be on the promotion of able people even if they are young. Managers and workers in these firms may see their espousal of the meritocratic principle as a weapon in their competition with big companies where the best men take years to get to the top. Moreover, when a company is growing, even those who are left behind can allay their disappointment. The firm will be paying higher salaries to everyone as it gets bigger. With new factories being built, even the less successful managers will have great responsibilities placed on them; and the constant influx of recruits will automatically confer seniority on those, however unsuccessful, who joined the company first. By contrast, in a large and well-established company which is not growing fast and providing many opportunities for promotion it is invidious to choose one or two out of many people in the same rank.

In a big company, too, there is less certainty about what constitutes merit, and whether it is possible to compare the abilities of men doing different jobs in different parts of the country. To try to make a fair test of ability, and to eliminate personal bias, some large companies, like the 'Electric Factory' studied by Professors Marsh and Mannari,[2] rely on a series of examinations which have to be passed before a man can be promoted. But examinations of an academic kind may not distinguish between a good manager and a bad one.

The compromise will also take a different form according to the nature of a firm's business. Where good management depends on understanding a difficult science, or in those businesses in which individual flair and talent are of great importance—trading or leasing might perhaps be examples— everyone may be moderately willing to accept that capable men should rise quickly through the ranks. Where the company's business is in a relatively simple industry, and where work depends more on steady teamwork than clever insights and inspired initiative, it will probably be easier for a company to promote people by age.

Age and ability will even be given different weights in different parts of the same company, in filling higher and lower ranks. At the top it is crucial that department heads and directors should be chosen because of

---

[1] James Legge (1861: 269).

[2] Robert M. Marsh and Hiroshi Mannari (1976: 160–4).

their outstanding ability. In the lower ranks no great harm need come from appointing men by age, provided that they are at least minimally competent. Passage through the standard ranks of a Japanese company is therefore rather like promotion in a civil service or army in the West. A man will rise through the first few ranks more or less automatically, but as he reaches the top of the company his progress will depend very much more on what he has achieved, and whether he is thought to be a good manager. Automatic promotion ends, and competition frequently begins, between the ranks of section head and department head. The competition is all the more intense because what is at stake is not simply rank and responsibility. In Japanese companies the mandatory retirement age is set very low, at between 55 and 60 for men. One reason for this is that base pay frequently increases with age and length of service, so that it is not in the company's interest to have too old a labour force. Those who retire at, say, 55 are either re-employed in the firm for lower salaries as 'non-regular staff' (*shokutaku*), or join smaller companies, or else become independent businessmen. In any event their incomes are likely to be less than before retirement. The only certain escape from this fate is to become first a department head and then a director. On reaching the board an employee retires from the company's employ, but stays on in the higher standard ranks until 65 or more. The competition among middle managers to ensure eventual promotion to directorships is very severe, and the emphasis on differences of ability at this level correspondingly great.

Another complicating factor is the question of how a company should differentiate between graduates and non-graduates in assigning people to the standard ranks. Graduates certainly have some kind of ability—at least if universities are selecting able people, which they are widely presumed to be in Japan. It is also probable that this ability will contribute towards making them better managers, especially when so many graduates have studied economics and associated subjects. Many and perhaps most of the graduates taken in by a company should, therefore, reach senior positions within it. When they first join it, however, at the age of twenty-three or twenty-four, they are quite without business experience and are less useful than their contemporaries who joined the company from high school, and who are now approaching the rank of team leader. Clearly, graduates have to be given an accelerated passage through the standard ranks, but without upsetting non-graduates of the same age.

Marumaru provided a particularly interesting example of how the demands of age and ability can be balanced, because the balance had changed as the company had grown, and was likely to continue to change in the future.

During Marumaru's early days, when the company was a small firm in the timber business in a remote prefecture, there had been little or no possibility of offering employees automatic promotion. Most of the employees had been taken in from other firms, and not from schools or universities, so that their ages were not correlated with length of service or experience, as they would have been in a large and long-established firm. Partly, perhaps, to make a virtue of necessity, but also from a sense of conviction (for the very able president was only a young man), the company made meritocracy its watchword.

As the company grew, however, it became increasingly difficult to promote people according to ability. The larger numbers alone meant that senior managers were no longer sure of being able to assess the ability of their juniors. An even more important reason was that in becoming a large company Marumaru had consciously adopted the personnel policies that befitted its new position in the society of industry. It made the utmost effort to recruit employees from school and university, and cut down on the numbers of recruits from other companies. Substantial sums of money were spent on the indirect benefits which a firm of moderate size ought to offer. Hostels were built for unmarried workers, and many of those in the middle ranks received company houses. The company provided sports facilities, and bought lodges where employees could take their families on holiday. Those who worked in Marumaru were encouraged to think that the firm was now strong and secure enough to be able to employ them, and indeed offer them as attractive a career as any other major Japanese company, until they reached a normal retirement age. But could such benign 'lifetime employment' really be combined with meritocratic principles? Now that there were recruits who might have to spend much of their working lives together, would it really be possible to choose some, and leave the rest behind? Would the employees, even the many who claimed to approve of promotion by ability, be able to endure being passed over by their friends and colleagues of long standing without becoming bitter?

The implicit answer given by the upper management of Marumaru was no. It was obviously safer to promote by age where there was a serious danger of upsetting a team or work force. It was accepted by most of the people in Marumaru that the company was turning more and more to the age-seniority system practised by large Japanese companies.

Even in those Japanese companies where the age-seniority system is most firmly established, the rule that promotions go by age only applies to a proportion of those working in a company, and then only for part of their careers. Japanese companies do not promote women. Promotion only goes by age for those men who have joined a company from school or college. Those who have joined from another company, 'mid-career entrants' (*chūto saiyō*) may not pass up the standard ranks at all, and certainly will do so more slowly than the 'school entrants' (*gakusotsu*). Moreover, as I have already explained, in the middle standard ranks the number of posts available diminishes progressively, and selection for them inevitably takes place more and more on the grounds of ability.

It was not surprising, therefore, that at Marumaru a new age-seniority system was only in partial operation. There were perhaps 1,200 people working in Marumaru in 1971. 250 of these would have been 'temporary employees'. Some of these were genuinely temporary, farmers working during the off-season, or students paying their way through college; others were more or less permanent labourers doing menial jobs. None of them, however, was a member of the company, and none was eligible for promotion. Of the 950 full employees, 120 were women. The management considered them as essentially short-term workers who would leave to marry after three or four years. If they did stay on, they stood only a very limited chance of becoming team heads or sub-section heads. There remained 830 male full employees. One-third of these were mid-career entrants. When Marumaru had been a small company it had not been able to attract recruits directly from schools, and most of its employees had come from other companies. In those days mid-career entrants were not discriminated against. Now that Marumaru had became a large company it was inconceivable that mid-career entrants should be treated on a par with school entrants. The longer a mid-career entrant stayed the closer his treatment approximated to that of school entrants of his age; but mid-career entrants would probably reach a given standard rank between two and ten years after coeval school entrants, and then only if they were able. Only the 500 or so male employees who had entered Marumaru from school or college could really expect promotion more or less automatically.

Automatic promotion did not mean that everyone moved up one standard rank when they reached a particular age. The correlation between age and promotion was in fact rather inexact, just as it was in the bank studied by Thomas Rohlen[1], a far more homogeneous and consistently ordered organization than Marumaru. Differences were becoming

[1] Thomas P. Rohlen (1974: 138-43).

apparent between the career prospects of graduates and non-graduates, as I shall explain later. Even those who had come in straight from university had actually entered the company at ages ranging from twenty-two to twenty-seven, because of the widespread practice in Japan of taking a year or two after finishing school to prepare for university entrance. Moreover, as Marumaru was ceasing to grow quite so fast, the age at which men were promoted was beginning to rise. It was certainly not possible for a man to assure himself that he would be a sub-section head by the time he was thirty, or a section head at thirty-six. What automatic promotion meant in practice was that most of the people in a school or university intake would reach at least the lower standard ranks within a year or so of each other. Table IV.2. gives an idea of how promotion ages varied among those who had reached the ranks of section head and sub-section head.

Table IV.2. Variation in age of promotion among graduate direct entrants in the standard ranks of Marumaru, 1970

Present graduate section heads (N = 16) became

Section heads at	31.1 ± 0.4 years; the youngest at 28; the oldest at 35
Sub-section heads at	27.9 ± 0.2 years; the youngest at 27; the oldest at 30

Present graduate sub-section heads (N = 16) became

Sub-section heads at	30.0 ± 0.5 years; the youngest at 26; the oldest at 34

The upper management looked on age-seniority as an organizational rheumatism, inevitable in older and larger companies, but always to be fought against and never succumbed to. Much effort was put into maintaining, despite the odds, the meritocratic tradition. It was relatively easy to give able people responsibility without status, simply by subordinating them to phantom managers in the way I have already described. A brilliant young sub-section head could find himself doing the work of a deputy manager, because the deputy manager and section head who were supposed to be above him did not exist. Yet such a device required ability to pay tribute to age, and hardly counted as unashamed meritocracy.

In the late 1960s, when similar schemes became fashionable in Japanese industry, Marumaru adopted a grade system. One of the chief advantages of this was said to be that it would allow for greater recognition of personal ability. All employees were placed in one of thirteen grades. The six lowest grades were assigned by job-content, so that despatch clerks, or those working on the complicated printer-slotters, were in higher

5

grades than receptionists or binding-machine operators. The top seven grades, however, were supposed to represent ability. Within each grade there were ten steps, to which an employee was also supposed to be assigned on grounds of ability. The monthly wage system was rearranged so that there were three main components of wages, a length of service payment, a grade and step payment (*shokunōkyū*—literally 'work-ability payment'), calculated in accordance with Table IV.3, and a responsibility allowance.[1]

Table IV.3. The grade system and associated allowances at Marumaru, 1970

'000 yen

					Step						
	1	2	3	4	5	6	7	8	9	10	
Grade											
1	11.2	11.7	12.2	12.7	13.2	13.7	14.2	14.7	15.2	15.7	
2	12.4	13.0	13.6	14.2	14.8	15.4	16.0	16.6	17.2	17.8	Job
3	13.8	14.5	15.2	15.9	16.6	17.3	18.0	18.7	19.4	20.1	Content
4	15.4	16.2	17.0	17.8	18.6	19.4	20.2	21.0	21.8	22.6	
5	17.3	18.2	19.1	20.0	20.9	21.0	21.8	22.7	23.6	24.5	
6	19.5	20.5	21.5	22.5	23.5	24.5	25.5	26.5	27.5	28.5	↓
7	22.2	23.3	24.4	25.5	26.6	27.7	28.8	29.9	31.0	32.1	
8	24.9	26.1 etc		increments of 1.2							
9	28.3	29.8 etc		increments of 1.5							Ability
10	33.0	35.2 etc		increments of 2.2							
11	39.2	42.4 etc		increments of 3.2							
12	47.4	51.6 etc		increments of 4.2							
13	59.3	64.5 etc		increments of 5.2 to 100.9				106.1	111.3		↓

←———————————————— Ability ————————→

The upper name grades were associated with the standard ranks, so that a sub-section head was placed either in grade 7 or grade 8, ostensibly according to ability. Those who were not in the standard ranks, but nevertheless had been placed in the top seven grades, were given grade names, with meanings roughly corresponding to 'assistant executive', 'executive' or 'counsellor'. The idea was that they would be called by their grade names, just as those in the standard ranks were called by their rank names. Those with grade names also received a responsibility

[1] I have omitted detailed discussion of the pay system at Marumaru because it was very similar to the pay systems described by Thomas P. Rohlen (1974: 156–75) and R. P. Dore (1973: 94–113). A comparative account of three pay systems, including that of Marumaru, can be found in Nathan Glazer (1976: 870–6).

allowance slightly lower than those paid to people in the equivalent standard ranks. The correspondence between grades, grade names and standard ranks is set out in Table IV.4.

Table IV.4. Grades, grade names and standard ranks at Marumaru, 1970

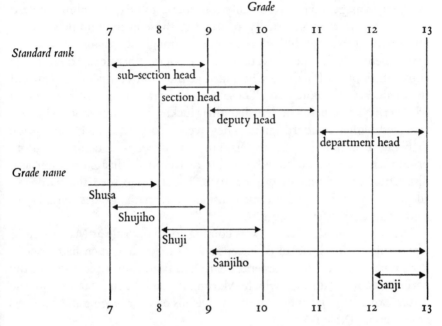

The grade system certainly made it possible to reward an able worker much more generously than a less able one, but only very rarely did the company use it in this way. Instead the system operated inconsistently. Though the steps within each grade were supposed to measure and reward ability, every employee automatically moved up one step at the end of every year. A man who had been doing a grade 5 job for six years would therefore be in the sixth step at least, regardless of whether he was better at the job than a colleague who was only in the third step. A further anomaly arose when a man in one of the lower six grades (where grade corresponded with job content) was moved from one machine to another. A man working on a grade 5 machine at step 4, for which he received a monthly grade allowance of 20,000 yen, might be moved, for reasons not concerned with his ability, to a machine placed in grade 4. Since it would be unreasonable to ask him to accept a loss of wages, he would enter grade 4 at that step which gave him an equal or greater grade allowance. In this particular case, therefore, he would have to be put in grade 4 step 7. Even if he knew nothing at all of the new work he would still be put into a step which was supposed to indicate great skill at it.

In the higher part of the grade system the grade names might have been (and very occasionally were) used to recognize the achievements of younger managers who were really too young to be given high standard ranks. They were more usually awarded to those in the middle standard ranks who were not likely to be good enough to go on to become department heads and directors. They were, therefore, honourable consolation prizes for those who failed at the most competitive stages of their careers in the company. Those who had grade names received good pay, perhaps five per cent. less than their luckier contemporaries who had achieved higher standard ranks. They were also able to take some pride in being a 'counsellor' or an 'assistant counsellor'—certainly far more pride than they would have been able to feel in the insipidly numerical distinction of a rating of 9–4 or 10–2. But no one used the names in address or reference, and no one considered the name grades remotely as important as the standard ranks.

Though promotion by age was coming to be the rule at Marumaru, it was a rule with a handful of exceptions. Some young men had reached high ranks early in their careers. There had been four rapid risers in the period 1960–70, during which Marumaru had begun taking on the features of a large Japanese company. Details of their origins and progress are given in Table IV.5.

Table IV.5. Rapid promotion at Marumaru

				Age at promotion to:			
Case	Education	Entry age	Sub-section	Section head	Deputy	Deputy head	Director
A	N——— University	25	28	29	30	33	35
B	N——— University	22	27	29	31	35	
C	N——— University	22	26	27	31		
D	Night School	19	26				
Average age of promotion for all male graduates:			30	32	37	41	50

All these men had risen far faster than the average at Marumaru, and left their contemporaries behind. The career of A in particular, which had taken him from recruit to director in ten years, would have been remark-able even in a Western firm of Marumaru's size. It was understandable that their fellow employees showed mixed feelings towards them. Only one of the four men inspired explicit resentment.[1] For the most part people expressed their bitter sentiments in a roundabout way. Some would shake their heads over the malign influence of 'university cliques' (gakubatsu). Three of the four men had come from N——— University, and there are said to be 'university cliques', alumni of the same university who help each other's careers, in many large Japanese companies.[2]

Yet Marumaru had not been taking in graduates long enough for 'university cliques' to be of significance, and disinterested informants denied that they existed at all: it was purely a coincidence that three particularly successful men should have been to N——— University. N——— University was the 'best' one from which Marumaru systematically recruited, and its graduates were likely to be pre-selected for ability. Another reaction to rapid promotion was that it was the reward for sycophancy. Those who got on were those who oiled their way (gomasuri) to the top. This sort of aspersion was very common at Marumaru, and one did not have to be particularly successful to be the subject of it. But while successful men were sometimes denigrated, at other times they were a source of pride. All four of the men I have mentioned were well known throughout the company, even in factories where they had never been; and their careers were frequently cited as examples of how one could get on in Marumaru (as opposed to stuffier companies) just on one's ability. Rapid promotion is not particularly uncommon in other Japanese firms, even large ones, and in some I have come across a similar sort of vicarious pride, as when an older department head pays tribute to the youth and energy of the director above him, who is only forty. The very fact that a man has beaten the age-seniority system constitutes proof that he really is gifted, and makes it an honour to work with him.

The four successful men had two characteristics in common. They were all graduates—D having got an engineering qualification at a night school. There had never been a formal distinction at Marumaru between staff

---

[1] The man was accused of having ingratiated himself with the top management by betraying the union. He had been elected secretary of the company union and had apparently taken the initiative in reducing the union's demands at the bonus negotiations. The man himself admitted the facts but put a different interpretation on them: a reduction in the demand for a bonus had obviously been inevitable, and he had suggested it in order to break a deadlock. The position of the senior officers of the company union was such as to make them liable to be accused of treacherous sell-outs to the upper management in order to advance their careers. The man was, however, universally acknowledged to be a very able manager.

[2] Cf. Thomas P. Rohlen (1974: 132–3).

(many of whom would be graduates) and workers, so that non-graduates did not have to cross a major barrier to achieve the highest standard ranks. In any case, in Marumaru's early days there had not been enough graduates to fill the upper ranks of a growing organization. There were therefore a number of non-graduates in the higher standard ranks: 5 out of 17 department heads and 8 out of 22 deputy department heads. Though there was still no official reason why a non-graduate should not rise from the shop floor to become a director, it was coming to seem more and more likely that the careers of non-graduates would end at the section head rank, and that the standard ranks above that would be the preserve of graduates. Equally, it was becoming much more difficult, and perhaps even impossible, for the company to promote a non-graduate ahead of other men of his age, especially if they were graduates.

The successful men also without exception came from the production side in the factories. In each factory there was an important division between the production and sales side, each of which was headed by a deputy manager, responsible to the manager of the factory. The production side consisted largely of shop floor workers, most of them non-graduates. A number of these workers had come into Marumaru from other companies, and were therefore ineligible for rapid promotion. Others were temporary workers, who were not even technically members of the company. Among all of these, and even among those who had joined Marumaru from schools, there was a high turnover rate. The heterogeneity of the production side, and the continual coming and going of workers, made it relatively easy for the upper management to promote a younger man. For able school leavers who took the opportunity to go to night school at the company's expense—D's was such a case—and even more for young graduates who had been assigned to it on entering Marumaru, the production side provided reasonable opportunities for getting ahead early. The sales side, by contrast, was staffed almost entirely by graduates. Most of these had come into the company straight from university and few of them ever left. There would be perhaps twenty salesmen attached to a factory, and they would arrange themselves naturally into intakes, the two or three members of the 1965 intake accounting themselves automatically senior to the younger men of the 1969 intake. Clearly, promoting a salesman ahead of his fellows was much more likely to cause dissension than putting a young graduate in charge of a production sub-section which might include only one other graduate. There may also have been difficulties in determining ability on the sales side. Whereas production managers did their work entirely within

Marumaru, the salesmen were out all day negotiating with clients, and senior managers had little opportunity to see them at work.[1]

At Marumaru, then, the simultaneous influence of the principles of age and ability made for the mottled effect that comes when light and darkness contend for a landscape. Here there were patches of meritocracy amidst great areas of the company where promotion was automatic. Elsewhere there were indistinct regions where no one could be sure which principle applied. Sometimes in a section where men had been promoted by age, a transfer or an unusual advancement would occur to reassert the claims of ability. This uncertainty was not a weakness in the organization but a source of strength. It encouraged people to do their best, for even if progress seemed to be automatic there was always the possibility that someone from an intake, perhaps oneself, would get ahead of the rest. The ambivalence of principle allowed people to interpret their own positions to suit their vanities. Those in high ranks could be sure that they were reasonably able; those in low that their time would come. The alloy of age-seniority and meritocracy also made the edifice of authority stronger than it would have been if built on either principle alone. Those high in the company were either abler or older and more experienced than oneself—or perhaps both. It was not unreasonable to obey them. Besides, for all the complexity of the ranks and grades, and all the equivocation about allocating them, there was, for those who wanted it, a rough but accurate test of how a man was doing at Marumaru: was he really doing important work, regardless of his rank; and did his opinion count for something in running the company? I shall turn now to the questions of responsibility and decision-making.

RESPONSIBILITY AND DECISION-MAKING

Japanese most frequently use the word 'responsibility' to refer to symbolic assumption of guilt, the responsibility that is accepted for failure when, for example, the president of a loss-making company resigns, or the board of directors of a bank in which a fraud has occurred dock their own salaries to pay for the default. The rules of this kind of responsibility are simple, for it comes automatically with high position. When something goes wrong the senior man or group of men presiding over the mistake will 'take responsibility' to lift the blame from their subordinates. Symbolic responsibility, which for the individual is simply the price of status, has

---

[1] Salesmen did, however, have individual pitches, and over a period good salesmen stood out from bad ones.

some value for the company community. It encourages a conscious mutual dependence of seniors and juniors. Those below know that those above will protect them. Those above must rely on their subordinates not to make mistakes that will lead to responsibility having to be taken. When a mistake is made the resignation, transfer or other penance of the leader of the group allows everyone to make a fresh start. Symbolic responsibility need not, however, have much to do with what one could call 'real' responsibility', the moral and practical accountability for decisions and events. Companies usually make a clear distinction in practice between the two types. The manager who is transferred because production was lost when someone misread the instructions on a machine and stripped its cogs will soon be given a new and important assignment. The manager who is transferred because he authorized credit to a client without taking elementary precautions will probably stay in the corporate equivalent of Siberia for four or five years. In this particular example the man's 'real' responsibility is apparent; but 'real' responsibility is not usually so easy to determine, because it is not simply called into existence by disasters but is ever present in the normal course of work. Perhaps the easiest way to begin finding out how 'real' responsibility is allocated in Japanese companies—and I shall drop the 'real' from now on—is to consider the way in which decisions are taken in them. For decision-making usually entails responsibility, and responsibility usually entails scope for making decisions.

There is a surprising degree of unanimity among the many writers who have dealt with how Japanese executives make decisions. Almost all of them say that decisions are taken not by one man with specific authority but collectively, by a group of managers.[1] The most frequently cited example of the actual mechanism by which decisions take place is the circulation of ringi. A ringi is a proposal which emanates from one manager or one department, and passes first around collateral departments and then to the senior managers of a company, the directors, managing directors, and the president. All those who see the proposal make their comments on an attached form. When it finally reaches the top of the company the president takes the decision to execute or reject the proposal on the basis of what his subordinates have said. Sometimes, however, the ringi is not used actually to make the decision, but rather to provide a record of a decision that has already been made, and to distribute the responsibility for it among the entire management.[2] The example of the ringi has

---

[1] James C. Abegglen (1958: 84); Herbert Glazer (1969: 88); Hazama Hiroshi* (1971: 39–40).

[2] R. P. Dore (1973: 227–8); Susumu Takamiya (1970: 99–102).

suggested to some authors that the initiative in decision-making comes from below, because the *ringi* is first issued in a unit of lower management, and by the time it has reached the upper management it has gained so much support and so many approving comments that the president and directors can scarcely reject it.[1] It is sometimes said, and more frequently implied, that the collective nature of the process of decision-making is partly or largely determined by Japanese cultural traditions.[2] By contrast, the implication goes, collective decision-making is rare in the West, and responsibility is much more clearly assigned to the individual.[3]

In fact, the comparison between decision-making in the West and in Japan is not at all simple. In Japan, as in the West, decision-making can be more or less collective according to what is being decided and in what context. But where in the West managers perhaps tend to emphasize those decisions, and those parts of the process of deciding, which are carried out by individuals, Japanese managers emphasize and extol the establishment of consensus. Their different views of what is done and what ought to be done may lead them to choose different idioms to make the same sort of decision, and so confuse the outside observer. What makes things even more difficult is that because the industrial context in Japan and in many Western countries is so different, the parts played by managers in apparently comparable positions may not be at all similar.

Let us begin with the practical reasons for making decisions individually or collectively. To the extent that decisions involve the selection, analysis and transformation of information, then the advantages of having a single manager make a decision are that he can make it quickly and explain his motives clearly. Where the decision depends on searching out and interpreting large quantities of information, choosing between complicated alternatives, and framing instructions so as to effect the chosen end with a minimum of disturbance, then it is best entrusted to many people. Usually, of course, decisions will be made in stages. Some stages have to be passed through very quickly, and others require the handling of a huge volume of material; the former will involve individual managers, the latter numbers of managers.

But decision-making is not merely a matter of transforming information. It is a political activity. Decisions change organizations and affect the standing of their members, including, of course, those members who

---

[1] M. Y. Yoshino (1968: 257–8).
[2] Matsushima Shizuo* (1967); S. Prakash Sethi (1975: 52); but William Brown (1966) is sceptical.
[3] R. P. Dore (1973: 228–9).

5*

initiated the decision. From a political point of view individual decision-making involves risk not merely for the firm but also for the decision-maker. The risks for the firm are that the decision-maker may be unable to persuade his nominal subordinates to follow his orders, and that he may be biased or dishonest. The risks for the decision-maker himself are that if he makes a mistake he alone will be responsible for the consequences, and that even if his decisions are right he may be accused of tyranny, dishonesty or bias. On the other hand there are advantages to individual decision-making. The firm is better able to tell good managers from bad ones, and the manager can expect rewards for good decisions, just as he can expect to suffer for mistakes. The converse of all this is that collective decision-making makes it easier to avoid dissension, by giving many people a chance to change a decision while it is still in the making. It also lessens the likelihood that a firm will be damaged by bias or dishonesty, for different managers will have different prejudices, and the honest men can be relied on to check dishonesty. The decision-makers themselves will be spared sole responsibility for their mistakes. But the firm will have the disadvantage of not being able to distinguish good and bad managers, and the managers may be inadequately rewarded for their efforts.

At the top of a company, whether Japanese or Western, the workload, the complexity of the decisions to be taken, and the continual and obvious conflicts of interest to be resolved, will act as inducements to the management to make collective decisions. This does not mean, of course, that decision-making has to be collective; merely that in the aggregate, and over a long period, collective managements should make fewer mistakes and run more smoothly, and so prosper, while relatively autocratic managements are replaced. To determine whether a company should diversify, for example, it would be prudent to gather material relevant to the decision from outside and inside the company; consult the opinions of large numbers of managers, some of them quite junior; spend a great deal of effort evaluating all this information; reach a complicated compromise between dozens of different departments; and incorporate or pretend to incorporate the views of many people in the final report or directive. But though this is what a well-managed firm in the West or Japan would have to do, there might be a considerable difference in appearances. The managers in a Western company might be expected to emphasize their ostensible specific responsibilities. The sales director of the Western company might think of himself as having sole responsibility for the sales of a new product, just as the management charts said he was;

even though in practice he would be spending all his time in meetings with other directors, market research departments, accountants, production supervisors and patent lawyers, and could scarcely move without their collective approval. His Japanese counterpart would almost certainly be inclined to think of himself as the head of a team of salesmen, and part of a larger team of senior managers, all working on different problems involving the new product.

There is in Japan, then, a willingness to recognize that responsibility is collective, that decisions necessarily involve numbers of people. This willingness is not simply the product of the Japanese political tradition that decisions should be unanimously supported by everyone affected by them. The idea that everyone may be involved in a decision is much easier to subscribe to in a Japanese company, with its relative homogeneity, its absence of extreme distinctions between management and labour, and its high proportion of graduates in economics, law, and other studies which emphasize social relations, than it is likely to be in a Western company with its differentiated work force, sharp distinction between management and labour, and dependence on specialized skills.

Perhaps the best indication of a general awareness that decisions are made collectively is the very thorough dissemination of information that takes place in many Japanese companies. Dozens of documents seem to be in continuous circulation, so that company members know a great deal of what is going on, even if it scarcely concerns them. There are, of course, the *ringi*, the suggestions and proposals mentioned earlier, which usually start in one department and are passed to collateral departments to be seen by relatively junior managers before being shown to the directors. There are rules and directives in the name of the president, managing directors, or department heads. There are daily or weekly pep talks or discussion sessions, at which salesmen will be told of the operating ratios on the shop floor as well as the sales figures, and production line workers will be given details of the efforts being made to get new recruits. The effects of this generous flow of information are great and good. The knowledge that he is worth informing at all improves a man's morale, particularly if his prospects are limited and his self-esteem depends upon his giving the impression that he is always in the know. Understanding what is happening elsewhere in a company helps people to take a greater interest in their own work, which they can come to see as part of an estimable whole. And, of course, by distributing information so liberally, upper managements ensure that no one who really needs to know something is overlooked.

Even if it is not really part of a company's intention, in keeping its employees informed, to allow widespread participation in decision-making, the very fact that everyone knows about an issue ensures that some degree of participation does occur. Decision-making at Marumaru was in some ways very autocratic, but when the upper management had decided on a measure it would appeal by means of lengthy discussions for the single-minded support of those in the middle and lower standard ranks. The scheme would be explained at committee meetings as an example of 'how the upper management is thinking', and everybody's co-operation would be requested. The middle managers would then talk about the proposed measures among themselves and with their juniors, so that within a few weeks every employee knew about it. If the scheme were to be unfavourably received, if it became the subject of wry jokes, or if it were held up as an example of how out of touch with events the directors were, then its implementation was often delayed until changes could be made in it. Sometimes, indeed, a decision would never be carried out at all, after it had failed to float on the exchange of management opinion.

Even though top-level decision-making in Japan usually appears collective there are occasions when it can seem the work of individuals. For the degree of emphasis a manager places on his own part in a decision is itself determined by political considerations arising from the decision. It is easy to see this principle at work in the West, where the idiom of decision-making may change from individualistic to collective as a decision proves to have been mistaken. Anyone who has worked through the files of a Western company dealing with a failed project will have seen Western analogues of the Japanese *ringi* as a mode of sharing responsibility *ex post facto*. There will be self-exculpatory memos, notes to seniors and collateral managers recalling times when 'if you remember, you and I agreed . . .', and references in minutes to earlier, half-forgotten warnings and presentiments of misfortune. Conversely, at Marumaru I noticed that every good decision always had an author—and sometimes two quite separate ones. No one, however, was entirely sure where a bad decision had come from. Perhaps one could say that in the West decision-making is presented as individualistic until adversity proves it collective. In Japan it is presented as collective until it is worth someone's while to claim a decision as his own.

What makes it even more misleading to talk without qualification of collectivist management in Japan is that there are so many Japanese companies where a senior director, usually the president, is running a large company more or less autocratically. In many of the companies I have knowledge of, Canon, Daiei, Kashiyama, Marui, Nippon Shinpan, Orient Lease and Sankō Steamship among them, I have had the impression that the direction of the company was under the control or at least the preponderant influence of one man. One reason for the persistence of autocracy in the midst of a collectivist 'tradition' (and, of course, Iwasaki is as much a part of Japanese commercial history as Shibusawa) is that there is a large number of rapidly growing companies in Japan. Many of those mentioned have only come to prominence in the last decade, and are still under the management of the founder of the firm. Another reason is that, for all the presumptions of collectivism, the president of a Japanese company is remarkably free of constitutional limitations to his power. The majority of those on the board of directors, to which he is formally responsible, are his juniors in the standard ranks of the company. There is also, as Professor Dore[1] has pointed out, a 'fiction of absolute central authority' in Japanese companies. It is the president who authorizes the execution of the proposals made in a *ringi*, even though these affect only one factory. It is the president who appoints or transfers even junior managers. Conversely, the president 'takes responsibility' for the successes and failures of the company. It is not surprising that occasionally a president with considerable drive and acumen can translate the fiction into something near reality.

Although there are exceptions, Japanese companies, like Western ones, turn to collective management methods as they get older and larger.[2] The change was evident at Marumaru, where the able young president had been in control of the company for fifteen years. The strength of his authority was still discernible in the workings of the *ringi* system. Where the normal function of *ringi* systems is to allow initiative to junior managers and to distribute responsibility for decisions, at Marumaru junior managers and even directors tended to put non-committal comments in the spaces provided for them on the *ringi* form, for fear, presumably, that if the president expressed his views forcibly they would appear on the completed form to be contradicting him. Nevertheless, with new factories being built nearly every year, and with large increases in the numbers of people in the various units of management, responsibility was gradually being delegated to directors and departmental heads. There were more and more meetings of middle and senior managers; and

[1] R. P. Dore (1973: 227), cf. also Kazuo Noda (1975: 137).
[2] For an assertion contrary to this common-sense statement see Matsutarō Wadaki *et al.* (1972: 11) who suggest that founder presidents are less autocratic and more concerned with developing their subordinates' ability than successor presidents, perhaps because the founder presidents rely on a small number of trusted subordinates.

some *ringi* proposals no longer went to the president, who was confining his attention to the more important issues. In the West the inevitable loss of influence of a founding entrepreneur, and his replacement by a committee, occasions mixed feelings. In Japan, where the collectivist tradition is stronger, and there is some suspicion of individualism, similar transitions are perhaps accepted more wholeheartedly. It is true that Mr Matsushita Konosuke is accorded profound respect and intense admiration —perhaps partly because he gives the impression of being a collectivist in spite of himself—and that the men who gave their names to companies like Honda are generally well-regarded. But the scandalous magazines continually harp on the demerits of 'one-man' presidents; and whenever a company goes bankrupt or suffers a great loss, the serious journals almost invariably diagnose autocracy.[1]

The difference between decision-making at the top of Japanese and Western companies may, then, be less a matter of antithetical principles than of emphasis and presentation. At lower levels, however, the contrast may be more fundamental. The ideal Western manager will have personal responsibility for a certain part of the company's organization, and he may be able to take rapid decisions on his own account on matters within his province. The Japanese manager will also be assigned responsibility for a part of the company's business, but he may not be so easily able to make independent decisions. His authority is frequently limited by statute. Companies prepare charts setting out how much expenditure a man in each standard rank may authorize without recourse to the *ringi*. The financial limits are frequently very low (and constantly being lowered in effect by monetary inflation). At Marumaru a deputy department head, ostensibly responsible for the production side of a factory, had to refer to his superiors before authorizing expenditures as low as 30,000 yen—then less than 100 dollars—in some circumstances. In practice, of course, the deputy would authorize an expenditure verbally and have the authorization validated by the *ringi* before the bill came in. It is not only these formal restrictions that limit the freedom of the Japanese middle manager to run 'his' part of the organization as he likes—and in Japanese a singular possessive pronoun would not be used. Informally, too, his decisions are subject to what might in the West be thought of as interference from superiors and colleagues in other departments, who may casually suggest

[1] As in the case of Kōjin, when the *Nihon Keizai Shinbun* remarked, 'What brought about this worsening of the situation? One can point, first of all, to the excesses of a management policy of diversifying, on top of Kōjin's rapid growth, and to the weakness of an autocratic (*wanman*) system'. *Nihon Keizai Shinbun* 27 August 1975, p. 7, '"Kōjin" de kinchō suru sangyōkai' (An industry tense after 'Kōjin').

improvements to his unit, or comment on the way he is handling a problem, with less diffidence or fear of trespass than they would in the West.

The comparative lack of delegation is only one reason why Japanese middle managers may tend to pool their experience and share their decision-making. Another is that few managers in Japanese companies have had specialized training before joining. Most enter with degrees in general economic subjects or commercial studies, but there are few accountants or operational researchers, men whose knowledge automatically validates their decisions within their particular field. When no one has an outstanding claim to expertise, it makes some sense to discuss a decision as widely as possible and obtain a measure of unanimity on it. A third circumstance which is perhaps even more conducive to collective decision-making is that Japanese managers are frequently not in charge of functional units. Because of the great dependence on sub-contractors and allies to do work that in British or American companies might be undertaken within the firm, a middle manager who wants to get something done may not be able simply to order a subordinate to do it. Instead he may have to negotiate for what he wants with the representatives of other companies. Thus even in the middle levels of a company, gathering information and getting people to act upon it may be a complicated political process, very like decision-making at the top, and as liable to be undertaken by the group.

Though much middle management decision-making may for these reasons appear to a Westerner to be slow and to involve an excess of consultation, there is one set of decisions which in the West would be thought delicate and to require much deliberation, but in larger Japanese companies are quickly handled, often by individual managers. These are decisions about assigning people to jobs. On the shop floor at Marumaru —and the same may have been true at Hitachi[1]—a sub-section head could move two or three men from one machine to another at a moment's notice. Similarly, a manager could be transferred rapidly at the discretion of a department head to another section or even another department. The reason why decisions about work allocation, provided that they do not involve promotion, can be made so quickly and simply is that they give rise to few conflicts of interest in larger companies. Japanese company unions rarely interest themselves in what they see as the management prerogative of assigning work. The wage and promotion systems in larger Japanese companies do not, on the whole, make it disadvantageous to be

[1] R. P. Dore (1973: 247).

transferred; so that employees are even prepared in many cases to accept that they themselves need hardly be consulted. Besides, to refuse a transfer might prejudice a man's chances of advancement. In bigger companies, therefore, work allocations and transfers may be sufficiently uncontentious to be decided upon quickly, and without too much fussy committee work or the need to collect signatures and opinions. In smaller Japanese companies, however, there is more piecework, and transferring a man may require more time and discussion.

One of the most difficult points to establish in the organization of the Japanese company is how far responsibility accords with status. There are so many types of Japanese company that the question may not be appropriate. Status is usually finely graded, but responsibilities tend to overlap in a complicated fashion. Then, as I have already mentioned, for a man to claim or disclaim responsibility is a political act; and those with high and low status may be inclined to claim or deny that they have real influence over decisions for different reasons and on different occasions. It has been suggested[1] that because in some companies relatively less competent men are promoted by age, their juniors take their decisions for them. No doubt this does happen from time to time, as it does in the West, but I am not sure that it is a common characteristic of company organizations, or that where it does occur it causes no difficulties. Most Japanese companies have sufficient regard for the need for good management, and for the ideal of meritocracy, to appoint men to the middle standard ranks at least on the basis of ability as well as length of service. Moreover, when appointments do go awry, and a senior manager is less able than his subordinates, he does not always know it, let alone have the grace to delegate much of his responsibility to a junior. Where, at Marumaru and elsewhere, I have come across management units in which the head of the unit was distinctly less able than his subordinates, I have not usually found relations between senior and junior to be consistent with a happy complementarity of status and responsibility. On the contrary, the fact that subordinates see so many of the documents their senior deals with, and go to so many meetings with him, can make them bitterly aware of his mistakes.

Company Aims and Managerial Authority

I have tried in this chapter to show how the organization and management of the Japanese company is a compromise between the rival claims

[1] Chie Nakane (1970: 69).

of age and merit for status and responsibility. The balance obtained at any time will only be temporary, for the demands of the parties to the compromise change from time to time and in different types of company. Moreover Japanese managements believe more avidly than most in the intrinsic value of change. In well-run Japanese companies innovations are continually being introduced. Some, to be sure, are minor adjustments to serve political rather than administrative ends, but others, such as the creation of new sections or the establishment of new methods of accounting, particularly profit-centre accounting in the Western fashion, may possibly alter the equilibrium of management.[1]

In describing the organization of the Japanese company so far, however, I have left two crucial questions unasked. The first is: what is the purpose of the Japanese company, to which this organization is presumably directed? Is it working for profit, to produce goods, to keep itself in existence, to serve society or the state, or all these things? The second is related to the first, and concerns the nature of the authority that must pervade the organization of the company and induce people to accept their places in it. Why exactly is it that men will obey their company seniors, and agree at least tacitly that their superiors should have a right to higher status and better conditions than they have?

The answer given to the first of these questions in the West is that the purpose of the firm is multifarious.[2] There is every reason to think that in Japan, too, the goal of the firm is determined much as R. M. Cyert and J. G. March[3] have pictured it, by a coalition of people whose interests differ, and who put a different emphasis on each of a number of aims, in accordance with their view of external circumstances and the internal

---

[1] Many Japanese firms have adopted profit-centre accounting; for a description of one see Kazuo Adachi (1965). I do not know of any study which examines the changes in management methods as a result of its adoption.

[2] There has, of course, been considerable disagreement as to what the purpose of the firm is. Part of the contention has been due to the fact that scholars with different interests have been talking about 'the firm' in different senses—cf. Fritz Machlup (1967). Many economists have been looking for goals which, if imputed to the ideal firm, explain the actual behaviour of firms in markets. Their various theories do seem to have in common the assumption that whatever the principal goal attributable to the firm—growth of sales, or increase of profits or net worth—other subsidiary goals must also be achieved. For a review of these theories see James B. Herendeen (1975: 35–47). The behaviourists, whose work is perhaps best represented by R. M. Cyert and J. G. March (1963), are also economists; but their interest has been more in resource allocation within the firm, over the shorter term. For them what appear as the purposes of the firm are the result of a complicated bargain between individuals. Both these complementary approaches provide evidence that firms do have a multiplicity of aims and motives.

[3] R. M. Cyert and J. G. March (1963: 26–43).

balance of power. In Japan, as elsewhere, a firm can only survive by making a certain level of profit, keeping a certain market share, achieving a certain operating ratio, paying wages of a certain standard, and so on. None of these is the unique aim of the enterprise, but failure to achieve any of them may unravel the coalition on which the success of the company is based, a coalition which consists of directors, managers, workers, shareholders, bankers, suppliers, customers and so on. As we have seen, the decision-making process in Japanese companies probably recognizes the existence of such a coalition, and the need for a variable and politically determined set of aims, rather more clearly than in the American or British company.

The many aims of the Japanese company will not, I think, be dissimilar to the aims of the American or British one; but differences in the context, in the form of the internal coalition, and in the prevailing opinions by which people decide their interests will cause the Japanese company to give those aims different priorities. Consider the degree of importance the ordinary Japanese company attaches to profit. Because it depends on its banks for finance, and banks hesitate to lend to loss-making companies for fear of not getting their loans back, it is extremely important that the Japanese company should make a profit. The size of the profit should be in line with profits in 'other firms in the same industry' of the same standing. But high *profitability*, a large return on assets or capital employed, is unlikely to be a very important goal. To begin with, the distortion which arises because company balance sheets are not revalued makes the measurement of profitability inexact. What good is the ratio of profit to capital employed, if the profit is in today's yen and the capital employed partly in the yen of 1952? Then the specialization of the Japanese company makes financial yardsticks less significant. In a Western conglomerate finance is the *lingua franca* of the firm; but managers and workers in more specialized Japanese companies can express their aims and successes in cars, or tons of flour. Again, the chief beneficiaries of high profitability are the shareholders of the company, who can claim the capital on which the large returns have been achieved. But the directors and managers of a Japanese company need only deal with the claims of the bigger shareholders, the banks, suppliers, or customers of the company, whose interest in it is not primarily their investment income from it. Finally, the influence of the Tokugawa merchants and of Shibusawa still persists. Service to society and the nation is laudable, but profit as an end in itself is suspect if not despicable. As an official of Matsushita (one of the most profitable of all Japanese companies) put it:

Service, not profit, is the objective. Profit is not what we can earn—it is given to Matsushita in appreciation of its services. If the company fails to make its profit, it has committed a social blunder or sin, according to our philosophy. The society to which Matsushita belongs entrusts it with capital and manpower for Matsushita to get results. Profit is the appreciation of society, the reward to Matsushita for what it has done.[1]

Just as ideologies, circumstances and interests combine to determine the level of profit a company should aim at, so they impel the company towards aims which are given rather lower priority in the West, such as the provision of welfare to employees. The effort put into this can be considerable. In March 1976, land and buildings allocated to welfare at Nissan Motors—principally, one may presume, company hostels and apartments—had a book value of 21,970 million yen, or eight per cent. of the total book value of the company's plant, property and equipment at that date.[2] The market value may, of course, have been substantially more,[3] but even at book value the investment in housing and welfare amounted to 427,000 yen for each employee.

Why has so much money been spent in this way? There is, without doubt, a prevailing ideal that companies should look after their employees, an ideal of indeterminate provenance, but one to which the merchant house, the Japanese discovery of European industry in the last century, and prewar 'familism' have all made a contribution. The ideal is all the more attractive because the people who can put it into practice are the employees themselves, who benefit from it. But the company's straightforward material interests are also served by investment in housing. Big companies recruit workers from school, both because that is what is expected of them in the society of industry, and also because young workers are paid less. For demographic reasons, however, young workers have in recent years been in short supply, and there has been fierce competition to recruit them. Because there is a shortage of good housing in Japan, company accommodation is an important inducement to recruits. In addition, the land on which company houses are built has usually been an excellent investment and has more than kept its value. The banks and trading partners which hold a company's shares have no objection to the company's building houses, for the company's

[1] Quoted in Rex Winsbury (1970: 20).
[2] *Ōkurashō Insatsukyoku Yūka Shōken Hōkokusho Sōran: Nissan Jidōsha Kabushiki Kaisha,* (March 1976: 20.)
[3] The average book value of 685,000 square metres of land was 8,271 yen per square metre, a figure which appears well below the market value of suburban land.

expenditure may benefit their businesses; and in any case they too have to provide houses for their own employees.

The expenditure on housing will not be beneficial to some of those associated with the company. Shareholders might have had better dividends if less money had gone into housing; but, as we have seen, the major shareholders are relatively unconcerned with dividends and the minor ones are without influence. Another category of people who gain little from company housing are a company's ex-employees. From their point of view a company is spending the wealth created by those like themselves who used to work for it, in order to attract those who do not yet work for it. These ex-employees would be better off if the company were to pay pensions—which relatively few Japanese companies do. As the average age of the Japanese population rises, there will be more ex-employees; and if they organize themselves so as to put pressure on their former employees, priorities may change.

The second unasked question, about the nature of authority in Japanese companies, is more difficult still to answer satisfactorily. The goal of a company may be a fiction, as the company itself is, in law; but it is at least a public fiction. Managers are always asking themselves what the company should be doing; and it is possible to determine what the company is indeed doing, and to relate its actions to the interests of the people who urged them. But the nature of authority is not often a matter for public debate (and when it is, it is frequently because authority has ceased to exert itself); and though its effects are obvious enough it works, like alcohol, on the private person.

It is easy enough, even at this preliminary stage, to suggest what the sources of authority might be. In Japan, as elsewhere, they are likely to be both moral and practical: people will obey because they believe they ought to, and because they believe it is profitable for them to do so; and sometimes for both reasons at once. Employees may accept the authority of a company because they approve of its goals—an important motive in Japan where companies place so much emphasis on the service they are providing the community. Subordinates may obey their superiors because those superiors are seen to have attributes that inspire deference not only inside the company but in the wider society outside it, and therefore seem to be intrinsically worthy of respect. Japanese managers are older, more able, or better educated than those they manage, with some exceptions and a good deal of variation, it is true, but with sufficient consistency to justify their positions in a nation which pays attention to age, merit and learning. At the same time, people may submit to authority out of self-interest. They are, after all, paid for their obedience.[1] They may expect to do well if they show themselves cooperative. Or again, they may obey for the sake of the company, for if that succeeds they will benefit. This last consideration is particularly significant in Japan because a man is known very largely by the size, quality and fame of the company he belongs to. Conversely, people may accept discipline because they know that if they do not their company will fail and they will be out of work. This is the discipline of the market, imposed all the more fiercely because of the way in which companies tend to be specialized and mutually dependent.

Yet though we may have guessed some of its ingredients, we are still some way from knowing the full recipe for authority. The reasons why people obey company directives, and accept orders from each other, are not only mixed—ideological and material, positive and negative—but differently mixed among different types of people and different sets of superior and subordinate. Before we can say more about authority in the company we have to consider who the people are who exert it and submit to it.

---

[1] Marumaru, like most other big Japanese companies, paid two large bonuses every year. Perhaps as much as one-third of an employee's annual income came to him in the form of bonuses. The bonus was calculated from the monthly wage by a complicated formula which rewarded or penalized an employee according to how his superiors assessed certain set qualities. One of these was obedience.

CHAPTER V

Joining and Leaving the Company

This chapter and the next will be concerned chiefly with the membership of the Japanese company and the behaviour and attitudes of the people who work in it. I am going to begin by examining how employees join and leave the company, because that is as good a way as any of illustrating what kind of people belong to the company at any time. Yet the study of these exits and entrances is far more than a mechanical exercise in demography. The Japanese company is a community of volunteers, a body of people who have willingly come together to share common aims, activities and values. When a man joins or leaves a company his action implies a moral choice of agreeing or disagreeing with those values, and indirectly expresses an opinion about what he is or wants to become. Conversely, companies choose some types of applicant for company membership and reject others, and induce some of their existing members to stay and others to go; so revealing preferences which are no doubt inspired by opinions and attitudes among the management, and perhaps the membership as a whole. Recruitment, resignation and dismissal do not merely provide an inverse definition of who is currently associated with a company; they are important indications of the aims and values of the company community.

One moral issue that a study of recruitment and leaving should help to clarify is that of the reciprocal commitment of employer and employee. The idea that there was 'lifetime employment' in Japan was originally put forward by James C. Abegglen:

At whatever level of organization in the Japanese factory the worker commits himself on entrance to the company for the remainder of his working career. The company will not discharge him even temporarily except in the most extreme circumstances. He will not quit the company for industrial employment elsewhere.[1]

Not only was 'lifetime employment', at least in so far as it existed in

[1] James C. Abegglen (1958: 11).

large Japanese companies, the result of a near-absolute moral commitment; it was also a commitment of traditional inspiration.[1] Much work has been undertaken to refute, correct, or qualify Dr Abegglen's thesis in the twenty years since he first advanced it. It is generally agreed that workers do in fact leave Japanese companies, even large ones, and it is also accepted that 'lifetime employment' is not a relic of traditional employment practices; even though the ideas involved in 'lifetime employment' and the related practice of 'pay by age' do have an affinity with the ideals of earlier Japanese eras.[2] Yet there remain problems, which I shall try to deal with, of what Professors Marsh and Mannari have called 'norms and values'. Does anyone think that there is 'lifetime employment' in Japanese industry—regardless of what happens in practice? Does anyone think that there should be 'lifetime employment', and if so upon what conditions?

A second moral question to be born in mind is that of the nature of authority in Japanese companies, a question that arose in the last chapter, and that I hope to consider more closely in the next. Joining a company implies submitting oneself to its authority. Recruiting someone usually involves assessing his willingness to submit. Leaving a company, at least in some circumstances, can be thought of as the final rejection of the company's authority. The mere fact that some people do leave companies limits the discipline that a company can demand of its membership.

While the study of recruitment and resignation gives us clues to the nature of the company community, it also reveals something about the relations between the company and the national society. Not only does a company make an implicit commentary on society in accepting or rejecting certain types of people; by its behaviour on the labour market the company actually influences society. The aggregate result of the manner in which companies employ people, and release them from employment, is to provide some citizens with opportunities for gaining wealth and power, and deny similar opportunities to others; and thus profoundly to affect the distribution of those commodities. And the labour market policies of companies, in doing so much to determine where the wealth and power of society shall reside, may elicit or necessitate changes in other important social and political institutions. Education systems, for example, are likely to have to adapt themselves to produce the sort of people whom companies want to recruit; while social security schemes

[1] James C. Abegglen (1958: 130-1).
[2] Cf. Robert E. Cole (1971: 114).

will have to be devised to help those whom companies do not want to employ.

At the same time, the company itself is affected by society through the labour market, as well as in other ways. The increasing or decreasing availability of certain types of people for recruitment causes changes in personnel policies and in the make-up of firms, and these changes in turn induce, or threaten to induce, changes in management methods, relations between different types of employee, and even the general aims of the company.

In much of my discussion of how the Japanese company takes in people and how they leave it I shall be relying on material from my study of Marumaru. First, though, I shall provide some details of the Japanese labour market; for it was from this that Marumaru, like other Japanese companies, drew its recruits; and it was to this that Marumaru released those who left it.

MOBILITY AND CHANGE IN THE LABOUR MARKET

For anything like a complete description of the Japanese labour market the reader will have to refer elsewhere,[1] for the subject is a large and complicated one. I shall be concerned chiefly with the section of the Japanese working population engaged in activities other than agriculture, and working as employees for companies or individuals outside their families. As Table V.1 indicates, perhaps 75 per cent. of men and 59 per cent. of women fall into this classification. I shall be trying to explain two things: how workers of different types move into the market and between firms in the market; and how the market as a whole is changing.

The Japanese labour market is best understood in terms of employees and firms, rather than jobs and skills. In Western labour markets employers offer jobs with particular specifications with the hope of attracting people with particular skills. So far is the activity of the labour market organized in this way, that we talk not of the entire labour market but of the market for secretaries, for unskilled labourers, for machinists, or for lawyers. In Japan, too, there are job markets of this kind. On the whole, however, firms seek employees: men and women of a variety of types, whose actual jobs will probably only be decided upon when they have been engaged by the firm, and whose jobs may, moreover, be changed

[1] For rather lengthier accounts of the labour market in English see Robert E. Cole (1976) or Walter Galenson and Konosuke Odaka (1976). My discussion is also based on Arisawa Hiromi and Naitō Masaru* (1973) and Hara Kensaburō* (1970).

Table V.1. *The Japanese working population by major occupational categories,*
  1974

	Men (millions)	Women (millions)
TOTAL	32.3	19.7
Agricultural	3.0	3.3
Self-employed or family workers	2.8	3.2
Employees	0.2	0.1
Non-agricultural	29.3	16.4
Self-employed or family workers	5.1	4.8
Employees	24.2	11.6
Full employees	22.5	10.0
Temporary employees	0.7	1.2
Day-wage employees	0.7	0.6

Source: *Rōdō Junpōsha: Nihon Rōdō Nenkan, 1976*: 64.

several times in the course of a company career. In the West, pay is associated with jobs; jobs requiring little skill being paid less than those requiring great skill. In Japan, as we have already seen, pay is associated with
size of firm. Larger firms pay more than smaller ones, partly because their
higher productivity enables them to do so, and partly because in larger
firms there are frequently labour unions campaigning for higher pay. The
variation of pay with size of firm can be seen in Table V.2.

Table V.2 shows that the extent of pay differences by size of firm varies
substantially with the age of the worker, at least for men. Young men
receive much the same pay until their early twenties whatever the size of
organization they work for. Men in their late forties and fifties are, however, very much better paid in large firms than small ones. A second
point becomes apparent when the table is looked at as a set of wage
curves determining the wage of a worker entering a firm of a particular
size. This is that in firms of all sizes men first get higher incomes as they
grow older, and then, after a certain age, actually receive less pay year by
year. The age of diminishing income is much lower in small firms than
larger ones. Evidently big firms are better able than smaller ones to
operate 'pay by age' systems, because they are more stable. Big firms may
also be under greater pressure to operate such systems because of the
activities of their labour unions.

The pay of women is strikingly lower than that of men of comparable
age in firms of similar size. This is but one indication of how different the

Table V.2. Variation in earnings with size of enterprise, and age and sex of employee, 1974

Size of enterprise	\-18	18–19	20–24	25–29	30–34	35–39	40–44	45–49	50–54	55–59	60–64	65+
						Average monthly contract cash earnings ('000 yen)						
						Men						
10– 99	56.4	69.3	89.9	110.3	129.6	137.6	138.0	135.5	132.0	118.6	107.2	94.4
100–999	60.0	74.7	91.8	114.4	140.1	155.4	160.5	161.9	161.1	137.1	116.7	101.2
1,000+	64.1	79.7	96.1	118.2	146.8	167.0	174.8	182.6	191.8	171.4	132.9	112.5
						Women						
10– 99	49.4	57.3	63.7	68.3	68.0	65.8	66.4	69.6	67.6	63.9	61.8	57.5
100–999	55.5	63.5	70.9	77.1	78.3	75.5	77.7	81.7	78.3	73.2	66.4	62.4
1,000+	60.2	69.0	78.4	88.4	93.8	100.1	108.7	117.1	116.1	108.8	104.3	84.9

Source: Japan Statistical Yearbook, 1976: 394–5: Table 284.

positions of men and women are in the labour market. A very high proportion of men go to work after finishing their education, and stay at work until their late sixties. The way in which women begin work, change jobs, and leave off working is represented in Table V.3. Many girls find jobs on leaving school or college, work for a few years, and then leave. They tend to resign on marrying, or at the very latest on becoming pregnant, for there is a strong prejudice in Japan against a woman working after marriage. The general opinion on the matter is reflected in the reluctance of larger firms to offer attractive careers to women. The women who do remain at work after the age of about thirty are frequently farmers' wives and the wives of small shopkeepers.[1] Some of the women who leave employment in their twenties return to work in their late thirties, after their children are in school. At this stage few of them have the chance (or, perhaps, the inclination) to pursue careers. Most of them are simply earning a little extra income for the family, often by working as part-time workers or on piecework at home.[2]

The work patterns of men are not, of course, so directly affected by

Table V.3. *Women in the labour force: participation, job changing, and resignations among women of different ages, 1974*

Age	No. of women in population ('000)	No. of women working ('000)	Percentage working %	No. who changed jobs in previous year ('000)	Percentage changing jobs %	No. who stopped working in previous year ('000)	Percentage stopping work %
15–19	3,987	996	25.0	44	4.4	32	3.2
20–24	4,878	3,071	63.0	290	9.4	439	14.3
25–29	4,985	1,971	39.5	135	6.8	401	20.3
30–34	4,657	1,877	40.3	67	3.6	183	9.7
35–39	4,175	2,111	50.6	69	3.3	119	5.6
40–54	10,661	6,165	57.8	130	2.1	246	4.0
55–64	4,752	1,956	41.2	23	1.2	123	6.3
65+	4,739	682	14.4	3	0.4	84	12.3
Total	42,835	18,829	44.0				

Source: Calculated from *Japan Statistical Yearbook, 1977*: 55: Table 37.

[1] In 1970, 49.5 per cent. of working women over the age of thirty-five were engaged in agriculture, forestry, retailing, or the wholesale trade. Only 36.8 per cent. of younger working women were engaged in those occupations. Sano Yōko* (1972: 173).

[2] In 1970, 22.5 per cent. of working women over thirty were temporary or day-wage workers. Kobayashi Takumi* (1976: 167).

marriage and child-rearing. It is probably most convenient to discuss the labour market for men in two parts: first, the primary labour market, in which those from school and university look for employers; and next the secondary labour market, created by men moving from one employer to another.

In the primary labour market for men (and for women), the advantages lie on the one hand with job-seekers with better educational qualifications, and on the other with larger firms. A good education is rightly seen as a passport to a big company, with its prospects of high pay and greater security of tenure. A middle school leaver will have less chance of working for a major engineering company than a high school leaver. A man from a 'poor' university will be unable to join a major bank. The education system can be seen as a pre-selection mechanism for the labour market. Its examinations have become intensely competitive, for by passing them children are acquiring not merely a scholastic testimonial but a measurably superior chance in life. As for the firms, large employers, because they offer better conditions than small ones, are more easily able to indulge the preference for hiring people straight from school and college. Small employers may not be able to attract very many recruits from the primary market at all, and will have to rely on workers from other companies. Large employers will be able to choose the better educated from their numerous applicants; smaller ones will have no choice at all. Table V.4 gives statistical expression to these considerable advantages of size.

Table V.4. Competition between firms of different size in the primary labour market

a. Workers newly employed in enterprises of different size, by experience, education, 1974.

Size of enterprise (employees)	No. of regular workers ('000)	No. of newly employed workers ('000)	with work experience %	without experience %	Of which percentage straight from junior high school %	straight from senior high school %	straight from college %
5– 29	5,392.6	887.1	69.5	30.5	1.7	5.4	2.6
30– 99	4,248.6	853.1	67.8	32.2	2.1	8.8	2.9
100–499	5,020.4	987.4	62.2	37.8	3.1	11.9	7.2
500–999	1,478.4	244.9	56.1	43.9	3.9	16.4	11.2
1,000+	5,825.9	814.8	40.9	59.1	3.3	24.8	12.4

Source: *Japan Statistical Yearbook, 1976:* 64–5: Table 44.

b. Vacancies and the employment of new school leavers in March 1976, by size of firm.

Size of enterprise (employees)	Middle School Leavers			High School Leavers		
	Vacancies	Number newly employed	Per cent vacancies filled %	Vacancies	Number newly employed	Per cent vacancies filled %
– 29	70,300	17,900	25.5	161,100	56,200	34.9
30– 99	57,600	10,400	18.1	246,500	81,100	32.9
100–299	54,400	11,300	20.8	247,900	95,000	38.3
300–499	18,100	4,500	25.1	82,400	47,400	57.6
500–999	28,300	8,200	29.0	90,200	51,400	57.0
1,000+	16,900	7,000	41.7	176,700	119,700	67.7
Total	245,500	59,400	24.2	1,004,700	451,000	44.9

Source: Rōdō Jihō: 29: 10 (1976): 26.
Note: figures for jobs have been rounded to nearest hundred.

Even the largest firms, as Table V.4b reveals, cannot fill their vacancies for middle and high school leavers. Young, less educated workers are in fact in short supply, and for two reasons. The age distribution of the population of Japan has changed remarkably over the last few decades. Both the death rate and also the birth rate (except during the baby boom of 1945–7) have fallen, and the result, indicated in Table V.5, has been a population with fewer young and far more old people. In 1975 there were fewer potential recruits to the labour market—that is, fifteen- to nineteen-year-olds—than in 1950; but the number of people over sixty-five had more than doubled.

Not only has the number of young people who might enter the labour market been falling since 1965, but, as Table V.6 shows, more and more young people are going on to higher stages of education, and so postponing taking up jobs. Now that ninety per cent. of those leaving middle schools are going to high schools, there has been a dramatic fall in middle school leavers entering the labour market. Unskilled jobs are therefore having to be done by high school leavers, who are probably over-qualified for them, or by older workers who have already been in employment for some time. On the other hand, the number of university graduates entering the labour market has risen very rapidly. The demand for better educated workers has undoubtedly been increasing, as industries requiring advanced scientific and managerial skills have flourished, but university graduates, unlike middle and high school leavers, have not been in short supply.

Table V.5. Changes in the age distribution of the population of Japan in selected years, 1920–75

Year	Total population (millions)	Pre-working age			Working age										Post working age	
		0–4	5–9	10–14	15–19	20–24	25–29	30–34	35–39	40–44	45–49	50–54	55–59	60–64	65–69	70+
1920	56.0	7.5	6.9	6.1	5.4	4.6	3.9	3.6	3.4	3.2	2.7	2.2	1.8	1.7	1.3	1.6
1940	73.1	9.1	8.8	8.4	7.4	6.1	5.7	4.9	4.4	3.8	3.2	2.9	2.6	2.2	1.6	1.9
1950	83.2	11.2	9.5	8.7	8.6	7.7	6.2	5.2	5.0	4.5	4.0	3.4	2.7	2.3	1.8	2.3
1960	93.4	7.8	9.2	11.0	9.3	8.3	8.2	7.5	6.0	5.0	4.8	4.2	3.6	2.9	2.2	3.2
1965	98.3	8.1	7.8	9.2	10.9	9.1	8.4	8.3	7.5	6.0	4.9	4.7	4.0	3.3	2.6	3.6
1970	103.7	8.8	8.2	7.9	9.1	10.7	9.1	8.4	8.2	7.3	5.9	4.8	4.4	3.7	3.0	4.3
1975	111.9	10.0	9.0	8.3	7.9	9.1	10.9	9.3	8.4	8.2	7.4	5.8	4.6	4.3	3.5	5.4

Source: Japan Statistical Yearbook, 1977: 26–7: Table 13.

Note: The principles by which censuses were undertaken varied slightly in different years, foreigners and Okinawans being included and excluded. The variations are unlikely to have had significant effects on the table as a whole.

Table V.6. School and college leavers entering the Japanese labour market, 1960–75

| Year | Middle School Leavers | | High School Leavers | | College Graduates* |
	Total ('000)	No. entering labour market† ('000)	Total ('000)	No. entering labour market ('000)	('000)
1960	1,770	748	934	774	150
1965	2,360	692	1,160	865	218
1970	1,667	298	1,403	1,063	356
1971	1,622	244	1,360	996	n.a.
1972	1,561	201	1,319	934	411
1973	1,543	163	1,326	913	423
1974	1,624	150	1,337	906	431
1975	1,580	127	1,327	874	454

Source: *Japan Statistical Yearbook, 1976*: Tables 385, 386, 390, 392.
  Japan Statistical Yearbook, 1977: Tables 394, 395, 399, 401.

* 'Graduates' include graduates of junior colleges, colleges, and universities.
† 'Number entering labour market' from middle and high school is calculated from figures given for those going on to higher educational levels. These figures include working students.

The outlook is that competition among firms in the primary labour market is likely to become even more fierce, provided that the Japanese economy continues to grow. The ageing of Japan's population also has other, rather more important consequences for the employment system. To these I shall return later.

The secondary labour market is created by people leaving firms to join new ones. I have mentioned that women leave their employers in their late twenties for marriage and child-bearing. While they are still in employment, however, young women do tend to change jobs frequently, as Table V.3 testifies. Their leaving for other firms causes no great agitation, since women are so often employed on the assumption that they are going to leave anyway. Nor is it difficult to see why they do leave, given that employers rarely offer them good prospects, and that the young women themselves usually consider their work as merely a prelude to marriage. Older women seem to stay with one employer, presumably because so many of them are working in family firms.

What is the state of the secondary market in male labour? It is probably convenient to separate two kinds of men who leave their jobs. The first kind is composed of men who retire at the set age, usually 55, but now increasingly a little older. Most of them will receive severance pay amounting to perhaps three years' salary, but only a few will have a company pension. They will of course be too young to qualify for a state pension and will not be sufficiently well-off to stop working. Some of them will be re-employed as special category workers in the firms from which they have retired, at rather reduced pay. Others will be placed with subsidiaries and affiliates of their original firms, and at these their conditions of employment will reflect the inferior status of their new employers. Yet others will make a clean break and will find jobs elsewhere. These men, too, are likely to experience a fall in income. Many of them, moreover, will remain unemployed for several months before finding a job at all. Retirement is at best an uncomfortable process, and the lot of the older worker in Japan is unenviable.[1]

The second kind of male leaver leaves his job before official retirement age. Men of all types leave companies of all sizes, including even the large companies at which 'lifetime employment' is said to exist in reality or as an ideal. Nevertheless, it is quite evident from Table V.7 that men in large companies do not leave as frequently as men in small ones, and that the older a man is, and the more highly educated he is, the less likely he is to quit.

Table V.7. Leaving rates for male employees by size of firm, and age and education of employee

a. Leaving rate of male employees from establishments of different sizes, 1971–5

Leaving rate (percentage)

Size of establishment (employees)	1971 %	1972 %	1973 %	1974 %	1975 %
5– 29	19.3	18.1	19.5	15.7	16.4
30– 99	18.5	19.9	20.5	17.1	15.7
100–299	18.3	18.0	17.0	15.3	15.0
300–999	16.0	12.9	13.7	12.0	10.4
1,000+	10.0	8.6	9.5	7.7	6.3

Source: *Rōdōshō: Rōdō Daijin Kanbō Tōkei Jōhōbu: Kōyō Dōkō Chōsa Hōkoku* (1975): 25: Table 4.
Note: leaving includes retirement and retirement and re-employment at the appropriate age.

[1] For fuller details of the grim circumstances of workers beyond retirement age see *Rōdōshō: Rōdōkijunkyoku: Teinen Tōtatsusha Chōsa no Kekka* (1975) (Ministry of Labour: Labour Standards Bureau: Results of the survey of workers of retirement age).

b. Job changing by age, education, 1974

Age	Education	No. of male workers ('000)	No. changing jobs in 1974 ('000)	Job changing rate %
15–24	Total	4,405	329	7.4
	Middle school	1,297	115	8.9
	High school	2,483	176	7.1
	University	625	38	6.1
25–34	Total	9,157	505	5.5
	Middle school	2,834	195	6.9
	High school	4,264	212	5.0
	University	2,059	98	4.8
35+	Total	18,760	515	2.7
	Middle school	10,329	280	2.7
	High school	5,496	150	2.7
	University	2,934	85	2.9

Source: *Japan Statistical Yearbook, 1977*: 55: Table 37.

So high is the leaving rate among less educated young workers that it can be said to be normal for a man to leave his first employer, and abnormal for him to stay with his first employer for any length of time. Moreover, young men, who are expected to stay with their firms, leave at much the same rate as women, who are expected to leave for marriage:

Table V.8. Proportion of school leavers of different years who had changed jobs by March 1973

Number of years since leaving school	Percentage of leavers who had changed jobs			
	Men		Women	
	High School %	Middle School %	High School %	Middle School %
5 years	58.6	72.0	77.6	73.2
4 years	52.1	64.5	66.5	62.6
3 years	42.0	52.1	50.1	44.8
2 years	30.3	39.5	33.2	31.3
1 year	19.6	24.7	17.3	15.9

Source: *Rōdōshō: Fujinshōnenkyoku: Nenshō Rōdō Shiryō 30-go. Kinrō seinen no genjō* (1975): 22–3.

As for what happens to men who do leave their employers before retirement, the evidence is that the vast majority join other employers,

6

rather than become farmers or set up their own businesses.[1] Where retiring employees tend to move from larger employers to smaller ones, employees who leave their employers before retirement may not necessarily move to smaller firms. A 1975 survey showed that just over half the workers who joined firms of more than 1,000 workers from the secondary labour market came from smaller firms, with less than 100 workers.[2] It is clear that young men in particular do not inevitably suffer as a result of leaving their jobs. As Table V.9 shows, the younger a man is, the more likely he is to do better after leaving his first employer. Indeed, only if a man leaves his employer after the normal retirement age of 55 is he statistically likely to receive less pay in his new job.

Table V.9. Increase and decrease in pay after job changing among those changing jobs at different ages, 1976 (first half)

Age of job changer	Receiving more pay %	Receiving no change in pay %	Receiving less pay %
−19	41.9	44.8	13.1
20–29	36.9	47.8	14.9
30–44	35.8	49.9	14.1
45–54	32.6	49.0	18.2
55+	21.6	40.7	37.3

Source: *Rōdō Jihō*: 30: 2 (1977): 7.

The pattern of male job leaving, combined with that of wage differences by age and size of company, suggest that 'market forces' are at work. The lower paid men, younger, less educated, and in smaller companies, are leaving their jobs and moving to jobs where the pay is better. The better paid men, older, more highly educated, and in larger companies, have less incentive to move, and so stay where they are. The reason why men leave becomes obvious. Labour markets in Japan behave in just the same way as they do everywhere else: workers move to get better pay.

[1] It is hard to find incontrovertible proof of this because the statistics do not always distinguish between men who retire and men who leave before retirement. But in 1974, for example, 88 per cent. of 1.23 million men employed in non-agricultural jobs who changed jobs during the year were still in employment (presumably with new employers) at the end of the year. *Japan Statistical Yearbook, 1976*: 54: Table 36.

[2] *Rōdō Daijin Kanbō Tōkei Jōhōbu: Rōdō Tōkei Nenpō* (Yearbook of labour statistics) *1975*: 32: Table 20. Most male job changers are shown to move from large firms to smaller ones, or between smaller firms.

There are two important objections to this explanation of why men leave Japanese companies. The first is that leaving one employer and joining another may be two quite separate acts, particularly in Japan where the system of employment exchanges and job agencies is less developed than in most Western countries. A man may leave a lower paid job for some reason quite unconnected with pay, look around for a new job, and eventually find one with a large and expanding firm which is willing to pay high wages. The mere fact that he has moved from a low paid job to a highly paid one does not mean that pay was his motive, or that it even entered into his considerations. A second objection is the implausibility of the idea that all Japanese employees are self-seeking 'economic men', whose aim is simply to get as much salary as possible for as long as possible. As we shall shortly see, men actually leave companies for a host of reasons, and frequently their motives are so mixed that they may not be able to explain them themselves.

Perhaps a more plausible hypothesis is that the labour market facilitates leaving but does not cause it. A man will be more disposed to leave, for whatever reasons, if he thinks that he has a reasonable chance of getting as good a job elsewhere as with his present employer; and whether he thinks this or not will depend on his position in the labour market. A young worker with no more than high school education who is working in a small company will have low pay and moderate prospects if he stays with his firm. On the labour market, however, his type of worker is in short supply, and big firms may be offering high wages to attract him. If he is aware of these circumstances it may not take very much to induce him to leave. An older graduate manager in a large company will be in a quite different position. He receives high pay, and may have accumulated rights to a separation allowance or pension, rights which are most unlikely to be transferable to any new employer. On the labour market, older workers are not in short supply and Japanese employers do not necessarily pay older mid-career recruits very well. An older worker will think hard before he decides to change jobs, and will only move for a very good reason.

Even this modified hypothesis has the disadvantage of tending to depict the relationship between companies and employees in a negative way. Employees are attached to their employers largely by inertia, because they are unable to leave. We shall see that within Japanese companies a rather different explanation is put forward of why men resign before retirement. Put briefly, it is that no one would normally join a company unless to stay with it, so that if a man does leave, then there must be some defect either in the company or in the man himself which causes him to go. This kind of explanation is much more consistent with the idea, held very strongly in Japanese firms, that the company is a community, in which everyone lives and works together for common ends.

This all too brief account of the Japanese labour market has left out of consideration a number of very important factors, such as regional migration and, perhaps more important, the changes affecting the economy and particular industries. In times of economic depression (to which most of these tables refer) competition for labour will be less intense, and differences between conditions in large and small enterprises will be more marked, than in periods of boom. The rise of some industries, like electronics or supermarket retailing, and the decline of others, like textiles or shipbuilding, will also affect wages and employment patterns. For all these omissions we do know enough about the labour market to make two sets of observations, about employees on the one hand, and employers on the other.

Certain types of employee appear better able or more willing than others to change employers. In fact it is probably fair to distinguish between immobile employees and mobile ones. There are three conspicuous categories of immobile employees. There are the older women, presumably in family firms; the older men, especially in large firms; and graduates. There are also three categories of mobile employees. Two of these, young women and younger, less educated men, we have come across. The third category, which has only been mentioned in passing, consists of the many temporary and irregular employees, both men and women. Some of these are students, some retired employees, some seasonal workers and some foot-loose day labourers; what they all have in common is a weak association with any particular employer.

The employers' behaviour on the labour market seems paradoxical. There are many older workers, and their number is increasing; and few younger workers, and their number is diminishing. Yet larger employers are paying older workers twice as much as younger ones. If the aim of the 'rational' employer were simply to obtain the cheapest possible labour, we should expect him to pay older men less and younger men more—in other words, to give up 'pay by age'. We should also expect him to make considerable efforts to recruit among older workers, who are in such good supply, even though older workers would naturally be mid-career entrants from other firms. This latter change of policy would, of course, be inconsistent with the practices sustaining 'lifetime employment'.

Many large companies are indeed modifying their pay systems. The introduction of work-ability grades during the 1960s not only made it easier for companies to pay and promote by merit, but also allowed companies to offer young men and 'mid-career entrants' better salaries than before. Large companies have also begun systematically recruiting older workers. These changes have, however, only come slowly, rather more slowly than the changes in the labour market they are partly intended to counter. The reluctance of companies to alter their policies too quickly is not, of course, a reflection on their 'rationality'. There are two reasons for it. In the first place, the purely economic aims of the 'rational' employer are hardly simple. He is certainly not interested merely in obtaining the cheapest possible labour, but in recruiting men and women of particular qualities, and then developing those qualities over a period of years. He has to allow for the fact that his employees think of their employment not as an arrangement to be made or broken instantaneously but as having some minimal duration. Paying employees less when they begin work than later, when they have acquired skills, may be a very sensible way of matching contributions to rewards, not an entirely 'irrational' practice to be abandoned as soon as possible.

Another important reason why changes in company policy take place only slowly is that just as employees are not merely automatons following wage curves, but people, with loyalties, expectations, predilections and dislikes, so companies are not merely consumption units in the labour market but communities of people, with traditions, values, and internal conflicts. Firms cannot act strictly in pursuit of narrow economic interests, but have to take all sorts of moral and political considerations into account. Some of these have to do with the position of the company in society, and particularly in the society of industry. A big and famous company cannot suddenly revoke a tradition of decades, and stop serious recruiting from the high schools from which so many of its present employees came. Everyone knows that big firms recruit from schools and not from the secondary labour market—it is almost part of the definition of a big firm. Other considerations arise from the internal politics of the company. Firms cannot bring in large numbers of mid-career entrants without risking the unhappiness of older workers who joined their companies straight from school. Though there would certainly be economic benefits if firms were able to make better use of women's talents, women cannot suddenly be promoted in the same way as men, for fear of complaints, however unjustified. The very idea that recruitment is, or should be, primarily an economic activity, an accumulation of labour, offends against the sense of community which Japanese managers and workers feel should be part of company life.

To see how moral and cultural influences weigh with a firm in its attempt to adjust to changes in the labour market, let us take the example of Marumaru during 1970-1. This was a period when the Japanese economy was booming and labour was in great demand, before business had been affected by the quotas on imports imposed by President Nixon and by the oil crisis.

JOINING THE COMPANY

In its early days Marumaru had taken on new people casually and unsystematically; but as the company had grown larger it had put more and more effort into 'traditional' means of recruitment: straight from school or college.

The directors of Marumaru, all but one of whom had themselves had chequered careers in a number of jobs before joining Marumaru, were convinced that it was best to recruit from schools for two chief reasons. The first was that because Marumaru paid workers roughly according to age, it was cheaper to employ as many youngsters straight from school as possible. The financial advantage of school recruiting was, however, diminishing rapidly because of the shortage of school leavers. Not only were their wages rising relative to those of older men, but it was costing a great deal of money to attract them. By 1970 Marumaru was spending 500,000 yen to recruit a single high school leaver. The second reason was cultural rather than financial. School recruiting was a customary practice among companies of Marumaru's size, and in adopting it Marumaru was declaring its newly gained position in Japanese industry. Moreover, now that Marumaru was substantial enough to have its own 'company way of life' (shafū), it was best to recruit young people without experience elsewhere which might prejudice their receptiveness to what they were told at Marumaru.

Unfortunately for Marumaru, no sooner had the company achieved the stature necessary to attract recruits from schools and colleges than changes occurred in the labour market to make school recruitment at least extremely difficult. Instead of being able to take in as many innocent and pliable youngsters as it wanted from the appropriate levels of the education system, Marumaru found itself recruiting three types of male employee, each of apparently different disposition, in three separate ways. There were the school entrants, the graduate recruits, and the workers from other companies. The proportion of employees taken in by each method can be seen from the figures for the 1970 entrants:

Table V.10. Male entrants into Marumaru, 1969–70

	Level of education		
	Middle/High School	University	Total
Straight from school	49	26	75
From other companies	81	5	86
Total	130	31	161

THE SCHOOL RECRUITS

The harder it became to find schoolboys who wanted to join Marumaru, the more energy and money the company put into school recruiting. Originally Marumaru had had its recruiting grounds in N——— prefecture to itself, and the company had been able to rely on schoolmasters recommending their better pupils. As the shortage of school leavers intensified, large firms with no particular connections with the province began to send their staff to the schools of N———. When I visited one school of six hundred boys, from which Marumaru had usually obtained two or three applicants each year, I was shown the visiting cards of more than nine hundred company representatives, many from well-known companies, and several thousand recruitment pamphlets. In the face of this competition Marumaru had to assign one member of the personnel department to full-time recruiting duties in the prefecture, and to send staff from the factories on periodic tours of N——— schools. The company also began trying to attract recruits from schools outside N———, in the adjoining prefectures and in the localities of the factories all over Japan.

At the same time the entrance qualifications were made easier and easier. At first Marumaru had required all applicants to sit an examination, but when it became clear that the company was no longer able to pick and choose, the examination was waived for school applicants, though retained for graduates. Instead schoolboys were merely asked to write a short essay about their families. Later even this requirement was dropped. Again, it had been the practice to have new school entrants pass through a period of probation before becoming full company members, so that if, despite the originally elaborate selection process, a recruit proved unsuitable, he could be got rid of. In 1970, at the union's instigation, though with some reluctance, the management ended the probation system.

Once the recruits had signed on, enormous trouble was taken over their welfare. They were brought down together from N——— at the end of the school year by three men from the personnel department. Marumaru also offered free passages to any parent of a recruit who wanted to see the conditions under which his or her son was going to work. The recruits destined for the Yokohama factory were met at Tokyo station and brought in a bus to the factory, which had been decorated for the occasion with bunting and notices of welcome. They and their relatives were met and welcomed by the factory manager, offered lunch, and shown round the premises.

Training was far more an introduction to the community than a technical course. It began with a ceremony at which all the managers of the factory and even a director from the head office were formally introduced to the new entrants. The first lectures, given by the factory manager himself, concerned the history of the company and its organization. They were followed by talks on how Marumaru employees should behave, the rank and pay systems, and on welfare benefits and the social life the firm offered. A recurrent theme of these and subsequent lectures was that the new entrants were now 'men of society' or 'citizens' (shakaijin). By gaining positions at Marumaru they had become full adults, and had a chance, in working for their company, to serve society and to earn its esteem. It was not until the third day of a ten-day course that the new employees heard about the machines they would be using; and the relatively few technical lectures were given by junior managers and were of poor quality.

The new entrants were introduced at the same time to the life of the company hostel. They were given into the care of a senior hostel member, who discharged his responsibilities by taking them on runs in the early morning and evening. Individual recruits were also assigned 'elder brothers' from among the older hostel members. The 'elder brothers' were not, however, able to take much interest in their charges, partly because of the shift system, but also because older men had little to say to boys six or seven years their juniors. A large party was given to welcome the new entrants to the hostel. At this they were required to introduce themselves, their hesitant pronouncements being greeted by good-humoured banter. Then each of the seventy hostel members introduced himself in turn, to the accompaniment of jibes which were quite incomprehensible to the bemused newcomers. Later in their first week the recruits were taken on an outing to Mount Fuji with their 'elder brothers', and on an evening trip to see the lights of Tokyo.

The attention lavished on the new recruits was almost entirely wasted. The festivities in their honour—no bunting was hung for the accession of a new factory manager, nor, indeed on any other occasion—the trips and excursions, the expense of management time, were all useless to prevent middle and high school recruits from leaving within a year or two of joining. For the fact was that the high school leavers were well aware that they had been wooed by dozens of companies before joining Marumaru, and that they could get another job somewhere else at any time without the slightest difficulty. They were therefore able to take a very nonchalant and even cynical attitude towards Marumaru's offer of security, contentment, and a place in society. One young man in the 1971 high school intake, and a man, moreover, who had a father in the company, arranged that his girl friend should meet him at Tokyo Station on the morning he arrived with the party from N———. Posing as an elder sister anxious to see how Marumaru would look after her brother, she joined the party of recruits and relatives going to Yokohama, and had herself entertained at the factory with the genuine relatives. Her boyfriend left the company within two months, dismissed for taking two days off work to go to Tokyo. Several other new entrants had attitudes to their new employer that were only slightly less cavalier. The reaction of older Marumaru workers and managers to the behaviour of the high school leavers was a kind of hurt contempt. Younger people were spineless and spoilt, always thinking of their pleasures and never of their responsibilities. Though it was obvious that the young people could only behave as they did because of their advantages in the labour market, it was the education system that received the most blame. A personnel department official in his thirties wrote in his report on a recruitment visit to a school in N———:

As the teacher was talking I fell to thinking of the defects of present high school education, which raises feeble people who wriggle out of everything they don't like. In my own field I'm always hearing complaints about overtime and night work; and there are young people who have never heard of endurance who come running along with their resignations. Of course working conditions have to be improved, but there are few enough even among the older and more senior workers who realize how much common effort and purpose is needed for just that. If there have been any gaps in the education they have received we shall have,

6*

here in the workplace, to raise their morale as workers. Even if we go in for a policy of having a few, well qualified people, that will be the starting point.

THE GRADUATE RECRUITS

The surest proof that the education system had little to do with the attitudes of high school leavers was that the graduate recruits,[1] who passed an even longer time within the system, behaved quite differently. Marumaru constantly needed to send visitors to high schools, but no company representative had to call at universities. At Meiji University, which had supplied more than ten per cent. of all Marumaru's graduates, the company's recuitment brochure was not even on the rack in the career officer's room. Marumaru was, in fact, still able to rely largely on personal contacts to recruit graduates. Sixteen of forty-seven graduate applicants in 1970 had identifiable 'connections' with the company, and fourteen of them were among the twenty-four graduates accepted for employment.[2] With the graduates, too, Marumaru could conduct a proper selection process. There was an examination, partly to allow comparison to be made between men from universities of varying standards, partly to eliminate men who had been doing little or no work at university. There was also a three-hour essay, always on the subject of 'My Family', from which a man's background could be gauged. Finally, and most important of all, there was an interview at which a candidate was required to deliver a two-minute report on some topic or other, and then answer the questions of the assembled directors.

The graduate applicants behaved just as the company expected them to. They viewed themselves as half-formed creatures waiting for company membership to make them whole. Only two or three of nearly fifty applicants wore ties and suits for the interview, the rest appearing in college uniforms or open-necked shirts, almost as if they were mere schoolboys. The predominant theme of the three-hour essay was of preparation for 'coming out into society' (a phrase which occurred again and again). The candidates were admittedly immature:

[1] Strictly speaking, the recruitment was not of graduates but prospective graduates, final year university students.

[2] Candidates with 'connections' were not favoured as blatantly as these figures imply. Some candadates without 'connections' took job offers elsewhere, perhaps at companies with which they were more closely associated. Most of the candidates with 'connections' did well in the examination and presented themselves effectively in the interview—evidence, perhaps, that sponsors within Marumaru did not lend their support to candidates who might disgrace them. Finally, the directors showed no hesitation in rejecting candidates with good 'connections' who were unworthy of admission.

In ability to get on with people, in positiveness and so on, I'm still a child beside my parents.

Perhaps because I have been over-protected I am a little spoilt.

I am a little too carefree; and I might be a little naïve.

But they were already overcoming these symptoms of parental indulgence:

At high school I spent my time on nothing but judo. I hoped to cultivate some qualities I couldn't get at home—positiveness, the ability to co-operate, patience.

. . . when I entered high school I wanted to do some sports and build up body and spirit. I discussed it with my parents, but they were very much against it. Up till then I had been pampered as an only child, and I knew that I had a rather weak character. So joining the boat club required a little courage. I argued my parents into submission, and when I joined the boat club I felt the weight of my responsibility pressing on me for the first time . . . I joined the boat club so as not to be over-protected by my parents, and so as to develop a strong spirit and body, but it seems to have become a source of worry to my parents. Perhaps they feel something is lacking. For myself I am quite happy and I intend to go out in the world in a prepared frame of mind. But with my parents I do worry a little about my academic record.

Most of the essays went on to say that the candidates were looking forward to making their contribution to society—if possible through their work for Marumaru.

As a product of the M——— family, I think that I can serve my family best by going out into the world and working as hard as possible to contribute to a company and to society.

There was one particularly interesting essay which I shall quote in full because it showed how its author had shifted his loyalties from his home to what he himself described as a surrogate family:

I only return home thirty days a year, and family life being what it is now, I should like to write about my life in the university hostel, which could be called my present home. It must be thirty years since the hostel I live in was built, and now it's a run-down building which looks as though it will collapse shortly. Anyone who saw it would ask, 'Do people really live here?' I adopt the policy, 'Wherever you live, that's the capital', and though I was surprised when I first saw the hostel, now it's home. My room has eight people, a family of eight. The composition is as follows: four fourth year, two third year, and two first year. There are four room leaders, so that things aren't very well arranged. I am fourth year too, and as I have been living with the other three fourth year men for three and a bit years I know a lot about them. Often we talk from bed-time till dawn of the problems of existence and of love. The room really is like a family, and though we are all going to have our own families, it is very useful. Because there are eight people altogether there are some problems when someone wants to work or someone has the radio on loud. Rather than solve these problems individually we work things out in a debate involving the whole room. We work hard at enjoying ourselves and often go drinking together. The most enjoyable thing of all was the farewell party for the fourth year. Every year we go on a trip. Because hostel life is like this I am lucky enough to have two families.

With the fewest of changes this piece could be taken as a description of life in the hostel for the male workers at the head office, most of whom were graduates. It was obvious that living in a university hostel, and learning to get on with the changeless group of seniors, equals and juniors with whom one shared twenty-four hours a day, was excellent pre-conditioning for a future in Marumaru.

It would not be right to attribute the striking difference between the demeanours of graduate and high school recruits entirely to their different positions in the labour market. For the graduates, many of them economists or lawyers by training, working in a company was the natural culmination of a long period of study, and they could look forward to joining Marumaru with an intellectual anticipation hardly to be found among high school leavers. Graduates were also aware that they would probably form the elite of any company they did join. Nevertheless, the primary influence was that of the labour market. Seven or eight years earlier, I was told, when high school leavers were still relatively plentiful, their attitude had been just as 'positive' as that of the 1971 graduates.

Although Marumaru received more graduate applicants in 1971 than ever before, and was able to turn half of them away, there were ominous signs that graduate recruitment might one day become as difficult as getting high school leavers. Instead of being able to restrict recruiting to the 'best' six or seven of the universities which had provided most of the company's graduates, Marumaru was having to take men from more and more universities, some of them distinctly inferior institutions. Engineering and science graduates from 'good' universities were particularly difficult to come by. Table V.11 shows the qualitative changes that were taking place in graduate recruiting as Marumaru's intake of graduates grew year by year.

Table V.11. Graduate recruitment at Marumaru, 1964–71

University	Alumni in company, 1970	New recruits in							
		1964	1965	1966	1967	1968	1969	1970	1971
A	25	–	–	2	2	2	5	–	–
B	22	3	–	–	–	2	3	1	–
C	21	4	2	1	1	–	–	4	2
D	18	2	2	1	1	1	5	2	2
E	15	2	1	3	2	2	2	–	–
F	10	–	1	1	–	2	2	–	–
G	8	1	2	–	–	–	1	1	–
H	7	2	–	1	1	–	–	–	1
I	7	–	1	–	–	1	1	2	4
All others	68	1	n.a.	5	–	5	7	14	14
Total	201	15	n.a.	14	7	15	26	24	23
Per cent. from top nine universities	66%	93%	n.a.	64%	100%	67%	73%	42%	39%

Table V.11 also provides some evidence about the existence or non-existence of 'university cliques' at Marumaru, a subject I touched upon in connection with promotions. In large Japanese companies which have restricted their graduate recruiting to a few universities, the graduates of those universities are said to form loose alliances to further each other's careers and to influence the policies of the firm. The main reasons why there were no university cliques at Marumaru were that the company was too young, and that too many of the directors had not been to university; and the table does show how universities with many alumni at Marumaru frequently failed to provide new recruits for years at a time, something that would have been unlikely if there had been powerful university cliques.

There was some controversy in the upper management over how graduates should be trained. Some senior managers took the view that graduates should work their way up through the company, so that they should be sent to work machines long enough to get to know the factories properly (and at the same time ease the problems caused by the labour shortage). Only then should they take up positions of some responsibility. Other managers wanted to have the graduates trained from the start as an élite. As a sort of compromise, different annual intakes were treated in different ways. In some years graduates had worked on the shop floor for up to a year, in others they had spent only a month there before moving on to a quick succession of other jobs in various departments. In any case training was far more pragmatic than in Thomas Rohlen's bank, Uedagin,[1] with its endurance walks, sociological initiative tests, and spiritual improvement sessions. The graduates spent a week at the company's lodge in the mountains, and each day did begin with a run; but most of the time was spent learning about the business. Less attention was paid to inculcating appropriate views of society in the graduates than in the high school leavers, presumably because the graduates already had them.

THE MID-CAREER RECRUITS

Finally we come to the people who joined Marumaru in an irregular fashion, not from school or college but after leaving other companies. A very small minority of these came in at the invitation of a Marumaru official, sometimes to do a special job, and their treatment might be most advantageous if their sponsor was influential. Two or three men of middle management status were invited to join Marumaru each year, usually from bankrupt or declining companies. They were not immediately appointed to positions of rank and importance, but within two or three years they might expect to be made at least section heads. At the shop floor level, too, there were employees who had been asked to join Marumaru from other firms, and these too received special treatment, not promotion but a subsidized flat or company house.

Most of the irregular entrants, however, and therefore most of the entrants of any kind, came to Marumaru after hearing from friends that the company was looking for workers, or after applying to labour exchanges or seeing advertisements in the newspapers. Marumaru spent little time or money recruiting men in their 'mid-careers'. The company did not advertise for workers on hoardings or posters in trains and buses— though a notice outside the Yokohama factory invited job seekers to enquire within. The advertisements it placed in the newspapers were dull and even secretive, offering little information about the work and none at all about the pay. The company's apathetic attempts at this type of

[1] Thomas P. Rohlen (1974: 192–211).

recruitment contrasted not only with the frenetic efforts to attract schoolboys from the schools of N———, but also with the recruitment campaigns of much larger companies, which seemed to have adapted themselves more readily to changes in the labour market despite, presumably, long habituation to 'lifetime employment'.

In common with most Japanese companies, Marumaru did not attempt to recruit skilled workers from its competitors. I was told that there were no skilled workers available—this in spite of the fact that Marumaru was losing dozens of trained young men every year and rival companies were thought to be suffering in the same way. The real reason for the company's forbearance was moral: recruiting skilled workers could be thought of as poaching from other companies, and that would be unfair.[1] Even when a man with experience in another corrugated board company came into Marumaru's hands, very little account was taken of his work outside the company. Skilled though he was, he would receive less favoured treatment than a man with no knowledge of the industry who had been invited into Marumaru by a senior manager.

Just as Marumaru took so little trouble over obtaining mid-career recruits, so it treated them with careless indifference when they joined. Without more ceremony than a brief introduction to a busy production section head, they would be taken on as temporary employees (rinji jūgyōin). They retained this status for several months, until the management was convinced that they were eligible to become full employees. Their disadvantages were compounded by the fact that mid-career entrants were given no systematic training, and often, because supervisors were overworked, no training at all. Yet so far as could be determined—for there were no figures for leaving rates among temporary employees—these mid-career entrants were at least as likely to stay with Marumaru as the high school recruits on whom such care was lavished.[2]

On the whole mid-career entrants were resigned to their treatment, and seemed prepared to accept that those who had served Marumaru since leaving school deserved greater rewards than they themselves did. Yet inferior treatment for mid-career entrants was inconsistent with the

[1] I did see one advertisement in the corrugated board industry journal Danbōru in 1970 offering jobs to experienced corrugator operators. The advertisement, which appeared to be unique, had been placed by an agency and I was unable to discover who the principal was.

[2] The personnel department estimated that only about forty per cent. of mid-career entrants, once they were registered as full employees, left the company within three years of joining. My own calculations put the proportion at thirty-two per cent. Seventy-five per cent. of school entrants left within the same period of joining.

meritocratic ideal, which the company made such great play of. The company itself used the principle of promotion by ability to justify the rapid rises of those mid-career entrants who had been invited to join Marumaru. For who would have invited them if they had not been able; and if they were able, was it not right that they should be promoted? The problem was, however, whether the same arguments applied to uninvited mid-career entrants who showed ability. There were cases of men who had entered the company casually at nineteen or twenty and had risen above other men who had earlier been recruited from schools. But these were rare exceptions. Most mid-career entrants never caught up, and one or two of them found the iterations of meritocracy irksome:

> I have been in this company four years and five months and I think I am as good as any of the older people at the work. When I joined the company [after two other firms] I heard that if one had ability one could be promoted rapidly and get a higher salary. With this in mind I myself worked hard. Last year, when the salary rises came round, the Yokohama factory put forward the names of those to be considered for promotion to the -th grade, and mine was among them; but after they had looked into it I wasn't promoted because I hadn't enough experience in the company. Everyone else as well as me thought that I would go to the -th grade, so the shock was enormous. You preach meritocracy, but I would like you to do proper, deep investigations [for promotion] which would satisfy everyone, so that meritocracy isn't just a pious word.

This man was remarkable for his bluntness in writing in this way, in reply to a certain questionnaire the company distributed—so remarkable that when I paraphrased his message and related it to some shop floor workers in another part of the company, to illustrate how men suggested themselves for appointments in British industry, they were genuinely shocked by its egotism and presumptuousness. Yet outspoken though he was, the writer was voicing a discontent which many mid-career recruits surely felt, and which may have contributed to the problems of discipline on the shop floor. Some of the team leaders in the factories were younger than the mid-career recruits it was their duty to supervise and train. They had to control men who not only might resent the age difference but who also lacked one important incentive to conform: the promise of semi-automatic promotion. The oldest team leader in the shift I associated with was a man of twenty-nine who had entered the company from a school in N——. He so disliked supervising older mid-career entrants that he would do his best to pass them on to the sub-section head above him.

Younger team leaders probably suffered even more acutely from the problem.

LEAVING THE COMPANY

Recruitment was only part of Marumaru's struggle with the labour market. If finding suitable workers was hard, preventing people from leaving once they had been recruited was just as difficult a task. Marumaru was a very young company, the average age of male employees being twenty-nine, and deaths and retirements were rare. Most of those who left did so voluntarily, the men because they wanted to find other jobs, and the women either for that reason or to marry.

Table V.12. Men and women leaving Marumaru, 1965–71

Company year	No. at beginning	Death	Retired	Leavers Married	Dismissed	Other	No. at end	Crude leaving rate*
Men								%
1971†	833	3	4		1	90	1,007	10.7
1970	781	–	1		1	99	833	12.5
1969	588	–	1		2	57	781	8.8
1968	541	–	–		1	57	588	10.3
1967	561	–	3		–	50	541	9.6
1966	528	1	2		–	48	561	9.4
1965	473	2	–		1	44	528	9.4
Women								
1971†	121	1	1	13	–	20	146	26.2
1970	134	–	1	12	1	36	121	39.2
1969	110	1	1	11	–	24	134	30.3
1968	89	–	–	4	–	18	110	22.1
1967	102	–	–	15	–	14	89	30.4
1966	109	1	2	13	–	15	102	29.4
1965	99	–	–	13	–	25	109	36.5

* Crude leaving rate = leavers of all types ÷ average number in company during year.
† These figures were compiled at the end of 1971, and since it usually took three or four months for reports on leavers to come in from the factories, the stated number of leavers for 1971 is almost certainly far too low.

Just as one would expect from the state of the national labour market, most of the male leavers from Marumaru were young men who had only worked in the company for a year or two. I was able to get details of sixty-four men who had left Marumaru between 1 September 1969 and

30 June 1970, the greater part of the 1970 company year. The distribution of age and length of service among them is given in Table V.13:

Table V.13. *Male employees leaving Marumaru by age and length of service, 1970 (ten months)*

Age	Length of service (years)								Total
	0–1	1–2	3–5	6–10	11–15	16–20	21–25	25+	
16–17	2	1	–	–	–	–	–	–	3
18–19	13	4	5	–	–	–	–	–	22
20–22	3	2	7	1	–	–	–	–	13
23–25	2	2	2	1	–	–	–	–	7
26–30	1	–	3	1	–	–	–	–	5
31–35	4	–	1	–	–	–	–	–	5
36–40	1	–	1	–	–	–	–	–	2
41–45	1	–	–	–	–	1	–	–	2
46–50	1	–	–	–	–	–	–	–	1
51–55	1	–	–	–	–	–	1	1	3
55+	–	–	–	–	1	–	–	–	1
Total	29	9	19	3	1	1	1	1	64

During the period in question two-thirds of the men who left Marumaru were under twenty-five, and had less than five years' service to their credit. Usually there were even more young men among the leavers, for the 1970 figures were slightly anomalous. During 1970 the company had kept its new graduates on the shop floor for a whole year, and some of them had fallen into despair and left. A second and more significant influence on the leaving rate was that in 1969 Marumaru had taken over a small company. Marumaru had been short of production capacity in the area north of Tokyo. It was proposing to build a huge new factory there, but to fill the gap before the new factory could be completed, Marumaru decided to take over a relatively small corrugated board firm with one rather antiquated plant in just the right area. The old plant would be scrapped when the new factory was ready, and the ex-employees of the smaller company would move to it. In fact, however, most of the ex-employees of the smaller company left Marumaru within a year of the merger. They were prompted to do so partly because Marumaru, unlike their original employer, ran a 24-hour shift system, so that night work was required of them (though their pay was much higher than before). An even greater incentive to leave, however, was the realization that few of them were likely to achieve much in the new organization. The smaller

company had had an old, poorly educated labour force with a high proportion of men who had changed jobs frequently. Such employees did
not stand much chance of promotion in a company like Marumaru, with
young, relatively well-educated employees, many of whom had come
into the company straight from school. For its part, Marumaru was not
sorry to see the ex-employees of the small company go. They were hardly
the right people for a firm in Marumaru's position.

The effects both of the graduate training programme and the merger
are apparent from Table V.14, where the sixty-four male leavers are
analysed by age and educational level. The five graduates under thirty left
because, presumably, they disliked shop floor work. I am not able to
explain why so many older graduates left. Seven of the thirteen men of
middle school education who were over the age of twenty-three had
come from the newly merged company. But for them the pattern of
leaving among those with middle school education would have been
similar to that among those with high school education.

Table V.14. Male employees leaving Marumaru by age and educational level,
1970 (ten months)

| | Level of education: | | |
Age	Middle School	High School	College/ University
16–17	3		
18–19	8	14	
20–22	1	12	
23–25	2	1	4
26–30	2	2	1
31–35	4	–	1
36–40	1	–	1
41–45	1	–	1
46–50	1	–	–
51–55	2	–	1
55+	–	1	–
Total	25	30	9 (64)

No one at Marumaru knew why young people left. The reasons the
leavers themselves stated on their resignation forms were usually obvious
excuses, 'family problems' being the most common; though fifteen per
cent. of male leavers said that night shift work was what was causing them

to resign. Occasionally, when leaving rates in a factory rose particularly high, the management would undertake an enquiry. An intensive enquiry would have been a delicate business, for it would have meant consulting the leavers or at least potential leavers, and so giving a chance to the young to comment on their elders, the spineless and irresponsible to criticize the people who were doing their utmost to make the company successful, and those with little interest in the community to pass judgement on what the community stood for. Understandably, therefore, the enquiries were restricted to a discussion among the managers about how best to prevent the spoilt youngsters from leaving quite so fast. Some improvements would be decided upon, and blame would be laid on circumstances beyond managerial control: on the education system; or on the fact that Japanese were having smaller families, so that young men tended to be only sons or even only children, and had no experience of the give and take of community life that came with having to get on with numbers of brothers and sisters. Marumaru did not even have the dubious satisfaction of knowing where the leavers went, for their new employers did not ask for references, any more than Marumaru asked for the references of its own mid-career entrants. Many of the employees who were about to leave talked of going into the 'water trades', of jobs in bars, cabarets, and restaurants where there was freedom, fun and companionship; but most of them probably found jobs in industry.

The truth was that men were leaving less because they were being driven out than because there was nothing to induce them to stay. Many of the high school entrants had never intended to devote their lives to Marumaru in the first place, having joined the company only to get themselves to Tokyo and look around. Those who had supposed they were entering a firm for life soon learned to wonder whether, given that it would take four or five years to become a machine charge hand, it might not be a good idea to try another firm. Marumaru was not a bad employer, and conditions at some of the factories were excellent; but there was nothing special about the corrugated board industry, and all sorts of interesting companies, some quite well known, others with no shift systems, and yet others with good sports grounds, were advertising for workers. Once they had achieved this state of mind young men were prompted to make the decision to quit by the most minor events. A man would leave because another member of his intake had resigned. Or, most exasperating for the management, a trivial upset at work would cause a man to leave. In every factory section heads and supervisors told the same stories: if you ordered an extra hour of overtime, or ticked off a worker for being careless, or even raised your voice to make yourself heard over the noise of the machines, the next thing you knew was that someone had resigned, and someone else was taking time off to look for a job.

It was very probable that recent influences, including the postwar education system, had made young people less compliant and heightened their sense of adventure. Even so, the argument that young people left because they belonged to a corrupt modern generation was vitiated not only by the behaviour of the young graduates, but also by the fact that the leaving rate had been high five, ten, and fifteen years earlier.[1] Many of the supervisors and managers who were so ready to berate young people for their 'selfish' modern attitudes, had themselves changed companies in their youth for what had presumably been selfish reasons. Evidently young people left largely because their youth allowed them to do so; their belonging to a new generation was of secondary importance.[2]

It is clear that the large proportion of voluntary leavers from Japanese companies makes the description 'lifetime employment' quite inadequate, even when applied only to bigger companies. Yet most of those who leave of their own accord are young, so that one can still reasonably talk of 'lifetime employment', with the provision that the 'lifetime' extends from the age of twenty-five, when an employee settles down, until his retirement at fifty-five—a period which does indeed constitute the bulk of his working life. But the idea that companies can and do dismiss their workers seems much more flagrantly against the rules of 'lifetime employment'. For this reason very few workers are ever formally dismissed. At Marumaru the management reserved the right to sack employees for a number of all-inclusive crimes: 'undertaking activities which the company could recognize as unsuitable' or 'performing acts equivalent to acts specifically proscribed'. In fact, however, those few men who had been dismissed in the seven years 1965–71 had nearly all been thieves. Their dismissals caused no resentment among employees. It was considered that the company had a right, if not a duty, to get rid of them. Even so, some

[1] I could find no convincing evidence that the leaving rate at Marumaru was rising with the worsening labour shortage. The leaving rates in the mid-1960s were not significantly different from those in 1970 (Table V.12), given that Marumaru had been a much smaller company, with inferior rates of pay, in the earlier period; and taking into account differences in the definition of 'full employee' over the years.

[2] Though this judgement should not be taken as a denial of the importance of generational changes. The attitudes of present-day young Japanese workers are significantly different from those of young workers in the early postwar period. For a discussion of the problem of differentiating between the effects of age and of generation see Robert E. Cole (1976) and Okamoto Hideaki* (1971).

of them had been treated very gently. Sometimes the police were not informed of the crime; and Marumaru seemed surprisingly willing to conceal the facts from a dismissed man's future employers. Occasionally Marumaru would dismiss a man who was persistently absent from work after repeated warnings; and, again, such dismissals were thought proper by the employees. More often, however, the company would 'ask the man to leave' *(yamete morau)*. Neglect of fire regulations was a third offence for which the penalty might be dismissal in practice as well as theory.

In less clear-cut cases of misdemeanour the company did not attempt to use the extensive powers it had given itself, but preferred to encourage an offender to tender his resignation.[1] This practice was a devious tribute to the principle that no employee should ever be dismissed. Sometimes it was possible to prevail upon a man to resign immediately, and so avoid controversy arising over his case, but sometimes subtle and complicated manœuvres continued over months.

On one occasion the company waged a campaign against a man who had been elected to a post in the company union by claiming that his presence on the union committee was damaging labour-management relations. By constantly repeating the claim the management persuaded the union to strike the man from the roll of membership. Soon afterwards the company suggested that he leave for his own good, because it would be impossible for someone who was not a union member to lead the normal life of an employee. After two or three months of hesitation the man finally resigned. Although the personnel department admitted having engineered the man's removal, the man himself was convinced that the management had been sympathetic to him, and that it had been the union which had forced him to go. There were various other, rather less complex cases, in which men were put into intolerable positions and so had to leave. There was also an instance of a woman who, having re-fused a transfer (women were very rarely transferred), also rejected all suggestions from her superiors that she should leave. After a month they gave up trying to persuade her.

These were examples of what the company might have viewed as dissidence, and it could be argued that no company, however genuine its commitment to 'lifetime employment', could permit employees to be disobedient and seditious. What impressed Abegglen[2] most was the

---

[1] This was also true at the factory Robert E. Cole (1971: 119–22) studied, and at Hitachi; R. P. Dore (1973: 34).

[2] James C. Abegglen (1958: 17).

apparent refusal to dismiss workers on *economic* grounds. Individual workers, he believed, were not sacked however little they contributed to the company; and even when a change of circumstances made an entire work force idle, management would continue to pay workers until times got better. In fact, firms do dismiss, or at least achieve the dismissal of, even full male employees. They do so with considerable reluctance, and only after trying other measures—not hiring new recruits, retiring employees slightly early, cutting back on orders to sub-contractors, and dismissing seasonal workers, 'temporary' employees, or women. Since the 'Nixon Shock' of 1971, and even more since the oil crisis of 1973, many Japanese companies have declared part of their supposedly permanent labour force redundant. Usually the company involved—and Tōyōbō[1] in the textile industry or Alps Electric[2] or Mitsumi Electric[3] in the electronics industry are good examples—made or was about to make serious losses. Usually, also, men were not 'dismissed' but 'caused to submit voluntary resignations' *(kibō taishoku saseru)*, so that they did at least receive separation allowances.

Even when circumstances are less harrowing than they were in those years, companies can find ways of reducing their work forces for economic reasons, just as they can rid themselves of individual dissidents without being seen to sack them. In the boom year of 1970 Marumaru's smallest factory, which was situated in a remote part of Japan, proved unprofitable for reasons that could not have been foreseen. The plant was closed and the workers, most of whom had been recruited locally, were transferred to another factory two hundred kilometres away.[4] Though the closure was known to be final, the transfers were said only to be temporary, and the workers were not given allowances to move their families, only their own fares home every fortnight. Naturally, the arrangement soon became unacceptable to most of the employees and they resigned.

[1] *Nihon Keizai Shinbun* (evening edition) 15 October 1974, p. 3, 'Tōyōbō: 2,330 nin ni asshuku: kibō taishoku de rōsō to gōi.' (Tōyōbō: agreement with the union reduces voluntary resignations to 2,330).

[2] *Nihon Keizai Shinbun*, 20 December 1974, p. 23, 'Nisen-nihyaku-nin jin-in seiri: Arupusu Denki gruupu sansha: zen-jūgyōin no niwari' (Two thousand two hundred people trimmed: twenty per cent. of all employees in three companies of the Alps Electric group).

[3] *Nihon Keizai Shinbun*, 18 December 1974, p. 7, 'Nihyaku-shichijū-nin no kibō taishoku teian: Mitsumi Denki' (Mitsumi Electric: a plan for two hundred and seventy voluntary resignations).

[4] For a similar example provided by a rather more famous company see *Nihon Keizai Shinbun*, 29 March 1975, p. 8, 'Hitachi no kyūhyaku-nin haiten taisaku: sanbyaku-nin-ijō taishoku' (Hitachi's plan to transfer nine hundred people: more than three hundred resign).

'Lifetime Employment' as Ideal and in Reality

At the beginning of the chapter I remarked that the study of how people joined and left companies revealed something of the nature of the company community; and particularly of the sense of mutual commitment between employer and employee which contributes to the strength of the community, and of the authority by which the community is directed. I also noted that the labour market was an arena in which the company and the wider society exchanged influences. These two themes, the nature of the community, and the relations between company and society, will be the subjects of the last two chapters, and in them the relevance of the labour market to both issues will become more clearly apparent. Even at this point, however, it is possible to say something about how recruitment and resignation reflect inner values, and the labour market conveys external influences.

Let us deal, in particular, with the question of commitment, of the extent to which employer and employee are bound to each other for moral or practical reasons, and the degree to which 'lifetime employment' exists in reality or as an ideal.

It is apparent that the term 'lifetime employment' describes the employment conditions of only a part of the Japanese labour force, and is even then a very imperfect description. As Abegglen himself knew, 'lifetime employment' is not offered by smaller companies, which still employ more than half of all workers. Nor does it apply to temporary workers or to women. It is enjoyed only by male full employees of large companies. Yet even in the largest companies men have to retire early, at fifty-five. 'Lifetime employment' does not last for life. Large Japanese companies take the best and most productive years of their employees' lives, and then leave them to look after themselves in their period of decline. Firms may dismiss workers openly or (more usually) by means of subterfuge, even before retirement age, for reasons varying from criminal activities to mere economic convenience; and though it is true that dismissals from big companies are relatively rare, neither employers nor employees leave them entirely out of their calculations. Finally, many of the younger and less educated workers in large companies leave their firms.

With all these qualifications admitted and exceptions made, what significance does 'lifetime employment' retain? Is not the abbreviated 'lifetime', between twenty-five and fifty-five, merely that period in a man's career when he is on the one hand able to stay with a big company, and on the other can no longer profitably change his job? Is it not true that companies try to employ young people and then keep them because young people are cheap to hire and easy to train? Is not 'lifetime employment' simply the result of universal economic forces, an artefact of the labour market? Presumably Professors Marsh and Mannari are right when they

> disagree with those who argue that there is a distinctively Japanese pattern of lifetime commitment. Insofar as Japanese employees in large firms do remain in one firm, this is due mainly to factors other than loyalty to the company as such. Japanese employees' motives for staying in one firm are essentially the same reasons that tie Western employees to a firm.[1]

It is salutary to point out that what 'lifetime employment' there is could be construed as the effect of a labour market consisting of essentially self-serving individuals and firms. But this sort of explanation does not invalidate the proposition that 'lifetime employment' is at the same time an ideal, and a very powerful one, entailing an obligation of mutual attachment between firm and employee. Sanctioned by what is seen as tradition, morally correct, and emblematic of Japanese culture, 'lifetime employment' is the goal towards which both firms and individuals have to direct their efforts—or their apologies.

One impressive proof of this was Marumaru's decision to change its recruitment practices and take in school and college graduates, a decision that may have been prompted partly by the fact that young people received low wages, but very much more by considerations of what was right for a firm in Marumaru's position in the society of industry, and of how a company community ought to be composed. The subsequent inability of Marumaru to come to terms with the changing labour market revealed how powerful the ideal was. Instead of behaving as our imaginary 'rational' employer might, and encouraging 'mid-career entrants', Marumaru spent tens of millions of yen trying to recruit high school leavers who were known to be unlikely to stay, and completely ignored its mid-career entrants. Another indication of the importance of the ideal was the deviousness with which the company dismissed employees. Marumaru had to be underhand because to be overt would be to admit a significant departure from what was right.

Nor is 'lifetime employment' merely an ideal for management alone.

[1] Robert M. Marsh and Hiroshi Mannari (1976: 253).

At Marumaru workers of all ages interpreted events as if 'lifetime employ-ment' was normal and right, and exceptions to it due to pressure of cir-cumstance or moral deficiencies. It was true that some high school entrants came into the company with no intention of staying longer than a few years or even a few months. Many, however, did intend to stay and saw themselves driven out by management failures and ineptitude, almost against their wills. When the foreman wanted ten or fifteen hours a week overtime, when 'good human relations' didn't exist in one's section, when so many other young people were leaving, then surely the company was doing something wrong and not keeping its side of the bargain? In arguing in this way, the young leavers were essentially agreeing with those managers who were so contemptuous of the moral fibre of the modern generation. The rightness of 'lifetime employment' was not at issue, only the reason why it didn't exist in practice. An even more impressive demonstration of the acceptance of the principle was the demeanour of the mid-career entrants. The example I gave of the forthright mid-career entrant was quite exceptional. Most men in this category were surprisingly ready to accept that they had set their own careers back by changing companies; and that it was reasonable that, for example, school entrants of their age should be preferred over them. None of them, not even the forthright one I quoted, appealed to the countervailing argument that, for example, mid-career entrants were actually better for the company than school entrants, because they had more experience of different types of work, and had got the *wanderlust* out of their systems before joining Marumaru.

Many workers went further than merely accepting 'lifetime employ-ment' as a principle. They even suggested that Marumaru, like most other companies, was practising it. Men who held this opinion tended to be older employees, and they were generalizing from their own particular circumstances. They knew, of course, that women and temporary workers were not employed for life, that young men were leaving in droves, that union members who opposed the management too violently would be got rid of, and that employees at the small factory were being strongly encouraged to go. They were able, however, to reconcile the actual insecurity of employment at Marumaru with the thesis that 'life-time employment' existed by reference to imagined conditions in the West. I was told by employees of all grades, including managers who had made trips to America, that any worker in the West who made even a tiny mistake would immediately lose his job. By contrast with these heartless Western practices, there was indeed a 'lifetime employment' system at Marumaru, however many people left the company for one reason or another.

In the long run it will become even more difficult for Japanese companies to operate 'lifetime employment' systems than it was for Marumaru in 1970. As the effects of the oil crisis diminish, the Japanese economy will probably grow with something of its former rapidity, and many firms which did little recruiting between 1973 and 1976 will start taking in workers once more. At the same time the proportion of young people in the labour force will decrease inexorably, making it impossible even for the most famous companies to attract all their new workers from schools and colleges. There are two, not wholly alternative ways in which Japanese companies can be expected to adapt. One will be to adopt the ways of the imaginary 'rational' company postulated earlier. Companies can deliberately set out to attract and recruit men who are already at work in other companies. Since it will make no sense to pay them by age and length of service, their new employers will offer them pay according to the jobs they are being hired to do. Thus individual skills will become more important in the labour market. Job seekers will have to have skills, and firms will have to reward them. To keep their workers, and also to meet the demands of labour unions, companies will raise the official age of retirement, and this, too, will make it impossible to pay workers by age or length of service. In addition companies may begin to offer better employment conditions to women; not only higher wages, but career prospects similar to those offered to men. There are already signs of all these developments. Firms are deliberately recruiting mid-career entrants. The official age of retirement has been rising slowly.[1] Certain bigger companies are improving the working conditions for women. All these tendencies, it needs hardly be said, will lead to the dissolution of 'lifetime employment' in practice.

The other solution, no less rational from the employer's point of view than the first, preserves the ideal of 'lifetime employment' rather better. Companies will confer the privileges of 'lifetime employment' on an even smaller proportion of the total labour force under their control. There will be a tiny core of full employees, and relatively large numbers of temporary workers, part-time women employees, and, above all, sub-contracting firms. It is already possible to see a progress towards this solution in

[1] Rather more slowly in big firms than small ones, big firms being more worried about the effects on the quality of their labour and the implications for their 'pay by age' systems. For details see: *Rōdō Jihō*: 27: 11: (1974): 6–8, '*Teinensei, sai-kōyōsei-kinmu enchō seido no genjō*'. (The present conditions of retirement, re-employment, and work-extension.)

companies like Uchida Yōkō and Kokuyo in the office equipment industry. Both these companies control manufacturing sub-contractors, whose activities they finance and co-ordinate and whose products they sell. Similar tendencies can be seen in the construction industry, in which companies like Kajima and Kumagai Gumi have, like construction firms elsewhere, reduced themselves to organizing and financing teams which supervise the sub-contractors undertaking the actual work of construction. The two solutions clearly have quite different effects on the standing of various types of worker. Which of the two is preferred, or more plausibly, how the two are combined in practice, will naturally influence Japanese society in the future; but I shall discuss that in the last chapter.

Now and in the next chapter I should like to consider the general nature, of which the commitment between employer and employee is only one element, of the community which forms around the Japanese company. We have already seen how a sense of community is fostered and the values of the community leaders expressed, in the way in which companies recruit and the type of applicant they accept. From the graduates who applied to Marumaru, for example, the company tried to choose men of at least a certain intellectual standard, but above all it was looking for those who would fit into the community. Successful candidates had to have the right sort of conventional family background, and perhaps most important of all, the right attitude of eager deference. Ideally, Marumaru would have liked to recruit high school leavers of similar disposition, intelligent, self-confident, but demurely naïve and obediently persevering. In fact, of course, recruitment was going awry, and the kind of people Marumaru did not set out to recruit, experienced men from other companies, were forming an ever larger part of the labour force.

The effect leavers had on the community was equally evident. The continual loss of high school entrants, the very people the company had chosen, naturally had a bad effect on community morale. Supervisors, exasperated by the resignations, grumbled at their young subordinates. Other young people were unsettled by having so many colleagues and team-mates resign—and leave them to do even more work than before. Even those who had nothing to do with the factories, from which the high school entrants were leaving, were affected. Salesmen, office girls, and research staff thought of the high rate of leaving as a sour comment on the quality of life to be found at Marumaru and on the standing of the company in industrial society.

Behaviour and attitudes in a company community may not merely be affected by the fact that people do leave, but also by the possibility that they *can*. I began this chapter by introducing a distinction, which was suggested by the statistics of the labour market, between mobile and immobile workers. The immobile workers were the better educated or older men, usually working in large companies. The mobile workers were younger, less educated men, especially those in small companies, and women. It is no surprise, given that the individual firm is a component of the labour market, that these categories of mobility and immobility could be applied—and to the same types of people—within Marumaru. We have come across two explanations of mobility, the readiness of people to leave companies. The first, most apparent in the context of the labour market as a whole, was that workers tend to be mobile if they think they can get as good a job elsewhere as with their current employer. The second explanation, found within Marumaru, was that those inclined to leave were morally at odds with the company community. Either they themselves were spineless and degenerate, or else the company had not been behaving in the right way. In practice, of course, the two explanations apply simultaneously. Leaving a company is bound to involve both practical and moral considerations. But whichever explanation is predominant in any particular case, we should expect to find a difference in the attitudes of mobile and immobile workers to the community and its values. To the extent that mobility is a question of outside opportunities, then mobile workers can presumably afford to take more casual attitudes to the demands of their employer and the rules of the community—as indeed the example of the high school entrants suggests. To the extent that mobility is determined by moral differences, then *a fortiori* the mobile employees should behave differently from immobile ones.

In the next chapter I shall try to explain how mobile and immobile employees of various types at Marumaru compared in their attitudes to their employer and to each other. Then, in the light of my findings, I shall put forward some views on the problem earlier put aside: the nature of authority in Japanese companies.

CHAPTER VI

Company and Employee

English speakers can choose to say that they are working *for* a company or working *in* a company, or even *at* or *with* a company. The degree of prepositional freedom is the result of the ambiguity of the idea of the company. The lawyer, we saw, thinks of the company as a corporation independent of the individual people associated with it; the layman, as a team of workers in a physical setting. The employee's view of the company combines both these. He is in a legally fixed relation to the corporation, but inside the team. Japanese employees manifest a similar ambiguity in a different way. Employees frequently talk of 'our company' (*uchi no kaisha*), and ascribe to it a character quite independent of management or any other group within it. Just as they will remark that 'our company's' share of the market is such and such, they will comment on the curious ways 'our company' has of naming its standard ranks, or its meanness over expenses, or its treatment of sub-section heads. Employees are both inside '*our* company' and helplessly under it.

Relations between employees of all types and their company are, therefore, a compound of relations with the company as corporation, and with the company as community. In this chapter, in which I shall rely largely on material from Marumaru, I shall start by considering separately the two elements that make up the compound, before assessing the properties of the final mixture.

At Marumaru, as in most other Japanese companies, there were many different types of employees: men and women, young and old, seniors and juniors, school and mid-career entrants, graduates and high school leavers, distributed throughout the various divisions of the company and doing different jobs. In one important respect, however, they could be divided simply into two categories. Among some types of employee there was a very high leaving rate, and among others a rather low one. There were, statistically speaking, mobile and immobile employees. The mobile employees were the younger men who had not been to university, and the women, nearly all of whom were young. The immobile employees were the young male graduates, and the men of over twenty-five, irrespective of education.

In the last chapter I argued that what made the mobile employees prone to leave was a combination of moral and practical circumstances. Their values were different from those of the company, but at the same time, under the prevailing labour market conditions, they were able to leave Marumaru without much likelihood of material loss. Other firms would offer them equally good pay and prospects. Immobile employees, by contrast, were more in tune with the company and were at the same time discouraged from leaving, because they had accumulated credit with their employer to the extent that they were unlikely to get a better job somewhere else. In this chapter I shall try to show how the same moral and practical motives that induced employees to stay or go influenced their attitudes to the company and to each other.

THE EMPLOYEE AND THE CORPORATION

My knowledge of relations between employees and Marumaru as a corporation derived from two sources, my own observations and the company questionnaire. Each year the personnel department distributed a confidential questionnaire to all employees. Many questions were asked, varying from the rents respondents paid and the sizes of their rooms, to their hobbies and whether they wanted transfers. But the most important unit of the questionnaire was that in which employees were urged to 'Write whatever opinions you have about any aspect of the company'.[1] Most of the remarks I quote below were made in response to this request.

The questionnaire forms were so complex that as the number of employees had grown the personnel department had ceased to have the time to analyse them, and merely filed them away for reference. I was therefore the only person to have scrutinized the 1969 forms, from which the quotations below are taken. I read all the eight hundred or so replies to that year's questionnaire, but concentrated my research on the forms from the head office and one factory. Details of the numbers of respondents at these are given in Table VI.1.

Given that there were 780 men and 130 women in the entire company at the time of the questionnaire, the respondents from these two places comprised about twenty per cent. of the men and twenty-three per cent. of the women respectively.

[1] *Kaisha zenpan ni tsuite no donna koto de mo kinyū shite kudasai.*

Table VI.1. Questionnaire respondents at Marumaru head office and Yokohama factory, 1969

	Questionnaire respondents (October 1969)	Payroll (September 1969)	Percentage response %
Head Office			
Men	41	77	53.2
Women	16	22	72.7
Yokohama			
Men	114	118	96.6
Women	14	15	93.3
Total			
Men	155	195	
Women	30	37	

The men of the head office were all either older men or graduates, likely to stay with the company. At the Yokohama factory 38 (33 per cent.) of the 114 men who responded were non-graduates of less than five years service and under the age of twenty-five. These, therefore, were the mobile male employees.

A further eight men (7 per cent.) were older but had only become full employees at Yokohama within the previous two years. They were not fully settled in at Marumaru, but were not very likely to leave. The remaining sixty-eight men could be counted as immobile. Either they were graduates, or else older men of sufficient length of service to be unlikely to find better jobs outside Marumaru. Virtually all the women both at the head office and in the factory were young and of short service, both past and prospective.

The significance of the questionnaire was that it provided direct evidence, quite uninfluenced by any interpolation on my part, of how people viewed Marumaru. It was, of course, an official document, and the opinions expressed in the returns were not always sincere, honest or complete. Some people wrote to ingratiate themselves with the company. Others were using an annual opportunity to make complaints, sometimes about very trivial matters. Many important problems that were the subject of continual gossip were hardly mentioned, because respondents thought it wisest not to put things in writing. Only one person on the hundreds of forms I examined admitted, in answer to a question, having poor relations with a superior. Again, the replies from the factory that had newly merged with Marumaru at the time the 1969–70 questionnaire was circulated were remarkably bland—though one-third of the work force at the factory left during the year. Yet if the questionnaire returns were silent on certain obvious issues, they did illuminate some more subtle ones, and opinions were expressed in them that I at least never heard anyone say.

THE IMMOBILE EMPLOYEES

All the immobile employees at Marumaru were attached to the company by considerations of their own interest, or because the company had offered or would offer them opportunities to do things they wanted. All of them were to some degree inhibited from changing companies by conditions on the labour market. They did, however, vary in the closeness of their association with the company and in their willingness to accept its demands. It was possible to distinguish the attitudes of three sorts of immobile employees, the younger graduates, the older employees (both graduate and non-graduate), and the non-graduates of between twenty-five and thirty-five years of age.

We saw earlier how strongly predisposed new graduates were to enjoy life in the company. Most of them had gone to university to read subjects like economics, law, or commercial studies, that would specifically prepare them for their work. Their social experiences at university could also be seen as a training for company life. It was not surprising, therefore, that young graduates appeared contented. Their questionnaire returns were free of complaints about pay and conditions, and displayed instead an informed concern with the organization of the company and its defects. Thus a computer programmer in his late twenties wrote: 'We have to think about moving into the next growth industry and not just stick to the corrugated board business.' A salesman at the Yokohama factory complained that:

There's no consistency in the company's policies. I think it is a very good thing to cut down on the production administration departments and put people into direct production jobs; but as a result the salesmen are having to do work that naturally should be done by production administration, and the sales effort is being limited. As for the introduction of the computer, far from office work being rationalized, the number of people has increased and the administrative work of the salesmen is growing.

The most frequent complaints in this category were that there was no

7

proper training, and that it was impossible for young people to participate in making decisions. The need for training, and the absence of an official training programme were deeply felt, for many of the young graduates gave as their interests and hobbies subjects connected with their work—computer systems, engineering, accounting or box design. Handbooks on these and similar subjects could be found on the bookshelves of most of the rooms in the head office hostel.

A new specialist training department is being established, but I should like effective training from top to bottom.

I am now learning sales but the company doesn't teach me very much. I would like the section head and others to give us lectures about sales.

The complaints on the questionnaire forms about being left out of decision-making and being made to do irrelevant work all came from one department, the production department of the head office, where the problem appeared to be acute; but in conversation young graduates in other parts of the company voiced similar grievances:

Although the company has grown so big, managers have received little power from the directors, so that work is done without any drive. Managers are doing work that anyone could do. Much of the work we young people do is of such a kind that it doesn't matter whether we do it or not. We should like to do work that is genuinely useful to the company; if we don't neither we nor the company can develop . . . I think that the time has come to look at this throughout the whole company. Only when we can trust the people above us, and when it has become possible for everyone to make full use of the abilities they have, will Marumaru become an enterprise of the first water in fact as well as theory.

The impression given by these quotations, of young graduates happily committed to the company and eager to learn and to serve, was broadly correct. There was, however, a common opinion among men of this type which did not appear in the questionnaire. Many of them were intellectually dissatisfied with modern industrial society, and particularly Japan's version of it. Their dissatisfaction often expressed itself in extreme left-wing views. I met perhaps five or six soi-disant Communists who were nevertheless much devoted to Marumaru, and as eager as anyone else to get on in the company. Very few Marumaru graduates had ever participated in student political activities, but many graduates, even some of the older ones, claimed sympathy with some of the aims of militant students. Two or three of the young graduates tried to give vent to their feelings by being active in Marumaru's rather feeble company union; but most confined themselves to private debate.

The responses to the questionnaire of the older male employees, both graduate and non-graduate, were far less effusive than those of the young graduates. Many of the more senior men did not want (or need) to confide in the personnel department staff, and of those who did fill in their forms only a few had anything special to say to the company. Their subjects were often technical, and always concerned with the company and its welfare rather than the individual himself:

> Generally speaking, the problems that are going to appear from now on are not going to be predictable, and we have to strengthen the management and information systems to deal with them. There is a feeling of imbalance between production and sales, and the people in charge of each of the executive units should resolve matters in mutual discussions. In particular, the top management of each factory should consider the results that will come of research and specialist responsibility.

Like the young graduates, these older immobile company members were genuinely engrossed in their work—though the questionnaire revealed them to be very much less interested in training and learning. The older men also had what their juniors had not yet had time to acquire, a great affection for and deep loyalty to Marumaru, together with a considerable pride in the company's achievements, for many of which they had themselves been responsible.

The older workers were also less troubled by the general questions arising from their attachment to Marumaru and its place in the world. They were, for the most part, confident that the company was making a valuable contribution to society, and that their own work was therefore of some worth. Many of them had been deeply influenced by war and early postwar experiences. By contrast with the unsettled existences they had been leading during and immediately after the war, their present lives were stable and successful, and they were very conscious of the advantages they and their families had gained from Marumaru. Nor was the benefit purely personal. Their company and firms like it had restored Japan to prosperity, and had assured her survival in the international struggle for existence. More times than I was able to take note of I was told that Japan had lost the war largely because of America's huge industrial power. Losing had, however, been a good thing because Japan could never have been so successful if she had won it. Now Japan herself was an 'economic great power', and the next century belonged to Japan and Germany. However much America tried to keep Japan down by imposing import quotas and surcharges, the Japanese, who always did best in adversity, would build the country up again. It must be remembered that the years 1970-1 were disturbing ones for American-Japanese trading relations, and events no doubt prompted more anti-American feeling than usual. But the comparisons between military and economic struggle were made so frequently that it was clear that, for some of these older employees at least, work was a war being fought by other means, and loyalty and service to Marumaru were a form of loyalty and service to the nation.

In spite of their affection for Marumaru, these older immobile employees resented being 'the pawns of the company', whose loyalty and dependability could be taken for granted. The personnel department took great care, for example, to meet the transfer requests of young shop floor workers. Some of the 1971 high school entrants asked for and were granted transfers to different factories within a fortnight of joining the company—though they left before the arrangements could be completed. Yet older employees were rarely consulted before being transferred. They were expected to go where they were sent and do what they were told. Again, though it was morally difficult for anyone at Marumaru to take his personal holiday allowance, senior employees not only had to waive their personal allowances but even, on occasion, their entitlement to national holidays. During the four day holiday at the New Year, most of the senior employees at the Yokohama factory went on holiday a day later, and returned a day earlier than their subordinates. There was no point in the senior employees' complaining at this treatment, because the company had so complete a control of their lives. They merely resigned themselves to their disadvantages, consoling themselves with thoughts of promotion or with dreams of setting up their own small businesses after they had retired and become their own masters.

The last group of immobile employees was that of the non-graduate men in their late twenties and early thirties.[1] Between twenty-five and thirty-five a great change took place in the lives of non-graduates. In their early twenties young men were only casually attached to Marumaru. They were very much the juniors in their shift teams or office sections, with little responsibility and not much knowledge of what was going on. Their colleagues would be leaving in large numbers, and they themselves

[1] My interpretation of the attitudes of this category of employee owes much to conversations I have had with Professor Okamoto Hideaki.

would probably have thought of moving elsewhere. After the age of twenty-five a man's value on the labour market declined sharply; and if, as was likely, he married and had a family he would be even less inclined to think of leaving. In any case he would now begin to receive recognition from the company and the community. By twenty-five or six he might be in charge of a machine if not a team, and his work would bring him into contact with the more senior managers of the factory. If he was still a bachelor in the company hostel, he would have been asked to sit on a committee or look after new school entrants. By thirty-five his position in the company would be established without question. Even if he were not a sub-section head, he would be one of the senior team leaders on the shop floor, running the corrugator or the boiler, or handling the despatch of goods. He would now be nearly indispensable. Things would become difficult for everybody if he took more than a day or two off. He would, of course, have to attend most of the meetings of the factory management, and he would be on easy terms with the factory manager and his deputies, from whom he would learn all the gossip from the head office.

The loss of freedom sustained in passing from irresponsible young shop floor worker to committed sub-section head was not easy to bear. What made the position of the newly immobilized employees even more unenviable was that, far from receiving material advantages in return for being tied to the company, they were very frequently worse off than before.[1] As bachelors in the company hostel they had paid only 5,000 yen monthly for board and lodging, from a salary of 50–60,000 yen. On marriage they had to leave the hostel, usually for normal rented accommodation. Though the company paid marriage allowances, the young couple would find themselves having to live on what remained of a salary of about 70,000 yen after paying 15,000 yen rent. Only much later, when a man was in his late thirties, did responsibility allowances and high grade payments bring salaries more comfortably into line with expenses. The employees of intermediate age therefore had the worst of all worlds. They lacked the relative freedom and prosperity of the younger workers, but had not yet gained the advantages that compensated their elders for being tied to the company.

The attitudes to the company of these employees of intermediate age reflected their preoccupation with commitment, freedom and welfare, and were frequently a fiercely illogical combination of loyalty and resentment. One striking example was the resignation of a particularly promising young shop floor worker of twenty-five at the Yokohama

[1] Cf. Robert E. Cole (1971: 157–8).

factory. He decided to leave immediately after receiving the company's offer of a night school course to enable him to get a degree. He made a conventional excuse for leaving to the authorities, but told his friends that he did not want to become too deeply obliged to the company. He would do the course later, at his own expense.

The company's annual attendance prizes also engendered violently mixed feelings in these employees. The prizes, which were very frequently won by team leaders and others of similar age and seniority, were given to those who had taken no more than their allowance of holidays, and who had given a full week's notice of their intentions before taking even a day off. The value of the prizes did not exceed three thousand yen. The prizes were, then, very minor rewards for behaviour convenient to the company. But a great many employees saw them as moral levers working against their freedom to take their paid holidays as they wished. I was told by several people, including some of the prize winners, that because of the prizes one wasn't able to take the day off if one had a headache.

Then there was the case of the team head who published an article in the Yokohama factory magazine *Cloud*, a quarterly which was supported by a company subsidy and given an admirable degree of editorial freedom. The author was a popular young man who was well thought of by his superiors. Both they and his subordinates considered him a good Maru-maru employee, diligently engaged in carrying out the very work his article satirized:

First and foremost a company must go for profits. This way or that it must make profits. If you don't sell you can't make profits, so the salesmen are given a kick in the arse. (There's no limit to sales. Sell, sell and sell again. Selling is war. Nothing but winning is good enough.) That's what Jack-of-the-nineteen-forties told me. Bit of aggro, because he was defeated? (Let's make it a duty to work twenty-four hours a day, three hundred and sixty-five days a year.) (No question of having the day off if your parents drop dead.) If you think it's a hard grind—the best salesmen *believe* in the value of the company's goods. Let's get rid of this habit of harping on their demerits rather than their merits—that's what they'll tell you. If you sell it you've got to make it, so on with production! (Keep down sedition. Don't allow complaints and grumbles to arise; and at the same time squeeze the utmost effort out of them. Extend the working hours!) Make each team compete in output in overtime and Sunday work. Produce, produce and produce again! Your belly hurts? Mind over matter! You mustn't think, just because you're sweating away, that you're working. Oh no! The result's the thing. Fulfil your norms! You can do anything you set your mind to, that's the attitude. Though Jack-who-pretended-not-to-know told me that he had thought that the time when you could do anything you set your mind to had ended. So that's the motto. The salesmen sell anything, even sell the rejects, that's the idea. And the shop workers go on and on . . .

It was interesting that the team head's seniors responded only mildly to the article. The factory manager called the man in and, in the course of a three-hour interview, suggested that if he thought so little of Marumaru he might like to leave; but no action was taken against him. Other managers thought that the team head had been ill-advised, but that the incident was nevertheless unimportant and would not prejudice the man's career. The team head's contemporaries generally approved of the article and thought it both funny and true.

The oldest of the men in this age group, those approaching thirty-five, were usually sub-section heads. Their position was the most difficult of all, and their attitudes were correspondingly equivocal. They worked harder for the company than any other group of workers, yet they were constantly complaining how 'cold' or 'mean' the company was. Sub-section heads counted as 'management' in the sense that they did not belong to the company union, so that they were not entitled to overtime or night shift allowances. Instead they received a responsibility allowance of 7,000 yen, several thousand yen less than they might otherwise have made. This was a cause of much resentment:

The pay of sub-section heads is too bad, and the various allowances are poor. Once or twice a month I have to leave the factory to do some business outside and I make a loss. The lunch allowance is poor. Sometimes I don't apply [beforehand] to the company, and when I go out on business without an appointment I have to pay for the meals myself. [Edited]

I don't understand why sub-section heads don't get allowances and overtime rates. Living has become more difficult than when I was a team leader.

Sub-section heads are not paid overtime, just meal allowances. Nor do they get night shift allowances. Problems like these are being calmly ignored and I think they should be dealt with.

Another problem for the sub-section head was that the upper management was always ready to find fault with him. There was often talk at the

head office of the (unspecified) defects of first line management, and most
of the very few training programmes that had ever been put into practice
at Marumaru had been devised for sub-section heads. In fact, management
difficulties probably arose higher up. Factories were divided into two main
units, sales and production, each headed by a deputy manager. The
salesmen were usually graduates, due to reach at least the rank of deputy
manager. The production workers were nearly all non-graduates, most of
whom would not exceed the rank of section head. It was becoming
common to promote sales section heads to the position of production
deputy manager. Salesmen transferred in this way knew very little of the
business of keeping machines running, and the task of training their
innocent superiors fell on the production section heads and sub-section
heads. Another problem for the sub-section heads was the constant
shortage of labour. An acting sub-section head (his appointment was soon
to be confirmed) wrote:

What I think, after ten years' work, is that the company has developed
with great leaps and bounds, and is now of some substance. I would like
to think that there will be growth from now on. In the ten years we
have been working on the shop floor the machines have become high-
speed, and the work methods and so on have changed. What doesn't
change is the labour shortage. Day labourers, part-timers and casual
workers are put on to shift work, and all they do is make up the numbers.
Although in certain jobs there are section heads and sub-section heads
with no one underneath them, we team leaders have to deal with ten
people (including those day labourers) all by ourselves. Then if mistakes
occur we are ticked off for having no administrative ability.

Another sub-section head took the offensive against his critical seniors
in an article in *Cloud*.

Today's managers seem to be very fond of new words. Just using words
like Self-Management, Management by Objectives, Such-and-Such a
Movement, Such-and-Such a Technique seems to make them happy.
There are, however, times when these words can have a bad effect on the
employees. If this sort of new word were to come from the first-line
employees then everyone would be able to agree it was the best possible
thing . . .

The position of the sub-section heads, technically managers but tending
to see themselves as subordinate to management, obviously had some

affinity to the position of foreman in Western companies.[1] Too much should not, however, be made of the comparison. At Marumaru the distinction between labour and management was very much less significant than would normally be the case in Western companies, because of the system of standard ranks. Sub-section heads were merely men at one point on a continuum. A few years earlier they had been ordinary employees; in a few years time many of them would be section heads. Moreover, the actual work of supervision, which in a Western company would have been done by a single set of foremen, was shared by employees in a number of ranks. There were machine leaders, twenty-five-year-olds appointed informally to look after medium-sized machines with three operators apiece; team leaders, and sub-section heads, each responsible for a part of the shop floor; and section heads, who were in charge of the shifts. All these people were to some extent 'marginal', in that they could reasonably see themselves as both managers and workers. The particular disadvantages of the sub-section heads at Marumaru resulted not from their holding a position analogous in its ambiguity to that of the Western foreman, so much as from their conditions of employment: the extent to which they were required to serve the company at personal cost, and the purely contingent difficulties caused by the labour shortage and the transfers of salesmen.[2]

THE MOBILE EMPLOYEES

The mobile employees of Marumaru fell into two main categories: young non-graduate men, who were not expected to leave but did; and women, whose mobility was part of the normal course of things.

The very fact that the young non-graduate men left in such large numbers suggested that they felt little loyalty or affection for Marumaru. The absence of both was confirmed by the way they answered the questionnaire. Few of the young workers who filled it in wrote anything more than a peremptory demand or complaint:

When the time comes for me to move to another factory I'd like you to make it the area I want. You might increase the number of clothes (especially trousers) you give us when we first join the company.

I was made to write the same thing last year but afterwards things neither

---

[1] Donald Wray (1949).

[2] Both Professors Cole and Dore have made comparisons between Western foremen and their Japanese equivalents. They, too, have been aware of the difficulty of finding the exact equivalent. Robert E. Cole (1971: 183 n).

got better nor worse. It's just the same as before. I don't suppose it would matter if people like me didn't write anything at all. Oh well, I'll write it anyway. I'm fed up with Yokohama and I want to go back to the country immediately.

Talking about sudden accidents, there is a lot of Sunday work, and with no managers over the rank of team leader there, there is no preparation and [*the machines*] stop for a long time. I am fed up with this sort of thing. I am doing night work, but I think health comes first. I want to do some exercise on Sundays but there's no ground. I'd like you to hire a ground.

Labour management is claptrap, and there's no proper system for placing people. Recently the overwork has been getting worse. You just say its a general social problem and do nothing but fold your hands. No steps are being taken to sort things out. Look at this opinion questionnaire. You get a person to write it, but it just remains writing and nothing happens the way we want it. I have my doubts whether you look into what we write or not.

But more usually the comments consisted merely of two or three words, 'Stop night work', 'poor lighting', 'sports ground', and above all, 'shortage of people'.

The young non-graduates evidently thought of the company in more contractual terms than any group of immobile employees, however discontented. You worked for the company mainly to earn a living. The company shouldn't work you too hard, and it should give you things you had a right to expect, reasonable working conditions, sporting amenities, and so on. But work was not life. One of the most impressive contrasts between young non-graduates and graduates in the questionnaire returns was the extent to which the former asserted outside interests. Where nearly all graduates mentioned a hobby or interest connected with work, scarcely any non-graduates did. Of forty-four young non-graduates who filled in the questionnaire at the Yokohama factory, fifteen mentioned some kind of hobby. The most usual ones were sport and travel, but some men admitted to interests in music, 'girls and human love', English, and Buddhist philosophy. One of the two men interested in Buddhist philosophy also mentioned an interest in labour relations. The only other interest which concerned the company was that of a young man whose leisure hours were spent wondering whether the questionnaire was going to be any use to him; for the remarks he had made the year before had had no effects.

One might have expected that certain types of young shop floor worker would have been rather more favourably disposed to the company than others. Men who came to Marumaru through 'connections' or those from the province of N—— might, perhaps, have shown some loyalty to the company from the start. Yet just as the most unmanageable middle school recruit in the 1971 intake (the one who had had his girl friend shown round the Yokohama factory) had come from N—— and had had a father in the firm, so many of the most vociferous complainants on the questionnaire were from N——. Maybe rural recruits, even though they were thought by the management to be most likely to fit into the company,[1] were seriously shocked by the contrast between the dirt of the city and the discipline of the company, and the freedom and clean skies they had been used to.

Though the attitude of the young non-graduates might be detached, it was not on the whole antagonistic to the company and its goals. There were no accusations, like those of the team leader writing in *Cloud*, that the company was interested only in profit and was exploiting its workers, no attacks on the capitalist system, and not even much criticism of 'the management'. There was an interesting example of how the young workers seemed to accept the company's view of a difficult situation. By far the most frequent complaint of the young shop floor employees was 'labour shortage'. The standard week at Marumaru was of six eight-hour days, but on top of that there would usually be seven or eight hours overtime, paid and unpaid, and Sunday morning work one week out of four. The lack of free time and the strain that so much work involved were very deeply felt. Marumaru could probably have solved the problem by turning down a few orders, or working the salesmen a little less hard. There might even have been something to gain by doing so. Yet the complaint was rarely of 'overwork', and much more of 'labour shortage'; as if the young workers, overworked as they were, and lacking much loyalty to Marumaru, still agreed with the management's policy of growth at all costs.

Of the other class of mobile employees, the women, only the smallest degree of loyalty and commitment to the company was expected. Indeed, Marumaru would have been embarrassed to find women wanting to live their lives in and for the company. The main principles of the employment of women were that arrangements should only be for the short term—

---

[1] Cf. James C. Abegglen's (1958: 100) supposition that relations in Japanese companies would inevitably change, with the influx of urban recruits to factories which had previously drawn their workers from the country.

though in fact young women high school entrants left at a slower rate than men—and that engagements should be relatively easy to dissolve. The company had to be able to dispense with women employees if times became difficult, and women had to be able to leave to follow their main interests, which lay outside the company, in marriage and home-making.

Most of the women working for Marumaru were young girls with high school education doing clerical jobs. There were no secretaries in the Western sense of assistants to particular managers. Instead the women worked in the sales and administration departments alongside the men, but at very much more tedious and less responsible jobs. They would add up figures while the young male graduates did the budgeting, or would fill in the sales invoices while the salesmen worked out the minimum areas of corrugated board required to fulfil an order. When visitors came, the women would bring tea while the men discussed business.

Nearly all the women employees took the attitude expected of them. Working in the company was merely a prelude to marrying. Though women worked hard, those in the factory sales sections doing two hours overtime on most days, they did not take much interest in their work, or in the progress of the company over the longer term. On the questionnaire forms the women showed themselves to be as absorbed in outside interests as the young non-graduate men. They amused themselves with handi-crafts, English, mountain hiking or foreign travel (of a hypothetical sort). Women made fewer complaints to the company than the younger male shop floor workers, but what they said was not dissimilar. They wanted shorter working hours, or better food. In addition several asked the company to provide an opportunity for girls to get together once a month.

Some of the slightly older women, aged between twenty-five and thirty, showed an interest in organizational problems, but only a very mild one, compared with that of men of the same age.

I would like you to set up a body like a grievance committee such as exists in many other companies. It would be better if there were more detailed communication between upper and lower ranks.

I think it would be better to have a separate place for photo-copying.

These older women, who included one or two graduates, might have been expected to resent their low place in the company, and their menial work. On the whole, however, they accepted it. When they did complain it was about the details of their work, not the principles by which they were assigned it. One graduate girl of twenty-nine wrote:

I should like you to make it clear whether we are to work on Saturday afternoons or not. To make Saturday work dependent on the convenience of our superiors is too much of an excuse, and we don't know where we stand. In particular I would like all the women put on the same footing. I should like you to consider allowing women to go home early because they have to come in early for cleaning duties. I don't think it would affect work.

The writer does not reject the idea that graduate women of her age should have to wash cups and bring in tea for young men. She merely wants special arrangements to correspond with the special nature of her work.

There was a tiny minority, perhaps two in a hundred, of women who were not resigned to their role. One of them, a woman of twenty-eight who had achieved a position of some consequence in a sales section, complained on her questionnaire form:

Though, because of the office rationalization, women are said to be given responsibility, I am dissatisfied because there is no means for developing the abilities of women. You join the company and are made to sit in your place, and that's it. Except for your own particular work you can't do anything at all. As for qualifications, men are sent to classes or on a course; but there's nothing like that for women. I suppose the fact that women leave the company for marriage means that it's a loss for the company, but under present social conditions and in view of the need to re-employ housewives, or to use part-timers to combat the labour shortage, I should like to see you develop women's capabilities and improve welfare and conditions.

I did hear one or two men say how badly the company treated women, or rather certain particularly able women; but there was as little feminist sentiment among the men as among the majority of women themselves. The union rarely concerned itself with the disadvantages of women, among the more concrete of which were their low pay and their very early age of compulsory retirement: forty-five instead of fifty-five. If there were few spontaneous demands for more equitable treatment of women, there were also few prospects of changes being forced on Marumaru by circumstances, at least in the short term. It was true that using clever women as skivvies was costing the company money; but the cost was concealed, and since all Marumaru's competitors were using women in the same way, the company suffered no disadvantage.[1] The effects of the labour shortage referred to by the feminist were not as yet discernible, for the shortage was of young production workers rather than office workers, and male office workers, older men and graduates, were not in particularly short supply. Even in 1971 women seemed a long way from enjoying company membership on the same terms as men. Since then, and in spite of the activities of the feminist movements in Japan, the cause of women's advancement in industry has probably been damaged by the oil crisis. Only over decades, and even then, perhaps, only in certain industries like banking or trading where there are few problems of discipline and where individual ability can count enormously,[2] are Japanese women likely to achieve employment on the same terms as men.

The Employee and the Community

We come now to the aspect of being *in* rather than *with* a company, to relations between employees, and the nature of the company community. I have referred on several occasions to the fact that Japanese companies are communities. It is time for an explanation of why this is so, and why the people working in a company like Marumaru were sufficiently cut off from the rest of Japanese society, and sufficiently involved in each others' lives to justify the use of that word.

As a company with about one thousand employees, Marumaru was still small enough for people who had worked two or three years to know many of their colleagues. The employees were spread over a number of factories in different parts of the country; yet distances were overcome by the effects of a highly centralized administration. The organization and control of the factories was made as standard as possible. Every factory had the same functional sections and sub-sections, and the same system of ranks and grades, and there had even been a directive specifying what factory managers should do every hour of the day. Most matters of concern to employees, wage rates, the standards of company housing,

[1] I have been impressed, in dealing with Japanese companies, at the gains in efficiency arising from having intelligent women in relatively *low* positions in the organization: receptionists and telephone operators who can handle visitors without referring to busy managers, and junior clerks who can deal with more than routine business.

[2] Mr Robert Thomas has drawn my attention to the fact that certain small insurance companies and stockbrokers employ sales girls to visit housewives at home and, in some cases at least, pay their sales staff commissions. A handful of girls are able, therefore, to earn comparatively high salaries. I do not think, however, that they are offered the same promotion prospects as men.

promotions and transfers, even the settlement of some local grievances, were decided upon at the head office. The organization of the company labour union was similarly centralized, with all the official information flowing from the centre. Employees in different parts of the company therefore had a great variety of interests in common, and carried out many of their activities in a common context.

Moreover, the way in which Marumaru was run enabled people from distant factories to remain in personal contact with each other. There were many conferences and committees requiring the attendance of representatives from different plants. Most of these were arranged for middle management, but shop floor workers and younger employees had an opportunity to meet their counterparts in other factories through the union. The union general meeting, held once a year, brought together sixty delegates from all over the company; and once a month there was a meeting of the union executive committee, to which each plant sent at least one member. There were frequent business trips to other plants, usually, again, for managers, but sometimes for senior workers; five or six workers from a factory work force of about 120 employees would be sent to look at one of the other plants of the company each year.

The administrative measure that perhaps contributed most to Marumaru's sense of community was the practice of transferring employees between factories. In many larger Japanese companies transfers are frequent,[1] men being recruited centrally and then moved to different factories in the course of their careers, just as executives are in Britain or the United States. At Marumaru the transfer rate was especially high because new factories were being built almost every year. Only a proportion of the workers to man them were recruited locally, the managers and senior workers all being transferred to a new factory from existing ones.

Table VI.2. Transfers of male employees at Marumaru, 1968–70

Year	Men transferred over year	No. of men in company at year end	Transfer rate %
1970	97	732	13.3
1969	49	580	8.4
1968	43	498	8.6

[1] The transfer rate for employees (both men and women) in 1974 was 7.5 per cent. into establishments of between 500–999 workers, and 5.6 per cent. into larger establishments. *Japan Statistical Yearbook, 1976*: 64: Table 44.

The cumulative effect of moving ten per cent. of the population of each factory every year was, naturally, to keep members of the company in touch with each other, and so to prevent any factory from establishing a social order independent of the rest of the company. At the same time, the high transfer rate meant that men were often working in parts of the country to which they had no particular ties. Strangers to the local community, they were all the more likely to direct their social activities towards the company. The Yokohama factory, where I did much of my fieldwork, had been established eleven years; yet only 24 out of 114 men working in the factory in October 1969 came from Yokohama. Thirty-two men were from the prefecture of N———, Marumaru's home area, and thirty-seven from other rural prefectures. It was true that women were usually recruited locally, and that there were fourteen of them at the Yokohama factory; but they were mostly young girl clerks who were continually coming and going, and they scarcely served to link the factory with the local area. At some of the new factories the proportion of transferred men was much higher than at Yokohama, and the relations between factory and town correspondingly more tenuous.

Another factor in the consolidation of the Marumaru community was that so many company members lived together in company houses and hostels. Originally the company had been too small to offer company housing, but the first company houses were built within six years of Marumaru's foundation, partly in order to attract recruits and discourage people from leaving, but also as an expression of the solicitous attitude a growing and successful firm should adopt towards its employees. By the time I arrived at Marumaru more than half the employees were housed by the company. Even employees who lived in their own apartments had usually spent several years in hostels before marrying and setting up house. In living together, men came to know their colleagues very thoroughly indeed. Most men knew the ages, dates of entry, and promotion records of everyone they worked with as a matter of course. They also knew a great deal about the personal lives of their work fellows, their hobbies, their 'connections' of kinship or friendship with other people at Marumaru, the details of their school or college careers, their foibles and their tastes.

Past recruitment policies also contributed to the cohesion of Marumaru. Because so many people had been recruited there more than one-third of the employees of Marumaru were from N———. The firm kept many sentimental connections with the prefecture, though individual employees from N———, once exiled, soon lost contact with the region. A flower from N———— formed part of the company badge; and the songs of the province were sung at drinking parties and company outings. The predominance of men from one prefecture could, perhaps, have had the effect of dividing the community rather than uniting it. But it was not thought that those from N———— had any great advantages over others in, for example, matters of promotion; so that there were few employees from other parts who found it unacceptable that Marumaru should have a mild regional flavour.

Another important aspect of past recruitment policies was the reliance on personal connections to attract new members to the company. Marumaru encouraged employees to recruit among their friends and relatives on its behalf, and some of the senior directors in particular recommended nephews, cousins and sons of old schoolfellows in profusion for entry into the firm. Perhaps two-thirds of the men at the Yokohama factory had what were known as 'kinship relations' (*enko kankei*) or 'connections' (*kone*) within the firm or in associated companies. Even an employee who came into Marumaru friendless was able, once inside the company, to enter into an association with a senior by asking him to officiate as a ceremonial 'go-between' at his wedding. Relations between go-between and bridegroom, like those of sponsor and successful applicant, were of mild patronage on the one side and deference and obligation on the other. The senior man would take a friendly interest in his junior's career. The younger man would consult his senior over difficulties at home or work, and would mark his respect by visiting the senior's home at the New Year. The kinship relations and connections naturally provided links between different parts of the community. In particular they had the effect of interesting old and young, seniors and juniors, managers and workers in each others' activities. However little a director, for example, actually saw of the shop floor, the fact that he had one or two protégés working on machines in the factories enlivened his concern for shop floor conditions. Conversely, his relations with a senior manager, even one he rarely met, gave a young factory worker a sense of involvement in what would otherwise have been the remote workings of management, enabled him to express the history of the company in personal terms, and lent significance to the gossip he would hear about the head office or other factories. As we shall see, however, connections did have a negative as well as a positive effect on the fellowship of the community.

Another unifying force was the general awareness that everyone was on the same side in a commercial war. It was realized that Marumaru was in relentless competition with other corrugated board companies, that there were plenty of rivals and few customers, and that no one owed Marumaru a living. Bankruptcies were common enough in Japanese industry. However successful Marumaru had been up to now, two or three mistakes, a change of attitude at the head office of the main bank, or a turn for the worse in the corrugated board market could halt the company's advance and at the worst begin a decline into bankruptcy. On the other hand, if everyone pulled their weight the company would grow; and as Marumaru became more powerful its employees, too, would count for more in the society of industry. Perhaps in ten or fifteen years time employees might be able to take the same sort of pride in belonging to Marumaru as the employees of Rengō presently took in belonging to that company, the biggest corrugated board maker in Japan, and a firm of which people quite unconnected with the industry might have heard.

Yet all these incentives to community—centralized authority, a high transfer rate, company housing, recruitment by connection, and consciousness of common economic interest—would have counted for nothing if most of the people of Marumaru had not been agreed that there should be a community, that relations between company members should not be superficial and simple but multifarious and intense.

The most obvious indication that people believed that the company ought to be a community was the constant emphasis on 'good human relations' (ii ningen kankei). This phrase, which in English at least is so ominously redolent of applied sociology, was used frequently in quite normal conversations, often when talking of the group to which the speaker himself belonged. Good human relations began with the work group. In the ideal factory sub-section or office department all the members would be on good terms with each other. Superiors would be firm, trustworthy and friendly. Subordinates would be polite and co-operative. Everyone would be amicable, not only in working hours but outside work. Responsibility for the maintenance of good human relations within the group rested with the leader. He had to look after the interests of his subordinates and to see that they all got along together. The company made available small sums of money to all those in charge of units of organization so that they could take their subordinates bowling or to a restaurant. In some parts of the company there were only three or four such outings a year. In others there was a tradition of monthly or even fortnightly visits to restaurants or bars. As well as these semi-formal outings there would be many occasions on which two or three members of a unit would go to a bar together.

Good human relations were also necessary between people in different units. Members of the head office production department had to be friendly with the production supervisors whom they aided and advised. The packaging engineers from head office had to be on good terms with the factory salesmen. Good relations were established between those from different units, as between those within the same departments and sections, by communal entertainment. A visiting engineer from head office would be taken out by the factory production staff he had come to help. He would join their drinking parties and become, for the duration of his visit, one of their number.

The same self-conscious gregariousness was to be found in all groups or associations of employees within Marumaru. The graduates from the head office hostel seemed to cultivate the most intense relationships among themselves. They worked in the same sections during the day, played mah-jong or went to bars together in the evenings, and visited places in twos and threes on Sundays. The union leaders marked their committee meetings with a frenzy of entertainment. During the bonus negotiations, the members of the union executive committee stayed together from early morning until after midnight, discussing matters of policy during the day, and drinking and going to cabarets or restaurants after work was over.

Though a casual observer would have been impressed by the eagerness employees showed for each others' society, and the remarkable ability they displayed for getting on together, nevertheless the good human relations everyone took such care to nurture were essentially superficial. Employees would often contrast family ties and old friendships formed at school and college with relations with colleagues. With his family and his true friends a man could be himself. When he was with his fellow workers there was always an element of strain and a need for circumspection.

The reason why genuinely good human relations were so difficult to attain was, of course, that Marumaru was not a social club but a highly organized and firmly disciplined industrial company. Employees were required to co-operate with each other; but they were also required to compete and to be each other's subordinates and superiors. Reconciling co-operation, competition, and hierarchy is a problem for workers in industry everywhere. Alan Fox[1] has written of the difficulties employees in the West have in combining loyalty and team-work with the struggle for advancement, both being equally encouraged by managements. At Marumaru the difficulties were particularly severe. The competition was

[1] Alan Fox (1971: 125).

intensified and the hierarchy made more complete by the system of ranks and grades. Because these applied across the whole company, and because there was so little emphasis on specialization, any two men were either rivals or subordinate and superior. But what made good human relations especially elusive was the very thing that made them so necessary: the presence of so many immobile employees.

THE IMMOBILE EMPLOYEES

The immobile employees, linked to the company by loyalty, self-interest, and the difficulty of leaving, were destined to live and work together for twenty or thirty years. Among these men, bound to get on with each other, competition was relentless. Success was all the more desirable for being won over an unchanging group of contemporaries and colleagues. Failure was correspondingly hard to live down. Resigning and trying a different kind of job was possible but very risky. It was difficult for a man even to escape into his interests outside the company, for after ten or fifteen years' service and several transfers he had probably lost his connections with any district or region he had previously known; and ten hours work a day, and two or three evenings a week drinking with colleagues and customers, left little time for hobbies. Beneath the superficial harmony, therefore, men were working to defeat each other to get ahead. Since promotion, at least in some parts of the company, was so nearly automatic, the gains and losses in the struggle were apparently slight. But so thoroughly did everyone know the biographical details of everyone else and so nice were the calculations of precedence, that to reach a grade a month or two ahead of one's contemporaries might be accounted a considerable success. In any case, even if the members of an intake rose through the standard ranks together there would be other marks of estimation to compete for, notably responsibility and the extent to which they were allowed to participate in the deliberations of upper management.

Combining co-operation and competition was perhaps made more difficult because employees had had no previous experience of it. Although the Japanese education system is extremely competitive, children are not encouraged to compete *within* a class. All class-mates pass through their grades together. It is only on entry to the next stage of education, getting into high school from middle school, or university from high school, that competition takes place. Then the entrance exams are open to candidates from a wide area, perhaps even the entire nation, and they are administered impersonally. A child therefore has no need to feel particularly threatened by other class members; nor subject to the discrimination of the teacher, who can appear instead as a friendly guide. It is not until a man joins a company that he has to learn how to get on with the very people he is trying to displace.[1]

The strain of subordination was quite as great as that of competition. In many ways authority pressed harder on the individual at Marumaru than it would have done in a Western company. A man who could not leave the company easily had little choice but to obey orders. There was no set process by which even a non-manager could appeal against a superior's decision, and for a manager to try to make such an appeal was unthinkable.[2] The company union was a very mild 'loyal opposition', and it rarely concerned itself with disciplinary problems affecting single individuals. There was only limited recognition of the authority given in the West to specialized knowledge—and not many people would have been entitled to that authority, had it been recognized. Just as the distinction between company and private life, work and leisure was less clearly made at Marumaru than it would have been in a Western firm, so the scope of authority was wider. The company's rules applied in the bachelors' hostels (though hostel members did have a certain degree of internal self-government) and in the company apartment blocks. There were occasions when it was in order for a superior to employ a subordinate on his private business outside office hours. When the mother of one of the directors of Marumaru died, three or four members of his department spent two days at his home helping with the preparations for the funeral.[3] Usually a subordinate would undertake these duties cheerfully, as a normal part of his job; but even if he resented doing them, there was little he could do about it.

Perhaps the most forceful representation of the absolute nature of superordination and subordination in Japanese companies can be found in the comic strips in newspapers and in television skits. Invariably the department head, portrayed with grotesque features, is to be seen shouting

[1] Cf. Robert E. Cole (1971: 166), who attributes the more genuine friendships workers develop with school friends to the lack of competition within schools. For details of how competition within school classes is avoided, and families and teachers are enlisted as a child's supporters, see C. W. Kiefer (1970).

[2] Alan Fox (1971: 140) has remarked how grievance procedures in British companies are not expected to be used by managers.

[3] An indication of how far public and private life were mixed was that most of the people attending the memorial service were representatives of Marumaru's suppliers, paper companies and the like. None of them, of course, had ever met the mother. On this public occasion a large number of relatively senior employees helped the director receive the mourners.

abuse and beating his prostrate subordinates on the head with rolled-up sheets of foolscap. No one, of course, would confuse these ogres with the real thing; but it is significant that the authority they exhibit is demanding, brusque and unfeeling; a world removed from good human relations and management familism.

To achieve good human relations, to co-operate, to compete, to obey and at the same time to preserve the most amicable appearances, needed remarkable sensitivity and self-control. If a man was too much at ease with the senior men in his work unit, he could be accused of sycophancy by his colleagues. If he paid his superiors too little attention he might be supposed insubordinate or at least unco-operative. If he was too reserved with his contemporaries, he would be suspected of being unhealthily ambitious. If he was too friendly with them, problems would arise when he or they moved slightly ahead in the race for promotion.

Such judicious moderation was not given to many individuals, and all sorts of dissensions and disputes did occur. There was frequently antipathy between a superior and a subordinate, often because a previous superior, with whom the subordinate's relations had been good, had been replaced by a man with a different style of management. There were fierce rivalries between men in the same standard ranks. Two sub-section heads, two department heads, even two directors were on such bad terms that they could hardly speak to each other. A common problem was that caused by an incompetent or, worse still, a lazy member of a work-group, who gave his fellows extra work, or let the side down in its dealings with other parts of the company.

Problems similar to these arise in companies everywhere, but at Marumaru the need for ostensibly good human relations caused them to be expressed in oblique and even devious ways. People were reluctant to admit that there was any competition in their own part of the organization, even though in other, less happy sections men were indeed trying to surpass each other.[1] They were more ready to talk about bad relations between juniors and seniors, but in vague and emotional terms:

Contrary to my expectations, the people above are warm, and that's very good. But in this section human relations are complicated and things are tough. Human relations are not particularly affecting the work, but it is simply that one wants to work in a good atmosphere. I am very envious of X section. I am still learning, and I would like things to be done strictly like C does them.

[1] Cf. Robert E. Cole (1971: 107).

The writer, almost the only immobile employee to complain to the company about problems involving 'human relations', was a young and rather naïve graduate. The actual difficulty was a simple one. One of the senior men of the section was apparently a misanthrope who did not much like the society of his colleagues. He also disliked and avoided going to places outside the company, even though his duties required it. When he was moved to another job a year later the problem disappeared.

By far the most common symptoms of tension and discontent were the continual and frequent allegations of sycophancy and favouritism. Men would constantly be accused—though not to their faces—of having risen by flattering (*gomasuri*) their superiors. Sometimes when a man was talking to his boss, one of the man's colleagues would surreptitiously make the gesture of grinding with mortar and pestle: the literal meaning of *gomasuri* is 'crushing sesame'. Another recurrent accusation was of nepotism. Men were said to have got on because they had relatives in the company or some 'connection' with a director. So many men had been recruited into Marumaru with 'connections' of one kind or another, though not necessarily close ones, that there were a large number of employees liable to be maligned on this account. There was no certain way of ascertaining the truth of these charges. One man's politeness was another's ingratiation. Who could tell whether a man had been promoted simply because he was related to a superior, or, conversely, deny that his relationship might have served to bring his genuine ability to the attention of upper management? My intuition, however, was that few of the accusations were well founded.

The contrast between the superficial impression of determined amity and the underlying contention and resentment among these immobile employees was very great. By the time I left Marumaru, departments that had once seemed to me models of 'good human relations' had been revealed to be full of animosities and spites. Sections whose members were always to be seen together in bars, and in which the senior men were continually inviting their juniors home, proved to be beset with bitter rivalries, or to contain boorish superiors or sly subordinates who caused difficulties for everyone else.

The strain of dissembling, self-effacement and ingratiation required in Marumaru life was eased by two processes: transfers and going to bars. I have already explained how the frequent transfers of managers and workers kept the company one and prevented any factory from becoming too independent, while at the same time tending to isolate employees from the local community. Transfers also brought new faces into a work group and removed old ones, dissipating acrimony by separating rivals and giving subordinates a change of superiors.

But the finest respite from the travails of the company was to be found in a bar. Perhaps, as many employees remarked, life would have been quite impossible without the amazingly numerous bars near every factory. There were a few employees who disliked night-life, but most men went to bars two or three times a week. They usually drank with men they worked with or those who lived with them in the company hostel. Perhaps because it was easier to forget competition than rank, the nearer the revellers in a group were to the same age and rank the more convivial the evening would be.

The world of bars was the antithesis of that of companies. A bar would usually be presided over by a motherly older woman (*mama-san*), sympathetic, willing to listen, but witty and capable of tart remarks. There might be bar hostesses. These would either be called '*nee-chan*' (elder sister) or else addressed by their personal names, a usage otherwise reserved for wives and sisters. The customers, nearly all of them company employees, were often given childish nicknames, usually ending in the infantile form, '*chan*'. To visit a bar was therefore to return to childhood, as indeed some employees explicitly recognized, seeking out bars where the *mama san* reminded them of their mothers or came from their own home regions.[1]

It was important for a man to go to the right kind of bar. Certain bars were frequented by men in their late twenties and early thirties, others by older shop floor workers, and yet others by senior salesmen. A man would go to the bars appropriate to his station, and change his allegiances as he rose in the company. After all, the whole purpose of going to a bar was to relax, and no one could relax in a place where a senior manager could come in at any moment. In the wrong bar, also, the conversation of the *mama-san* and the hostesses would jar. I remember an evening turning sour when my companions, most of whom were shop floor workers of about team head level, tried out a new bar. The husband and wife who ran it knew Marumaru, but they only knew the deputy manager in charge of the sales side and his section heads. After listening in silence to two or three of the wife's anecdotes about 'Rin-Chan', and the way he had achieved some new customer, we left hastily. It was to avoid episodes like this that

[1] Not all bars fit the description I have given. Recently a new and very different type of bar, catering for office girls, has become popular in the big cities. These bars are huge, noisy, and garish, with cosmopolitan pretensions. The staff are not women but young men in evening dress. The fantasy purveyed in this sort of bar was not, however, attractive to older men of the kind I have been talking about.

Marumaru employees at the Yokohama factory distributed themselves over as many as thirty or forty bars.

In the right bar and on the right occasion a man was expected to get drunk. Nothing that he said or did then would be held against him.[1] It was not uncommon for someone suddenly to announce himself the best worker present, or the only man of his year with any real knowledge of sales. The assertion would provoke raucous laughter, or a maudlin denial and a counter-claim from one of the other employees present. Sometimes an office argument would be reborn in a bar conversation, and the protagonists would abuse each other in a manner quite intolerable in the work place. As the evening went on the debate would lose its logic, and finally the parties would carry each other home, muttering incoherently. By the next morning everything would be forgotten or at least forgiven, and though the issues might remain they would at least be less rancorous.

THE MOBILE EMPLOYEES

By comparison with the behaviour of the immobile employees, that of the mobile employees, the young, less educated men and the women, was free and frank.

So many men were coming and going on the shop floor that the young workers there scarcely had time to know each other. A salesman might work two or three years with the same handful of colleagues, but a shop floor worker would have a new team every few months, and the seasonal and temporary workers attached to his shift would change still more frequently. Where men saw so little of each other they could treat each other more casually and with less circumspection.

Young workers also competed less fiercely. Indeed, there was very little for them to compete about. A man would not reach the lowest official rank, that of team head, until he was twenty-six or more, and would not become a semi-official machine head until twenty-four or five. It was not even possible to compete for better pay, because the work-ability ratings at this level were determined largely by the work a man was doing, and this changed when, as frequently happened, he was moved to a different machine. Last, and most important of all, authority weighed rather more lightly on these young mobile workers. They did not have to put up with demanding section heads or irritating rules. There might be gentler superiors and more congenial personnel departments elsewhere. Just as it was only the younger men who could refuse to do overtime or Sunday work, and only the younger men who could put in for a holiday at a day

[1] Chie Nakane (1970: 125) makes this point.

or two's notice, so it was only younger men who could make it obvious that they did not like their bosses.

Social relations on the shop floor were, then, open and without affectation by comparison with those in the rest of the company. A man associated with his friends, avoided his enemies, and was prepared to say what he thought of other people.

Women, like the young graduates, were spared the rigours of competition. In the case of the women, however, it was not simply that there were no immediate rewards to compete for; there was no promise even of eventual rewards. Like the young men, also, women were able to regard authority lightly. The girl mentioned earlier who refused to be transferred was an extreme example of women's independence; but girls frequently came late for work when it suited them, or disappeared into the office kitchen when their sections were particularly busy. On the questionnaire forms only women went so far as directly to criticize their superiors. A confident older woman, who worked in the same section as the misanthropic senior man who disliked going out, came close to bluntness:

I don't dislike my work; in fact, it's work I've been given to do for a long time and I like it. But with my present superiors it's somehow impossible to work reasonably. The junior people are much to be pitied. Aren't they ignoring the people below too much? Everyone in this section wants work to be done properly, but for junior people to put their hearts into it I would like it to be a happier workplace with superiors who can be relied upon.

If the behaviour of women was partly conditioned by their mobility, it (and, indeed, that mobility itself) was largely a reflection of the position of women in Japanese society. In few industrial countries are the roles of the sexes more clearly differentiated than in Japan. Certainly men and women seemed to live almost separate social lives at Marumaru. During the lunch breaks the women tended to gather together in the switchboard room, while the men played games, or left the company premises for a meal. In the evening the men would go to bars of the kind described above. The women would usually go straight home, but if they did go out it was to the cinema to see foreign films (men preferred samurai or gangster dramas), or to cocktail bars or restaurants. No woman had ever visited the Yokohama factory hostel—at least as far as any of its inmates could remember. Only once or twice during my stay did women go to the head office hostel. On one of these occasions an incident took place which revealed how firmly even young and educated men believed in the social segregation of women. One of the men of the hostel, a member, as it happened, of an ascetic Christian sect, put his fiancée up for the night in his hostel room while he slept with a friend. When she had left, a meeting of the hostel members was called at which he was censured, only two other residents taking his side.

Even when men and women took part in the same social events they seemed to remain apart. On the head office outing men and women sat separately in the bus on the way out. On the way back a man of thirty sat with a woman of twenty-eight, to the amusement and admiration of the less courageous. The highlight of the outing, for the women at least, was a dance which took place immediately after supper. Within two hours, however, all the men had gone off to play mah-jong, leaving the women to go back to their rooms.

Though the reserve and shyness which men and women showed each other owed something to Japanese etiquette, the men especially were made cautious by their circumstances in the company. The men of marriageable age were usually immobile employees for whom the company was or should appear to be the first consideration. A man who showed too much interest in the women he worked with risked being thought slightly frivolous. Moreover, it was very difficult in so closed a society for a man and woman to enter into a private relationship. One man who took a company girl out found himself receiving well-intentioned advice from his superiors on whether he should marry her.

It was very remarkable, considering how little men and women appeared to associate with each other, how many 'company marriages' (*shanai kekkon*) there were. Perhaps as many as one-fifth of all the married men in Marumaru had married fellow workers; or, to look at it from a woman's point of view, marriage to an employee was one of the most likely reasons for her to leave the company. Ten out of the sixteen women who left one large factory in the five years 1966–70 had married men they had met at work. A few couples 'dated' in secrecy. Yet the lack of gossip about romance, at least among the men, in comparison with the enormous volume of slander and speculation about company politics, seemed to suggest that there was very little 'dating', secret or otherwise, and that many men proposed to women whom they knew only as workmates and as a result of company functions. The reason why even casual relations between young men and women could be an immediate prelude to marriage[1] was, perhaps, that wives were thought of more as complements

[1] Cf. Robert O. Blood, Jr. (1967: 59).

than companions to men. Few employees at Marumaru went as far as the man who told me that any woman would do as his wife. (He was true to his word and engaged himself to a woman after no more than a two-hour interview.) Yet most men, when they talked of marriage—which was very often, though only as an abstract state—were thinking more of a congenial person to keep a home than of a unique soulmate. Few of them thought that there was a pressing need for a man and a woman to explore each other's personalities before marrying.

On marrying a workmate a girl would retire and set up a home. In her early married days she would continue to see those of her girl friends in the company who were not yet married, but as these left Marumaru she would cease to have any contacts with the company beyond those provided by her husband. Marumaru men were very anxious to keep company and family separate, and husbands discouraged their wives from interesting themselves in company affairs. I was frequently told the cautionary tale of a man either in Marumaru or another company who had heard of his promotion from his wife, who in turn had learned of it from the wife of his superior. Often, therefore, a wife who had met her husband at work would, within five years of marriage, know as little of his job as if she had never been in Marumaru.

Authority and Mobility

This analysis of the two aspects of company membership, attachment to a corporation and involvement in a community, reveals, as one might have expected, that the more an employee works *for* a company the more he finds himself *in* it. Those employees who are most committed to a corporation are also most deeply implicated in each others' lives. Those who are less closely tied to a corporation are also more independent of their fellow employees.

The degree of attachment to both corporation and community is, I have implied, closely correlated with an employee's labour market mobility or immobility. If an employee has little to lose by leaving and stands some chance of gaining by doing so, he or she tends to have casual attitudes towards a company. If an employee has much to gain by staying and is unlikely to get an equally good job elsewhere, then he (for there are few or no women in this position) will almost certainly be more intimately involved with the company. A similar tendency would, in all probability, be observed in a Western firm. In Japan, however, the organization of the company and of the labour market make mobility and immobility more a matter of age and education than of skills or trades.

The correlation between mobility and degree of involvement does not mean that attachment to a company can be explained entirely by reference to the labour market. The questionnaire returns at Marumaru show the graduates and older men to have been morally and intellectually engrossed by their company; and the questionnaire, which was, after all, an annual invitation to complain, greatly under-represented the extent to which employees were intensely absorbed in each others' lives. It was a matter of intrinsic interest that one man was doing well, that another had got married to a girl in the personnel section, and that a third appeared to be getting on better with his seniors. Employees also genuinely loved the work. They would scan trade papers to learn more about the industry, to see what competitors were doing, and to find out what the world thought of Marumaru. They would enthusiastically follow the decisions of higher management, as those were represented in *ringi* proposals, and they would argue passionately about the merits of each issue. Of course there were self-interested reasons for some of this behaviour. A wise man kept up with the latest gossip; and men were gregarious and enthusiastic because they thought it would bring them success. But merely belonging to a community can be fulfilling; a rapidly changing industry exerts its own fascination; and an efficient and successful company, like many other well-run organizations, inspires admiration and allegiance simply by being what it is.

If the labour market is not the sole determinant of an employee's relations with the company, it is nevertheless an extremely important one. We have seen how among the non-graduate men of Marumaru mobile and immobile employees, who came from very similar backgrounds and were separated only by a few years' service, were nearly indifferent to the company on the one hand and utterly absorbed in it on the other. The absorption in and with the company caused painfully mixed feelings. Men who for the first time in their careers were enjoying a little authority were among all employees the most resentfully conscious of their sub-ordination. Elevated to a secure place in the community, they were all too aware of the relentless competition that prevented the community from being one of genuine fellowship. And the principal reason for these mixed feelings was surely the recognition that their position on the labour market had changed, that they could no longer leave the company on favourable terms.

An important implication of this argument is that the relations between whole work forces and the companies that employ them are likely to be very different in firms of different size. In a very large firm nearly all the employees will be immobile. Large firms pay high wages and offer increases of pay with age and length of service. Employment with them confers considerable prestige. Few employees have anything to gain from leaving. In large firms, therefore, we should expect employees' attitudes to be similar to those of graduates and older shop floor workers in Marumaru. In small firms, however, a high proportion of the work force is likely to be mobile. Small firms pay low wages, do not offer pay by age to the same extent as large ones, are insecure, and confer no prestige. Very few employees will have great incentive to stay or much to prevent their going. One would expect that relations between companies and employees in these firms would tend to be as casual and contractual as they were between Marumaru and its young shop floor workers.

I should like now to end by considering what the preceding analysis tells us of the nature and exercise of authority in Japanese companies. In any firm, or indeed any other organization, there are two types of support for authority: opinion and interest. People may believe that a superior should be obeyed. They may also obey him because they will benefit themselves by doing so. These two considerations are not entirely separate. Opinion determines interest; for a man's view that he will gain from obedience is conditioned by his ideas of what is right and desirable, which will be influenced by general opinion. Interest, on the other hand, very often encourages opinion. A man half-way up the ladder of promotion will accept and even purvey ideas about authority which were much less attractive to him when he was junior. Nevertheless, it is reasonable to think of the justifications for authority in the firm as ideological on the one hand and pragmatic on the other.

In a Japanese company, at least in so far as Marumaru can be taken as representative, the ideological support for authority is nearly unanimous —though there are anti-authoritarian strands of thought. The practical incentives to obey are also very great, but they are markedly less for mobile than for immobile employees.

Japanese employees are no more philosophers than Western employees are, but if they were to be inveigled into a philosophical defence of why they recognized authority and did what their superiors told them, they would, perhaps, rely on three propositions. The first would be that work was a good and proper activity. The second, that companies were useful and respectable bodies which, on the whole, looked after their employees. The third would be that within the company, administration was in the hands of the most suitable people, and that they made their decisions in the right way.

The first of these propositions seems trivially obvious, until one considers how attitudes to work in some Western countries, especially Britain, have been endowed by religion and history with penal associations.[1] In some contexts, it is true, Westerners think of work as a creative activity leading to material success and spiritual fulfilment; but in others work is the unpleasant interlude for which pay is received, the thing a person has to do to maintain himself. In Japan, where the predominant influence on social thought has been Confucian, work is not something that is imposed on the worker, as it was originally imposed on a disobedient Adam, or as it was demanded of indigents and vagrants as the price of charity. On the contrary, in the Confucian view, work is honourable and decent, the hall-mark of the responsible adult. Exactly such an idea was represented in the suggestion that those who had joined Marumaru and were about to begin work had become 'men of society' (shakaijin). We have come across other evidence that work was seen as a wholesome and useful activity rather than a penance. The young shop floor workers who talked of 'labour shortage' rather than 'overwork', the graduates eager to learn their business, the evident concern of the older shop floor workers for getting things done, the generous flow of information about the company's progress, all testified to an assumption that work was worth doing and interesting. Such an assumption naturally justified authority, for if work was meritorious so was the authority that directed it. The assumption also made authority easier to administer and to bear. Since reasonable people wanted to work, managers no more had to force their workers to labour than the committee of a chess club would have to insist that the club members played chess. Workers need not look at their bosses as extortionate oppressors. Managers could make what R. P. Dore has called an 'assumption of original virtue'[2] in their subordinates.

In the long run the idea that work is good and rewarding in itself may possibly be infected by the increasing interest in leisure.[3] When I was at Marumaru, Japan was engaged in what some called a 'leisure boom'. There were new bowling alleys everywhere. Sports equipment of all kinds was selling well, and car ownership was becoming common. Many of the younger employees bought their first cars during my stay. As Japanese employees are given rather more leisure time—and the two day

[1] Reinhard Bendix (1963: 42–3).
[2] R. P. Dore (1973: 238).
[3] By 'leisure' I mean the pursuit of private interests. In Japan much of the time outside working hours is spent getting to know work-fellows better. For an elaboration of this point and a review of surveys on the Japanese use of spare time see Sepp Linhart (1975).

week-end is still not fully established—work may come to be seen as something that intrudes on one's own more pleasurable activities. But Japan is still far from being a hedonistic country, and in any case a better use of leisure does not necessarily entail a revulsion against work.

The second proposition, that companies serve both society and their employees, was also widely accepted by those at Marumaru. The idea of service to society was most frequently put into words by an older generation of employees who had seen war and reconstruction for themselves; but it had its appeal for younger workers educated to appreciate the importance of economic growth, and to understand the means of achieving it. The lack of support in the questionnaire returns for any contrary hypothesis—that, for example, the company's true aim was to support a political establishment, or to give the directors opportunities for self-aggrandizement—was very remarkable. The only manifestations of a Marxian view of capitalist industry I came across at Marumaru, besides the private musings of the young graduates and the satirical article in *Cloud*, were the union bulletins at the time of the annual wage negotiations and on a handful of other occasions. These pitted 'we workers' against 'top management' in the relentless labour struggle. But the union was held in some contempt by its membership, and I do not think that its fierce language was taken seriously.[1] The suggestion that companies look after their employees was viewed with scepticism by older shop floor workers, aware of the inadequacy of their welfare benefits, and conscious, perhaps, that they would not be as well treated in the future as they had been in the past. Even so, there were no complaints that parties other than the employers were taking an unjustifiably large share of the company's wealth, that too much was being paid to banks or shareholders, at the expense of those who deserved it most. In such a tight and homogeneous community few people could seriously have supposed that their factory manager, or even the board of directors, represented outside interests, or had any reason for wanting to make shareholders and banks richer and employees poorer. Most of the employees, therefore, seemed to find it possible to believe that they were doing something useful for the world and for themselves in working for Marumaru. This belief no doubt made it easier to accept the company's considerable demands.

Even in 1970–1, however, there were signs of a change in the regard in which companies were held in Japanese society. During my time at Marumaru there were a number of appalling cases of industrial pollution,

[1] Robert E. Cole (1970) has described the Marxist ideology of Japanese unions as a 'moral armour' designed to fit them for battle with employers.

some of them grotesquely mishandled by the managements of the companies involved. Matsushita Electric Industrial was subjected to a most effective boycott by women's organizations, because it was considered to have over-priced its products, some of which were selling more cheaply in the United States than in Japan. A similar campaign was directed at cosmetic companies. There were also constant complaints from Japan's trading partners that Japanese companies were 'dumping' their goods in export markets, so that it seemed that her great industrial firms, which had done so much to raise Japan in the esteem of the world, were now seriously harming her foreign relations. Some of the criticisms levelled at companies both by foreigners and Japanese may have been unfair, but that did not make them less significant as refutations of any assumption that companies were always right.

The third proposition was that those in authority were the best people acting in a reasonable way. We saw that one of the main differences between Marumaru and a Western industrial company was the lack of a clear distinction at Marumaru between managers and workers. Employees saw themselves as placed on a comprehensive scale of standard ranks. Those in any given standard rank were obviously superior in status to those in the standard ranks below, and they also had more authority. Those at the top of the scale were largely recruited from those at the bottom, and in theory anyone—or, more accurately, any man—could move up the standard ranks and acquire increments of both status and authority as he did so. Authority, then, was not the preserve of one group of employees (the managers) who exercised it over another group (the workers). It was distributed evenly over the company, and there were means by which those who did not yet have much of it could increase their portion. The conditions for promotion were, of course, age and merit. Most employees would surely have agreed that both these qualities constituted reasonable grounds for selection, and that those who had them were entitled to privilege and influence. Not only were those above selected from the lower ranks on sound principles, but authority itself was exercised with careful discretion. Although the president of the company was 'one-man', most managerial decisions were thought to be collective. Authority was therefore validated by the suitability of those who held it, and the consensus they achieved before applying it.

There were, as we have seen, some doubts about this third proposition. The continual gossip about connections and nepotism might have indicated that many people thought that the best men were not being promoted. In fact, however, the talk of nepotism was, like the intimations

of witchcraft in a primitive community, a strong inducement to everyone
to behave correctly. Few managers, knowing how liable they were to be
maligned for favouritism, would have dared to advance a man for
inappropriate reasons. A more troublesome uncertainty was how to
apply the criteria for selection. Was age more or less important than
merit? Those who lacked age or length of service naturally supported the
claims of merit, while practical considerations were causing the company
to promote by age. What exactly constituted merit? It was true that to
become a graduate a man had to pass through a very competitive education system, but did that fact justify the promotion of graduates within
the company? Should not allowance be made for abilities of different
kinds? The graduate salesmen who were promoted to deputy managers
on the production side were certainly meritorious. They were, after all,
both graduates and good salesmen. But were they the best men to keep
machines running? These doubts and inconsistencies worked to the
detriment of authority at Marumaru, but their effects were largely local,
chips at the gloss which did not weaken the body. In no human organization can the ideal of the best men ruling by perfect methods ever be
achieved. Few organizations could have made a very much closer ap-
proach to the ideal than Marumaru; and the company's obvious concern
with improving still further the ways by which men were selected for
office itself constituted a justification for authority.

Apart from these moral and ideological reasons for obedience there
were some obvious practical ones. Everyone at Marumaru had a strong
interest in the success and well-being of the firm. If Marumaru grew,
employees would be very likely to gain in pay and security. The company
would be able to afford better salaries, and it could offer new amenities:
sports grounds and health insurance, company housing and resort
accommodation. If Marumaru were ever to become the leader in its
industry, then employees would be able to carry themselves with extra
pride when they visited other companies, or obtain credit at the flourish
of a name card in shops and restaurants. The girl employees might gain
a slight advantage when it came to arranging marriages: better, after all,
to marry a girl from a company of the first water than one from some
local workshop. Even the wives of employees would be able to take a
slightly more assertive stance at the meetings of their parent–teacher
associations. If, on the other hand, Marumaru were to decline, then pay
and benefits would be diminished, and shame would replace pride. If it
were to go bankrupt, then many employees would suffer greatly, not
least because of the poverty of the Japanese social services, and the shame

would be all the worse. The material and social stake that everyone had in the company, therefore, constituted a powerful encouragement to cooperate, and therefore to obey.

Obedience and discipline were all the more essential because, as the management insisted in its monthly and weekly pep talks, and as the readily available information about internal and external conditions confirmed, the company's position was perpetually precarious. The salesmen would bring back news that the rivals were lowering their prices. Customers would ring up to complain about the quality of binding or smudged printing. There would be prognostications in the newspapers about rises in interest rates or the prices of paperboards. News would circulate about the bad effects on a factory of the bankruptcy of a customer. It was all too evident that there was no room for complacency. No one could guarantee Marumaru's future except the employees themselves.

The stake in the company of the mobile employees was, however, very much smaller than that of the immobile ones. If a young shop floor worker or a woman wanted to work in a big and notable company, he or she did not necessarily have to go to the trouble of making Marumaru one. Nor would Marumaru's decline have affected such mobile workers as disastrously as it would have done a section head or, worse still, an older man waiting for his separation allowance. It followed that mobile workers had rather less incentive to discipline themselves for the corporate good than immobile workers did. The sub-section head who tried to encourage his sub-section to accept an extra hour of overtime work might well suppose that his own sacrifice would be worth while, because of the effect that his work would have on the factory's profit margin, therefore on the factory's ability to take a loss on a pioneering contract with a big new customer, and eventually on Marumaru's future and his own. The young men whose enthusiasm he was trying to arouse had less reason to agree with Marumaru's priorities.

The mobile employees also had fewer personal as opposed to collective reasons for co-operation. The clearest example of this was that of the woman who refused to be transferred. The reason for her refusal was simply that the move proposed, from the head office in central Tokyo to a factory on the outskirts, would have meant spending much more time in trains and buses every day. If she had been a male graduate (and supposing that a male graduate would ever have failed to respond to such an order) her superiors would have been able to offer better chances of promotion and to threaten some kind of managerial oblivion to induce her to go. But a woman? Women were scarcely eligible for promotion in any event, and they could hardly be made to do more tedious jobs than they were doing. In the case of the young shop floor workers, promotion and demotion were not theoretically impossible; but the extent to which considerations of age entered into promotion made that remote and demotion meaningless. A young man required to transfer could well wonder whether his acceding to the request would be held in his favour in five years' time, when his turn for promotion would come. He already knew that no immediate harm could come to him if he refused. The age-seniority system, which helped in some cases to validate authority, here weakened it by making it almost impossible to reward obedience.

It might have been expected that the resistance to authority shown by the mobile workers would have been reflected, and even magnified, in the activities of the company union, to which everyone beneath the rank of sub-section head belonged. In fact, however, the union was under the control of older men, usually of the team leader rank, who were just on the point of becoming sub-section heads, and therefore managers. Their position was a difficult one. If they opposed the company seriously they jeopardized their careers. If they failed to oppose the company they risked being branded as traitors by the union membership, which consisted of so many young men and women. On the whole the union leadership did acquiesce in management decisions, but it had two important weapons of resistance at its disposal. The union leaders, all of them loyal company men, did enjoy the sympathy of the middle managers who were just above them in the standard ranks, and were, as we have seen, themselves dissatisfied with their treatment by the company. If the union leaders took up an issue, therefore, they would be listened to, and more or less surreptitiously supported, by the managers who were constitutionally supposed to be opposing them. The other weapon of the union officials was the ominous threat that if the management took no account of union demands, co-operative leaders like themselves would perhaps be replaced by leaders drawn from among the younger people, who cared rather less for the future of the company. In this indirect sense, then, the mobile employees did contribute to the strength of the union; but it could not be said that the union was of prime significance in limiting the authority of the company.[1]

The support for authority at Marumaru came, then, from nearly unanimous opinions and powerful interests. No one seriously challenged management's right to command on moral or political grounds, even

[1] For a more detailed account of the union see R. C. Clark (1975).

though alternative ideologies were readily available. At the same time a large number of employees had every practical incentive to obey. What resistance there was to authority came largely from those with positions on the labour market which gave them the facility of leaving the company. Since the labour market was organized not by jobs and skills, but by age, sex and level of education, the contrast between those who had to submit to discipline and those who could demur was a contrast, not between people doing different types of work, but between young and old, men and women, and the more and less educated.

And because the support for authority was so firm, Marumaru was by any standards an extremely orderly company. A British foreman or manager would have been amazed at the discipline of the employees. Absenteeism was very low, quite as low as at Hitachi,[1] where fewer man-days were lost for any reason than would have been lost if everyone had taken their full holiday entitlements. Individuals certainly grumbled, but work teams worked hard even under the most severe conditions: doing an hour of early morning overtime at the end of the midnight shift, when the temperature of the Yokohama factory might fall to near freezing point in winter, called for considerable self-restraint. On the rare occasions when indiscipline did occur, it was usually the result of a momentary aberration rather than a premeditated assault on authority. A man might lose his temper and refuse to work after lunch, or a girl might sulk when she was asked yet again to check her figures. Even when managers were morally in the wrong, their authority remained intact. Because the source of a decision was often so obscure, employees were able to curse 'our company' for being 'mean' and underhand, while continuing to respect their immediate superiors and to do as they were told.

It is probable that in a majority of Japanese companies of Marumaru's size similar conditions apply, and managers do not in normal circumstances need to doubt their abilities to get their subordinates to do things. But industrial discipline is not the birthright of every Japanese employer, nor, as some of the questionnaire returns suggest, are all Japanese employees inherently docile. In small firms, where the quality of management is not high, and there are a large number of mobile employees, many of them older men in junior positions, or part-time housewives working for a pittance, the problem of authority may be more pressing than it was at Marumaru, where only fifty per cent. of the employees were mobile. There are also large firms with autocratic owners, or histories of labour difficulties, and in these, too, the authority of company and management

[1] R. P. Dore (1973: 188).

may more often be challenged. Nevertheless, it is probably true to say that authority in industry is at least as firmly established in Japan today as in any other major industrial country. Nor is it likely to decay or crumble in the near future. Over decades, however, it may be that the changing attitudes and new employment practices I have referred to will weaken authority or confound its exercise. I shall consider this possibility and other potential changes in the final chapter.

CHAPTER VII

The Company, Society and Change

In the preceding chapters I have described various features of the context and workings of the Japanese company. It is now time to consider how these features fit together coherently to form a system, and to discuss how the company system is related to a changing society.

THE JAPANESE COMPANY SYSTEM

The easiest way to perceive the logical consistency in the arrangements of the Japanese company is to set out its more obvious characteristics side by side with those of the generalized Western company, as in Table VII.1.

Table VII.1. The Japanese and Western company systems

Japan	The West
The Industrial Context	
Company part of one industry.	Company covers many industries.
Company not functional unit, depends on sub-contracting.	Company more nearly a functional unit, higher degree of self-sufficiency.
Shareholders principally associated companies, not primarily interested in profits and dividends.	Shareholders primarily interested in company as financial investment.
Financed by debt.	Financed by equity.
Relations with other companies hierarchical.	Relations with other companies more nearly egalitarian.
Market share a major measure of success.	Profit a major measure of success.
The Labour Market	
'Lifetime employment' an ideal.	No ideal of 'lifetime employment'.

Japan	*The West*
Company recruits people of particular age and education to fill general vacancies.	Company recruits people with particular skills and types of experience to fill specified jobs.
Size of company correlated closely with employment practices.	No close correlation between size of company and employment practice.
Size of company correlated with quality of work force.	Size of company less closely correlated with quality of work force. All companies contain representatives of all sections of the wider society.

Internal Organization

Company ideally a community.	Less emphasis on community ideal.
No major distinction between managers and workers.	Frequently sharp distinction between managers and workers.
Standard ranks, strong emphasis on hierarchy.	Management positions not standard, related to particular function, less emphatically hierarchical.
Age and length of service explicitly recognized as promotion criteria.	Age and length of service only marginally relevant to promotion.
Authority and responsibility ostensibly diffuse.	Authority and responsibility ostensibly specific.
Attachment to company correlated with age and sex.	Attachment to company weaker, associated with skill as well as age and sex.
Enterprise unions.	Trade unions.
Managerial authority limited in practice by labour mobility.	Managerial authority challenged ideologically and practically by trade unions.

It hardly needs to be repeated at this stage that the comparison in Table VII.1 between the Japanese and the Western company is a very gross one. There are dozens of different types both of Japanese and Western companies, and not all of them have the characteristics attributed to them. Moreover, the characteristics themselves are more complicated than the brief descriptions of them suggest. The purpose of the table is not, however, to show how Japanese companies differ from Western ones in each particular respect, but to reveal how the characteristics on both sides can be resolved into a difference of systems.

If, instead of reading across the table, we read down the Japanese and Western columns, we see that any one attribute of each company is more or less closely related to many of the others. On the Japanese side, for example, the fact that firms are so often part of one industry makes market share a natural measure of success and an obvious management goal. To the extent that managers are not aiming primarily for profit, something that benefits only one group of people, but for growth of sales, which benefits everyone, management becomes not coercion but leadership. The distinction between managers and workers may be insignificant, especially when so many managers start out as workers and rise to management in the course of their 'lifetime' of service to their firms. The company can be a community in which everyone has interests in common, and work can be seen as at least partly a matter of self-interest. Similarly, there is an association between the firm's dependence on bank and trade credit, and the development of hierarchical relations between companies. A continuity exists between the ranking of companies in the society of industry and the ranking of company members within each company, because so many firms have standard ranks. Again, all these features are consistent with the predominance of enterprise unions. These obviously fit better into companies engaged in one industry than into companies involved in a number of different businesses. Enterprise unions help give rise to industrial gradation by encouraging their firms to pay higher wages than smaller enterprises can afford. The existence of an ideal of 'lifetime employment' is partly an historical result of the activities of enterprise unions. Within each company, the enterprise union contributes to the cohesion of the community by discouraging the differentiation of employees by skill or type of job; for the union itself depends on being able to represent the interests of workers doing every kind of work.

Reading down the right hand column of the table enables us to see the similarly consistent, but differently ordered, logic of the Western company. The firm, frequently involved in several industries, undertakes its business in the language of finance, which is common to all industries. Partly because of this, and partly because of the nature of its shareholders, it makes profit one of its most important goals. Within the company managers and workers alike fill more or less specialized positions relating to the function of the particular firm and, ultimately, to the achievement of financial success. The degree of interest managers and workers have in this success is different, and is widely assumed to be different. Managers are placed in a position of authority by the shareholders and they are expected to accept the goals of the company. Workers are to be cajoled

8*

and exhorted to contribute to those goals, which, it is implicitly admitted, are less directly beneficial to them. The involvement of the employee in the company is limited by the likelihood that he will change jobs, by his membership of a union, and by his participation in institutions outside the firm.

It is certainly remarkable that modern industrial countries can have developed apparently different ways of organizing industry; so remarkable that there is a temptation to suppose that the Japanese company, which appears, after all, to be the odd man out, will change so as to become more like the Western one. Later on I shall discuss 'convergence' hypotheses. I should like here, however, to examine the reasons why the Japanese company does *not* change, whether in a Western direction or otherwise.

The first reason, which scarcely needs labouring, is the success of the Japanese company. The resurgence of the Japanese economy after the Second World War was the result of many things, but one of them was surely the way Japanese industry was organized and the constitution of the company. One can see the progressive recognition of this in Western writings about Japan. Bemusement at the illogical nature of the Japanese company, with its disregard for universal principles of rationality and its precarious financial arrangements, has given way to respectful discernment of some of the Japanese advantages. Western businessmen are now aware, for example, that 'lifetime employment' and 'pay by age' make it easier to introduce new machinery without having to renegotiate wage rates or allay fears of dismissal. Industrialists everywhere are envious of the harmony which appears to be found in Japanese companies between management and labour. In countries like Britain, and in industries in which Japanese companies have become dominant, respect has been overtaken by fearful admiration. A converse process has occurred among the Japanese. In the 1950s the Japanese were modest about their own institutions and eager to learn. By the mid-1960s, when Japanese companies had become as productive as those in the West, their managements showed a new confidence in 'traditional' methods. By 1970 their pride in those methods was sufficiently well justified to permit them to deride the less efficient Western producers they were displacing for slapdash quality control, poor labour relations, or outdated technology.

Now it is true that not every Japanese company is a Matsushita, a Canon, or a Nippon Steel. It is also true that the formidable competitive power of such companies is partly derived from the sacrifices they can impose on smaller companies and, as I shall shortly explain, on the Japanese population as a whole. Even so, large Japanese companies, though they may be privileged, are also intrinsically efficient. They could hardly make goods of such high quality and deliver them on time if they were not. No one, Westerner or Japanese, need be in any doubt that the Japanese system works; that it is able to co-ordinate and even inspire thousands of men and women to make and sell things; and the fact that it works is a powerful argument for not tampering with it.

Another reason for the stability of the company is systemic inertia. So many of the important characteristics of the company are logically inter-dependent, or at least closely adapted to one another, that it is difficult to change one without changing the others at the same time. The company cannot, for example, adopt profit as its supreme goal without adjustments to its relations with shareholders, a reconstitution of manage-ment ideals, and changes in the behaviour of its employees and in the attitude of the company union. Nor can a company suddenly introduce detailed job specifications without altering the relations between company and employee and modifying the nature of authority; with further impli-cations for the strength of the distinction between managers and workers, and for the cohesion of the company union.

There is, however, an important corollary. It may be true that change is inhibited because it cannot occur in one respect alone. Yet if the com-pany is forced to change merely in one respect, that apparently limited change may bring about many other alterations. We have already noted one instance of a seemingly minor change having very extensive consequences. The rapid ageing of the Japanese population makes it diffi-cult for even the biggest firms to recruit employees straight from school, and allows younger people to change jobs easily. As a result, employers are having to modify pay by age systems, to extend the age of retire-ment, and to recruit from the labour market. It is not difficult to imagine how the need for better methods of recruiting mid-career entrants could lead to the growth of a job market based on skills rather than age, and how the new emphasis on skill within the firm could affect employees' attitudes to the company and to each other.

A third reason why the company remains as it is could be described as political, using that word in the widest sense. The company and Japanese industry as a whole confer their benefits on enough people for there to be considerable support for the status quo; while those who do not benefit from the company and from industry either do not realize it, or are unable to do anything about it.

To understand the nature of this political support, this implied bargain between the company and its beneficiaries, we shall have to consider at some length something that has only been mentioned in passing so far: the relations between the company system and society.

THE COMPANY SYSTEM AND SOCIETY

I intend to discipline the mass of questions that volunteer themselves for service in explaining the effect of the company on society by subordinating them to a naïve preoccupation: who gains and who loses from the activities of companies and the way they are organized? We shall have to consider the matter in three stages. To begin with, how does industry as a whole impose itself on and contribute to the rest of society? Next, how are wealth and power distributed within industry, between different types of firm? Finally, how does the organization of the company affect the individuals concerned with it?

At the beginning of Japanese industrialization, as we saw, the prosperity of the peasantry was sacrificed for the development of industry. After the Second World War, too, Japan recovered from her devastation by placing all available resources at the disposal of industry. Even today, when Japan has a formidable industrial economy and many of her firms dominate world markets, business and industry continue to be favoured at the expense of the private citizen.

Consider, for example, the sources and uses of taxation, as set out in Table VII.2. Japanese companies (which are not, of course, the only source of business taxes) provide a surprisingly high proportion of all government income. But the proportion of national income taken in tax is low by international standards. In most of the major West European countries government revenues represent more than thirty per cent. of the Gross National Product, while in Japan they represent less than twenty-five per cent.[1] Moreover, in Japan a rather smaller share of government revenue is distributed to private households than in other industrial countries.

Another piece of evidence is the flow of funds between the main sectors of the economy: personal, business (Table VII.3 deals only with business corporations), and government. Each year the personal sector surplus, the bank deposits and savings accounts of private individuals, has gone to make up the business sector deficit. Industry has, in fact, borrowed on a vast scale from the private citizen, while the government until recently has been more or less self-sufficient. The scale of this transfer of funds is less significant than the terms on which the transfer has taken place. Most

[1] For a comparison see Joseph A. Pechman and Keimei Kaizuka (1976).

Table VII.2. General government income by source, and government disbursements to individuals, in relation to Gross National Product, 1955–74

(million million yen)

	1955 %	1960 %	1965 %	1970 %	1971 %	1972 %	1973 %	1974 %
Gross National Product	8.9 (100.0)	16.2 (100.0)	32.8 (100.0)	73.0 (100.0)	81.6 (100.0)	94.8 (100.0)	115.6 (100.0)	136.3 (100.0)
General government revenue	1.6 (18.0)	3.3 (20.3)	6.7 (20.4)	15.9 (21.8)	17.6 (21.6)	21.0 (22.2)	27.4 (23.7)	32.6 (23.9)
Government income from corporations	0.2 (2.2)	0.7 (4.3)	1.2 (3.7)	3.4 (4.7)	3.5 (4.3)	3.9 (4.1)	5.8 (5.0)	8.2 (6.0)
Government income from individuals	0.4 (4.5)	0.7 (4.3)	1.7 (5.2)	4.0 (5.5)	4.8 (5.9)	6.2 (6.5)	8.2 (7.1)	9.1 (6.7)
Government income jointly from corporations and individuals*	1.0 (11.2)	1.8 (11.1)	3.6 (11.0)	8.2 (11.2)	9.1 (11.2)	10.7 (11.3)	13.2 (11.4)	15.9 (11.7)
Government disbursements to individuals†	0.4 (4.5)	0.6 (3.7)	1.4 (4.3)	3.2 (4.4)	3.6 (4.4)	4.5 (4.7)	5.6 (4.8)	8.1 (5.9)

Source: Japan Statistical Yearbook, 1976: 475–6: Table 329A, D.
* Indirect taxes + social insurance contributions.
† Includes social insurance benefits.

Table VII.3. Flow of funds between sectors, interest rates, and inflation, 1968–76

('000 million yen; fiscal years)

	1968	1969	1970	1971	1972	1973	1974	1975	1976
Net surplus funds of personal sector increase in personal bank deposits, etc.	4,475 (100)	5,355 (100)	5,767 (100)	7,877 (100)	10,936 (100)	9,393 (100)	13,750 (100)	17,138 (100)	18,006 (100)
Net deficit of government sector increase of borrowings by central and local governments, etc.	1,153 (26)	850 (16)	499 (9)	1,592 (20)	2,270 (21)	2,501 (27)	6,685 (49)	11,992 (70)	11,969 (66)
Net deficit (surplus) with rest of world funds passing out of (into) Japan from abroad in loans, investments, etc.	530 (12)	736 (14)	846 (15)	2,141 (27)	1,881 (17)	−1,127 (−12)*	−639 (−5)*	42 (0)	1,362 (8)
Net deficit of corporate sector increase of borrowing, etc. by companies	2,792 (62)	3,769 (70)	4,422 (77)	4,145 (53)	6,785 (62)	8,019 (85)	7,740 (56)	5,279 (31)	4,675 (26)

(percentages: calendar years)

	1968	1969	1970	1971	1972	1973	1974	1975	1976
Increase in consumer price index	5.3 %	5.2 %	7.7 %	6.1 %	4.5 %	11.7 %	24.5 %	11.6 %	9.3 %
Maximum available interest rate on bank one year term deposit	5.5	5.5	5.75	5.75	6.25	6.25	7.24	6.75	6.75

Source: Bank of Japan, Keizai Tōkei Geppō (Economic Statistics Monthly): 316, 325, 340, 364 and other official sources.

* In 1973 and 1974 there was a net inflow of funds into Japan to finance industry and government.

of it has been borrowed through the banking system, at interest rates which have been artificially set by the government at or below the inflation rate. Individual depositors have therefore received a negative real return on their bank deposits. Industry has been lent money at little or no real cost. The disadvantage of the depositor and the advantage of the industrial borrower have been compounded by tax, the depositor losing a percentage of the nominal interest due, and the borrower being able to charge the nominal interest expense against taxation. The cumulative effect of the movement of funds has been, therefore, a transfer of wealth from the individual to industry.

It is perhaps too early to say whether the increase in government debt in the years since the oil crisis, and the present reluctance of companies to borrow money, are indications of a permanent change in the direction in which funds flow. It is, however, possible that in the near future the government will benefit even more than industry and commerce from the willingness of the Japanese to save assiduously at low interest rates.

Another form of transfer has taken place in those industries where the government has used its influence to enable producers to take advantage of consumers by raising prices beyond those that would obtain on a free market. Government interference of this kind has perhaps been more conspicuous in agriculture rather than in industry. The Japanese consumer has to pay well above world market prices for rice and other crops in order to support the farming population. In a host of industries, however, the government has protected domestic manufacturers from cheap imports until 'liberalization' was deemed possible. Some industries are still protected or strictly controlled by the government, and in certain of them, notably the food industry and finance, the consumer is clearly supporting the producer. The official price rigging in the meat industry has recently been explained to the public in a celebrated book.[1] In the world of finance (in which the manipulation of bank interest rates could be considered a form of price fixing), the customer gets poor value for his money from the insurance industry and, even more significantly for the future, from pension fund administrators. Government rules about the disposition of pension funds ensure that industry gains while the beneficiaries have little chance of receiving an adequate pension. No great

[1] Yokota Tetsuji, *Gyūniku wa naze takai ka* (Why is beef expensive?) Tokyo, Saimaru Shuppankai, 1977. For an account of the reaction to this publication see *Asahi Shinbun*, 13 July 1977, p. 3, 'Takai gyūniku: kaigai de mo akuhyō' (Expensive beef: notorious even abroad).

effort is made to prevent trust banks, which share a monopoly of pension fund administration with life insurance companies, from generating profit for themselves from the funds they handle.[1]

The result of this transfer of wealth has been that those immediately engaged in industry can live comfortably, while those outside it are at a disadvantage. Factories and company apartments are grand and imposing, but private houses are cramped and very expensive. The restaurants of Japan are full of those conducting the world's business on tax-allowable expense accounts, while food prices in the shops are extremely high. In the hill resorts of Mount Fuji and the fashionable seaside towns the terraces and streets are crowded with lodges owned by large firms. For those not eligible to use them the cost of a holiday will be very considerable.

To recount these economic advantages of industry, and those within it, over the rest of society is to tell only part of the story. Ordinary people have given more than their wealth to industry. In some cases they have given their health and welfare and even their lives. For industrial pollution, for which Japan has become so notorious, is largely the cumulative effect of the priority accorded to the needs of industry over those of individuals, in a country where people have to live together in crowded conditions. Such an explanation seems bland and unsatisfactory when applied to the terrible tragedies which have now become so well known: the Minamata disease, caused by organic compounds of mercury contained in the waste products discharged from the chemical plants of two companies, Chisso and Shōwa Denkō, which has killed or paralysed hundreds of people; and the cadmium poisoning case involving Mitsui Mining & Smelting.[2] It would be hard indeed to excuse the heartless behaviour of some of the parties to these affairs. The Chisso management withheld its co-operation from the team of university medical researchers looking for the cause of the Minamata disease. It then tried, with the connivance of the Ministry of International Trade and Industry, to dissuade the victims from seeking legal redress, and finally employed 'general meeting men' gangsters to intimidate victims who came to a

---

[1] By the rules of the Bank of Japan, a high proportion of pension fund money must be lent, rather than invested in land or shares, which have a better chance than loans of keeping their value. The rate of return on pension trust funds tends, therefore, to be below the rate of inflation. Trust banks systematically benefit by requiring companies to which they have lent money from their pension trusts at a low nominal rate of interest to deposit 'compensating balances' in the trust banks' banking accounts. This money can then be lent on to other borrowers, to the advantage of the banks.

[2] For an account of these and similar cases see S. Prakash Sethi (1975: 77–93).

company meeting as shareholders.[1] Most pollution cases, however, are less apocalyptic and much easier to interpret as a mere misapplication (as it now appears) of policy.

Take, as a rather more typical example of a pollution problem than Chisso, the experience of the Osaka factory of Marumaru. The factory had been built in 1962 on an irregularly shaped plot of land surrounded by fields, within the jurisdiction of the suburban town of K————. In the summer of 1968 a second corrugator was put into the factory to increase production. This was an event that would not have concerned outsiders, except that in the autumn of the same year a number of houses were built in the vicinity of the factory. Almost immediately the town hall began to receive complaints about the intense and penetrating noise of the corrugators.

By rights, the neighbouring houses should never have been built, because their site was a piece of waste land between Marumaru's plot and a Hitachi factory, and was not officially recognized as suitable for housing. Some of the houses themselves contained factories, small workshops with one or two workers which were open to the street and no doubt caused as much nuisance to the other residents as Marumaru did, at least in the daytime. Unlike Marumaru, however, they did not work at night. The rest of the houses were shoddy blocks of flats, two stories high, with walls of grey corrugated iron. Between them ran unpaved roads.

In 1969 a second dispute arose. Until then the effluent from Marumaru's factory, which included waste corn starch and printing ink, had been drained away in an open unlined ditch. (Similar wastes from British corrugated board factories are collected in special containers and taken away by the local authorities.) The residents complained to the town hall of the smells carried past their windows, and the company built a new concrete ditch to drain both the factory and the houses. But nothing was done about the major problem of noise, even though the mayor of the town called several times at the factory to ask the manager to eliminate the nuisance. Nor did the company make any effort to discuss the matter directly with those who were being discomforted. Only in 1970, when the mayor sent official notice to Marumaru that the factory would be closed if the noise was not reduced, was action taken. The story of the mayor's threat was passed to the newspapers, and customers began to telephone Marumaru to find out whether their supply of boxes might be

[1] *Asahi Shinbun* (evening edition), 29 November 1971, p. 9, 'Ichi-kabu kabunushi o katasukashi: Chisso Sōkai' (The Chisso general meeting: dodging the one-share shareholders).

cut off. The company quickly enclosed the noisiest parts of the corrugators in sound-proofed boxes, and took certain other measures to bring the noise down to just above the official limit. The work was finished by February 1971, nearly two and a half years after the first complaints.

In this case, as in so many others, the pollution was not caused by a malevolent act on the part of a greedy company. Instead it was the consequence of the inadequacy of appropriate legislation, and the poverty of social services—both of which, however, reflected the priority historically given to industry. Marumaru's moral position was scarcely a strong one, but in a sense it too was a victim of the episode. The company had to pay for drains and for sound-proofing, so as not to inconvenience people who had illegally put up houses in an industrial zone. It was having to shoulder burdens for the whole community, even though, as a newcomer to the area, it had never benefited from the absence of restrictions and the low level of local taxation which had contributed so much to the cause of the problem.

The minor episode at Marumaru also illustrated how the isolation of a company from the local community and the strong collective sentiments within many firms can, in more serious cases, allow managements presumably composed of normal people to behave with such cruel indifference towards pollution victims. At the Marumaru Osaka factory there had never been much contact between anyone in the factory and those in the surrounding houses. The Marumaru employees lived in distant company apartments and did their shopping and found their entertainment near them. Since no one had had any cause to know the local people, when the problem arose it became all too easy to think of them as remote outsiders. Within Marumaru there was little or no controversy over the issue. Union leaders, workers and managers all took the same view. The situation was bad, but it was scarcely Marumaru's fault. The township could have prevented the problem's arising but, inevitably, 'our company' would have to pay out of its own pocket. In cases like that of Chisso, too, where a company has stood accused of perpetrating acts with the most hideous consequences, remarkably few employees or groups of employees have chosen to criticize their firms, at least in public. Company members, particularly immobile ones, see their interests as lying with their companies and are at the same time emotionally committed to their firms and their fellow workers. Enterprise unions balk at jeopardizing their members' livelihoods.[1] It is significant that the few

[1] For a lucid discussion of the Japanese labour unions and pollution see Shirai Taishirō* (1971).

employees who have 'betrayed' their companies in the interests of the community have tended to be mobile employees, and particularly women, who have less commitment to their employers, less to gain from company careers, and greater attachment to local communities than other company members. In the second outbreak of Minamata disease, for example, it was women employees at Shōwa Denkō who made public certain of the company's activities which bore on the investigation into the disease.[1]

So far we have been discussing the distribution of wealth between industry and the rest of society. The next question, how wealth and influence are distributed within industry, is answered easily. Companies have the advantage of unincorporated businesses, and (which is partly the same thing) large firms dominate small ones.

The company has become pre-eminent in Japan for the same reason as elsewhere. Because it is a legal personality, the company is able to engage the co-operation of many people, shareholders, employees, lenders, suppliers and customers, in a way quite impossible for an individual entrepreneur; and because it is or can be of unlimited duration the company can plan and conduct business on a time scale beyond the range of any single human being. Companies also tend in most countries—and Japan is no exception—to be taxed much more lightly than individuals. Their marginal tax rates on income are lower, and they are allowed to charge expenses such as interest against tax; besides being immune, of course, from inheritance taxes.

The dominance of large firms over small ones is also seen to some extent in other industrial countries, but it is probably more marked in Japan than anywhere else. We have seen that the bigger a firm is, the more efficient it is (in certain respects at least), the better the equipment it possesses, the more satisfactory the sources of its finance, and the greater its ability to attract able employees. Just as nothing succeeds like success, so the superiority of large firms adds to their advantages. Their cheap finance allows them to undercut their small competitors and become bigger firms and safer borrowers still. Their able graduates run them ever more efficiently and make them yet stronger and more attractive to good recruits. As they turn in these virtuous circles, bigger firms can make use of another advantage. They can depend on small firms to keep them safe

[1] *Asahi Nenkan** (The Asahi Yearbook) *1972*: 236. This source also gives an account of a campaign by an enterprise union against pollution by a company. In the spring of 1970 the union of an oil refining company, General Sekiyū Seisei, incorporated demands that the company cease polluting the environment into the programme for its 'spring offensive'. In the course of the union's campaign nine workers were dismissed, and the company tried to found a rival, docile 'second union'.

in adverse conditions. When a recession comes, Hitachi, Toyota, and Nippon Steel can keep their profit margins high by offering harsher terms to their suppliers and sub-contractors, and in extremities even deprive dependent smaller firms of their livelihood by making for themselves components they previously bought from outside. The primary suppliers and sub-contractors can in turn press hard upon their sub-contractors. The larger an enterprise is, therefore, the more economies of scale and market influence allow it to prevail over smaller rivals, and control and exploit subordinate firms.

The final consideration is how wealth and influence are distributed within the firm. If we take Marumaru as typical, it seems that women are paid lower wages than men, and are effectively excluded from authority in the firm. Among men pay and authority increase to a certain point simply with age, but beyond that they are conferred on those with ability, of which higher education is thought of as a precondition and an emblem.

What, then, is the combined effect of these three component influences? Who does gain and who loses as a result of the position of industry in society, the disposition of firms within industry, and the internal organization of the company? It is clear that the company system favours men over women, the educated over the less educated, and those of middle age over the very young and the old.

The difference between what men and women are offered by the company system is very marked. Women bear more than their share of the burden that industry imposes on the consumer and the citizen. Married women, it is true, need not be dismayed by high prices and low welfare benefits while their husbands are at work. Unmarried women, divorced women and (most significant for the future) widows do not always have male breadwinners to protect them. At the same time, within industry women are paid less than men for doing the same jobs, and have the poorest chances of ever achieving wealth or power. It is admittedly true that no industrial society gives women genuine parity with men in economic affairs, but Japanese women are more rigidly discriminated against than their Western counterparts. In addition, their position is made worse by the fact that skills are of such little account on the labour market, so that they cannot find better jobs by acquiring special expertise.

If the company system gives all men an advantage, it rewards more highly educated men far more generously than men of lower educational standards. Those who stay longest in school and college and go to the 'best' schools have the greatest chances of getting into the biggest and most influential companies, and then of rising within their chosen firms. The less educated a man is the more modest his prospects within industry. If he does enter a big company he will lose in the competition for promotion beyond a certain level. If he joins a smaller one he will be most unlikely to reach the very pinnacle of industrial success, though he may have the consolation of moderate achievement.

To be fair, a man's life-chances are not entirely determined by his education. There are several ways in which he can improve his lot even after he has left school and begun work. There will always be some possibility of a man's being promoted within his firm in spite of his poor academic record. He can go to night school to make good any educational deficiencies—many firms offer night school training to their less educated workers as a matter of course. He may change firms advantageously, a method of progression which has become more common with increasing labour shortage. He may also be lucky enough to be caught up in the success of a small firm, like Marumaru, that manages to become a big one. But all these paths to success are narrow, hard and, all too often, disappointingly short. The ten years of schooling between nine and nineteen provide far more opportunity for advancement than the thirty years of normal working life, from twenty-five onwards. It is incomparably easier for a schoolboy of eleven who is clearly on the way to Tokyo University eventually to become Chairman of Nippon Steel than for an eighteen-year-old high school entrant to Marumaru, or even to Nippon Steel itself.

The degree to which industry rewards education and punishes the lack of it has had a formidable effect on the education system. When examinations mean so much, schools have to become crammers and their teachers coaches, while the curriculum reverts to its origin in a race track. It is now becoming essential for candidates for the 'best' universities to go to night schools or special tutors; for if they do not they will not be up to the standard. The physical strain on children of so much work is bad enough, but the moral one is worse. Children, who are anxious enough at the prospect of chancing their own futures on an exam, are often handicapped as much as encouraged by their parents' interest in their success, which will confirm that the whole family is rising in the world—and in their failure. Similar distortions of the education system have occurred in many countries, and for similar reasons. The well-educated people administering the powerful institutions of modern societies recruit to their ranks well-educated people like themselves, largely because well-educated people are genuinely necessary, but also out of self-esteem. Universal and compulsory education systems must select those to be given the highest training, and the selection process once established, selection for higher education becomes a crucial preliminary for selection into the powerful institutions. Because industry is of such moment in Japanese society, because of industrial gradation, and because of the Japanese preference for recruitment from school and college, the influence of industry on education is perhaps more marked in Japan than elsewhere. It should be added, however, that the influence is not entirely malign: the insistence of employers on high educational standards must surely be one reason why Japan does not have the problems of illiteracy that vex the United States or Britain.

It must not be forgotten that there are dangers to industry, too, in the fact that the education system has become its recruiting sergeant. When they commit themselves to taking only graduates and high school leavers from certain institutions, for example, companies put their trust in a process of selection they cannot easily check. If for any reason—and I shall offer one in a moment—the selection becomes biased, then the companies may be badly affected without even realizing it, or, if they do realize it, without being easily able to repair the damage.

The last of the three criteria by which industry chooses its favourites is age. Within most firms, but especially large ones, the older a man is the more his authority and dignity, and the better his pay. But to all except the handful of men who go on to become directors of their firms, retirement brings a decline in power and wealth. At eighteen a man has no authority and little pay. At forty he will be a sub-section head or a section head, with ten or twenty respectful subordinates and something on his name card to impress outsiders. At sixty, if he has a job at all,[1] he will be a superannuated worker in the same firm, poorly paid and subordinate to his erstwhile juniors; or else a section or department head in a small subcontractor or associated firm, uncomfortably settled among the native employees. The arrangement of pay and retirement in this way is certainly beneficial to larger firms. They are able to promote younger, more able men in place of less able superannuated workers; and at the same time avoid having to pay higher salaries and to accumulate greater liabilities for separation allowances. Smaller firms gain people with first-class

---

[1] Though most older workers do find jobs after retirement some cannot, especially during slumps. See *Nihon Keizai Shinbun*, 18 September 1976, p. 3, 'Kōreisha no shitsugyō kyūzō' (Rapid increase in unemployment of old). A Ministry of Labour survey conducted in 1974 showed that just over a third of a sample of more than 5,000 men who had retired had been out of work at some stage, usually immediately after retiring. Most of those who had been out of work had had no job for more than three months. *Rōdōshō: Rōdōkijunkyoku: Teinen Tōtatsusha Chōsa no Kekka.* (1975): 12–14 (Ministry of Labour: Labour Standards Bureau: Results of the survey of workers of retiring age).

experience, but in taking on outsiders they risk lowering the morale of their younger existing employees. The disadvantage of early retirement on these terms for the superannuated employees is obvious: while they still consider themselves to be in good physical and mental condition they must lose both salary and position. Nor do they benefit in their declining years from the success of the large companies to which they gave the best part of their lives. Yet there are advantages as well. In some ways adjustment to inferior work at the age of fifty-five may be easier than adjustment to no work at all at the age of sixty-five. Moreover, if we allow that firms can only pay their middle-aged workers relatively well because they can superannuate their older ones, then the arrangement does not seem quite so unfair. Each man is borrowing from his old age, when expenses should be limited, to meet the greater expenses of his middle life. It is interesting to note how, in spite of the apparently illogical payment scheme within the individual firm, there is a close correlation between a man's contribution and his rewards over his entire working career. He receives most when he is at the height of his powers, and least when he is either too old or too young to give of his best.

INDUSTRY AND CLASS

This analysis of the differing effects of industry on people of different sex, education and age is hard to accommodate to the more usual interpretation of industrial society which relies on the concept of 'class'. Whatever the origins of the word 'class', its use today both by sociologists and by ordinary people has probably been most profoundly influenced by Karl Marx. The context for Marx's discussion of the subject was the passage of European societies from feudalism to capitalism, and the anticipated supersession of capitalism by socialism. He conceived of industry, the principal 'means of production' in the advanced capitalist countries, as the source of a distinction between antagonistic capitalist and working classes. The former owned property and thereby controlled the 'means of production'. The latter owned only their capacity to work, which they sold to capitalist employers on an impersonal labour market. Although the labour market appeared to be free and therefore fair, the wages received by the workers were always less than the value of the work they did. The capitalist class exploited the 'surplus value' of labour and used it to perpetuate the capitalist domination of society.

If this formulation was ever wholly applicable in Marx's time, events since then have made it less and less adequate as a guide to understanding even the Western industrial societies Marx himself was concerned with.

Marx's general historical predictions have not been fulfilled, and his specific observations on the economy and society of capitalist countries now appear outdated. Within industry there has been, in Professor Dahrendorf's words,[1] a 'decomposition' of both capital and labour. The individual capitalist entrepreneur has given place to the joint-stock company—an institution Marx himself recognized as weakening the control of the capitalist over industry, and considered to be a stage towards the capture of the 'means of production' by the proletariat.[2] Managements, too, have altered. Instead of a handful of stewards supervising each enterprise there are large and intricate bureaucracies, whose members comprise a burgeoning middle class. If the undifferentiated working masses ever existed, they have been transformed into a heterogeneous assortment of men and women engaged in different kinds of industry and possessed of different levels of skill; and in some countries workers have to be further distinguished by national origin and culture. There have been significant changes outside industry. Workers have won political and legal equality with their employers. They have used their votes to make governments responsive to their demands, and to institute tax and welfare systems to compensate those subordinate in industry for their inferiority. Partly as a result, the very nature of property, the institution on which the Marxian analysis relies so much, has changed. The rights of ownership over the older forms of property have becomes less absolute; and new forms of property like pension rights and insurance policies—conditional, social and not transferable—have come to comprise a large proportion of the national wealth.

Such developments have made it less plausible to talk about class in the sense in which Marx used the word. Those sociologists who feel they have to follow Marx at all costs have kept the word and the concept and reorganized reality to fit them. Sociologists who are not Marxists but who have been impressed by the facts that Marx drew attention to, that control over property and superordination and subordination in industry are of great importance in determining a person's position in society, have continued to use the word 'class', but with qualifications. They have cut its part and made it share a dressing-room with similar words such as 'status' or 'stratum'; or they have altered its definition, so that it no longer has

[1] Ralf Dahrendorf (1959: 36–71).

[2] 'This result of the highest development of capitalist production is a necessary transition to the reconversion of capital into the property of individual producers, but as the common property of associates, as social property outright.' Karl Marx (1909: 517). Marx goes on to mention, however, that the mechanism of the joint-stock company enables individual entrepreneurs to raise outside funds, and so greatly increases their influence.

exclusive reference to property or industry. In doing this they have risked making the word private, intelligible only to sociologists, or factions of sociologists.

Recently Anthony Giddens[1] has made a subtle and successful attempt to deal with modern European and American societies in terms of class; and to make use of Marx's insights without defending his misconceptions, or perpetuating those of his views that have become outmoded. For Giddens, as for Marx, there are classes because there are labour markets. People sell their labour or, more accurately, their skills on the market in return for wages and benefits. The differences between the market capacities of various types of people are, potentially, the origins of class differences. But every difference of market capacity does not constitute a difference of class. There are no separate classes of dustmen, machinists, farm workers and lawyers; for people can only be said to be aware of a limited number of classes.[2] The question is, therefore, how the differences in market capacity give rise to relatively simple class systems. They do so as a result of two sets of influences. The first set makes it easier or more difficult for people of one market capacity to adopt another. If dustmen and the sons of dustmen often become machinists but scarcely ever become lawyers, then dustmen and machinists may well belong to one class and lawyers to another. Normally there are three sorts of market capacity: ownership of property in the 'means of production', possession of educational qualifications, and ability to do manual labour. Mobility between those with each sort of market capacity tends to be limited: hence a common division into upper, middle and lower classes. The second set of influences on the class system of a given society consists of those arising from the organization of industry (and particularly the division of labour and the nature of authority within it), and from the way in which goods and property are distributed. All capitalist societies, however much they have changed since Marx's time, are 'intrinsically' class societies simply because they have highly developed labour markets; but in each of them classes differ in appearance and significance as a result of political and economic conditions.

The great advantage of Giddens' method of analysis lies in its flexibility. Classes no longer come in a standard, pre-conceived form. Instead they define themselves in each society, and differ from one society to the next.

[1] Anthony Giddens (1973: especially 100–12).

[2] It is not entirely clear from Giddens' main discussion of the subject why there are only a limited number of classes (106). It is only later (134) that we learn that 'class structuration always presupposes at least class awareness'. I have therefore, perhaps unjustifiably, filled in the missing term of a syllogism.

And Giddens' observations by induction from these differences are interesting and sometimes very plausible. He can, however, be criticized for making too rigid a distinction between capitalist societies, intrinsically divided by class, and state socialist ones, which he claims to be potentially and perhaps even actually classless.[1] His argument is also weakened by his failure to discuss the growth of institutional ownership, and the associated changes in the nature of property; so that his account of the upper class in capitalist societies is inadequate.

Now, the peculiarities of the Japanese case are two-fold. Industry remains more important in society than it does in other countries of comparable economic stature; and the decomposition of capital and labour, while in many ways more complete than in the West, has taken place in an unusual way. Industry has retained its influence because the state has done so little to qualify its effects. So uneven has been the distribution of wealth and power through the industrial labour market—consider the difference between the directors of Hitachi and the shop floor workers in a tiny sub-contractor—that one is immediately tempted to apply a Marxian analysis. The temptation is all the greater because it is clear that those at the top enjoy their wealth and power partly at the expense of those at the bottom. But Marx's original formulation is no longer useful. Capital has lost its integrity not by dilution among thousands of shareholders but by introversion: industry has come to own itself. In any case, the bulk of industry's capital comes not from shareholders but from banks; and these in Japan, perhaps more than in any other country, are under the control of professional managers. Labour has been dissociated not into categories of workers of different skills but, more conclusively, into groups of workers attached to different companies. Within each company labour and capital are hardly antithetical. The Hitachi directors are not the representatives of a class of capitalists so much as of the collective interests of the Hitachi employees from whose ranks they came. The shop floor workers in the sub-contractor are not Labour personified. Their position is weak because they belong to a powerless small company. If they were doing the same jobs in Hitachi itself they would be among the more privileged members of society.

It might be possible to preserve the Marxian scheme by assimilating the division between large and small firms to that between upper and lower classes,[2] if it were not for two obstacles. In the first place there is a grada-

---

[1] Cf. W. G. Runciman (1974: 110–11).
[2] Cf. the attempt made by Ōhashi Ryūken* (1975: 105–13) to determine whether people in firms of different sizes belong to a ruling or a subordinate class, defined in Marxian terms.

tion of firms of all sizes, rather than a simple division between the large and the small. Secondly, people move between firms of different size. Most industrial employees who start in larger firms retire to smaller ones; and some employees of small firms join larger ones as mid-career entrants.

If Marx's original methods of diagnosis seem to bring indistinct results, does Giddens' more delicate technique work better? Is it more helpful to consider not class itself but the way in which classes form and the reasons why they persist? Japanese society proves almost as intractable to Giddens as to Marx, and for a simple reason. Marx and Giddens share one fundamental assumption, an assumption which is more justified in a European or American context than a Japanese one. Both of them derive class ultimately from the operation of the labour market. But the labour market they both have in mind is one where individualistic skills search for impersonal vacancies. The Japanese labour market, where employees of different ages and levels of education find employers, is of a different disposition.

There is no need to spoil a strong argument by over-emphasis. The word 'class' is not meaningless in Japan, and the concept is not without application. Within small-scale industry owner-entrepreneurs and those who work for them can easily be put into classes. In large-scale industry, too, the shop floor workers of Hitachi are not always closer to the directors of Hitachi than they are to the shop floor workers of a sub-contractor. In Japan, as elsewhere, the very fact that people can sometimes see society in terms of classes makes class important, whatever the justification for their perceptions.[1] The workers in large companies specifically attract attention to an identity of class interests with other workers when, during wage negotiations, they call themselves 'wage workers' and direct their imprecations against the capitalists who are keeping their wages low. Yet people often exercise an ability to think in circles and move in squares. After all, when the employees of a big company have been inspired by their slogans to win a wage claim which it is beyond their company's immediate ability to pay, the result of their action is to put two or three hundred of their fellow workers in sub-contracting companies out of a job.

There is also some possibility that in the future Japanese society may have more clearly defined classes than it does today. If mid-career job changing becomes more common, and if skills become more marketable

[1] A good explanation of how the Japanese themselves conceive of a class is to be found in Yasuda Saburō (1973). Japanese tend to be less willing than people in many Western countries to think in terms of classes, or to divide society into 'them' and 'us'. Dr Yasuda's discussion of the increasing complexity of antagonistic relationships in Japanese society (206–8) parallels many of my arguments.

—and there are signs that they may—Japan, too, may become 'intrinsically' a class society. If appropriate changes in the labour market were to occur, the extent to which classes did become distinctive and significant would depend largely on the ease with which individuals and families could change their labour market positions. In the past the impartial administration of the education system has made it relatively easy for the sons of the poorest and least educated people in Japan to rise in the world.[1] In the last ten years, however, it has become obvious that children with richer parents are rather more likely than children of poorer parents to go to university, and especially to a 'good' university.[2] The entrance examinations to high schools and universities are as fair as before; but it is easier for the children of the well-to-do to go to the cramming courses that are now necessary to meet the required standards, or to wait a year after failing the exams once in order to sit them again. Attempts to make the state school system more egalitarian, by preventing children applying directly to the famous public high schools which appeared to offer the best chance of entering Tokyo University, have had the perverse effect of encouraging the development of private high schools of excellent academic standard. The richer parents of gifted children, because they cannot be sure of having their children go to a good state school, now send them to these good private schools. As a result, private schools are taking an increasing proportion of the places at Tokyo. We have seen how within industry education increases a man's chance of money. If money can in turn buy education there are prospects of a new class system, one based less on the labour market than on schools and universities. The immutability of such a system could even be enhanced by the workings of heredity. The educated class might become more intelligent than the uneducated class. There is, perhaps, a greater chance of an hereditary intelligentsia in Japan than elsewhere because of the Japanese practice of arranging marriages. Arrangements may facilitate more thoroughly than romantic chance the matching of rich, educated and intelligent men to the daughters of other rich, educated and intelligent men.[3]

[1] An account of the way in which education contributed to the careers of Japanese business leaders active in 1960 can be found in Hiroshi Mannari (1974: 64–82). A subsequent survey of business leaders in 1970 showed that though they were more highly educated than their 1960 counterparts, yet there was a smaller proportion among them of men of lowly origin. The sons of clerical and manual workers seemed to be finding it harder rather than easier to reach the top of industry. It should be noted, however, that if changes in educational selection are partly responsible for this tendency, they are changes which must have taken place thirty or forty years ago.

[2] Much of this paragraph is based on Thomas P. Rohlen (1977).

[3] The point is made by R. P. Dore (1975).

Well within the period required to confirm or prove false these apocalyptic predictions, however, the way in which the education system is ceasing to be a mass transport to success, and is becoming instead a private vehicle of inheritance, may affect the workings of the Japanese company. At present the promotion of graduates to the higher ranks of firms is justified ideologically by the fact that graduates have been pre-selected for ability. The more entrance to higher education depends on being able to afford fees, and the expenses involved in sitting exams twice, the less justification there is for thinking that graduates are necessarily more able than others. At the worst, the rigidity which would result from an education system increasingly at the service of the rich, combined with a labour market which failed to allow employees to improve their positions by changing jobs, might lead to rather more uncomfortable social relations within companies, and encourage antagonism between those in the increasingly discrete categories of manager and worker.

But for the present, the question of who gains most from the organization of industry and of the company is best answered in terms not of class but of sex, age and education. The company system is to the advantage of men, the better educated, and the middle-aged. It is reasonable to suppose that people in these categories will want to conserve it. They will use their influence, which is considerable not least because of the power and wealth that flows to them from industry, to keep the company in its present state.

THE FORCES FOR CHANGE

I have argued that three conditions have maintained the Japanese company as it is. Its organization has been validated by success. It has been protected from change by the logical consistency of its arrangements. It has been endorsed by those who benefit from it. This argument suggests an obvious inversion: that the company will change as a result of failure, or of events which confound the logic of the company system, or of a loss of political support.

Japan has achieved economic greatness so recently, and enjoys it with such confidence, that the possibility seems far-fetched of any universal failure: of her industries being outclassed or her manufacturers and merchants in wholesale disarray. But events during and since the oil crisis suggest that there may yet be failure of a comparative kind, failure to be quite as successful as before, with some effects at least on industry in general and on the company.

The recession which began after the major oil exporting countries raised petroleum prices in 1973 was more severe than any other within the last twenty years. Earlier business recessions in Japan tended to be like summer squalls. They were fierce and even dangerous for those not prepared for them, but they were soon over and quickly forgotten. As the demand for goods and services within the country fell, the position of companies became very uncomfortable. Most of them had borrowed from banks the greater part of the funds they needed to run their businesses —and to invest for an apparently rosy future. Unlike dividends to shareholders, which can be reduced in troubled times, bank borrowings are at fixed interest, which must be paid whether the borrower is doing well or badly. Companies were unable, therefore, to diminish the cost of their capital. They also found it difficult to lessen labour expenses. Firms could cut back on overtime and pay off temporary workers, but they could not easily dismiss their permanent employees. Company profits would fall very sharply and many firms would make considerable losses. Companies would adjust to the harsher conditions in two main ways. Firms of all sizes would increase exports, partly in order to keep production lines busy, and partly because exports were usually paid for more quickly than sales to domestic customers. At the same time, large firms would give less business, and on more rigorous terms, to smaller companies, with the result that hundreds of the smallest sub-contractors would go bankrupt. As exports rose, and as domestic interest rates fell because industry was borrowing less money, so the state of the economy would begin to improve. The recovery would be as rapid as the fall into recession had been. Firms would be able to do more business without borrowing more money or employing new workers; and because income would be rising faster than costs, profits would increase quickly. Soon regular employees would be earning overtime payments, and temporary workers would be back at their jobs. They would spend their increased earnings on the goods companies produced, and so encourage industrialists to invest in new factories and equipment and to recruit new staff.

The severity of the 1973–5 recession can be conveyed in a few simple figures. Between 1963 and 1973, a period which included the recessions of 1964–5 and 1970–1, the Gross National Product rose at an average annual rate of more than ten per cent. In 1974 the scale of the economy actually diminished, and even in 1975 the Gross National Product only grew by 2.4 per cent.[1] Equipment was made idle to an extent unparalleled in previous recessions. For most of 1973 firms were working at about

[1] OECD (1977: 6).

ninety per cent. of capacity; by the winter months of 1974-5 they were working at only about seventy per cent.[1] Company profits were vastly reduced. In the first half of fiscal 1973 the profits of large firms represented 3.76 per cent. of their turnover. Two years later the ratio was 0.84 per cent.[2] In fiscal 1973, 9,349 firms went bankrupt. Two years later there were more than 13,000 bankruptcies, and the debts involved had doubled, to more than 2,000 billion yen.[3] Unemployment statistics are not very reliable in Japan, but according to official sources the average number of men without jobs rose from 440,000 during 1973 to 740,000 during 1976.[4]

The 1973-5 recession was more than simply harsh. Its origins in the rise in the price of oil made it qualitatively different from earlier depressions. Previously, when the economy was in difficulties prices fell, or at least ceased to rise quite so fast, in obedience to the laws of supply and demand. As goods and services became cheaper, firms and ordinary individuals would be tempted to spend more money on them, and so demand would be resuscitated. In 1974, however, prices were forced up very rapidly in spite of falling demand because of the new price of oil. People responded by spending less of their money and saving more. On this occasion, then, industry was not to be helped out of trouble by consumer buying.

Again, the increase in the price of oil affected certain types of industry far more profoundly than others. Some industries, such as man-made fibres, suffered badly because oil was their main raw material. Others, like shipbuilding—and most of the ships built in Japan have been oil tankers—had grown with the oil industry itself, and suddenly found their prospects altered for the worse. Clearly, for these industries the oil crisis brought not temporary discomfort but lasting agony. Their decline is likely to continue to have debilitating effects on the whole economy.

Another major difference between the 1973-5 recession and those before it lay in matters relating to foreign trade. As on previous occasions, Japanese companies turned to exports when domestic demand fell. Exports rose from 12,126 billion yen in 1973 to 23,838 billion yen in 1976,[5] this latter sum being enough to cover the greatly increased cost of

[1] Calculated from the index of operating ratios published in *Keizai Tōkei Geppō* (Economic Statistics Monthly), on the assumption that the true operating ratio in the base year of 1970 was about ninety per cent. Cf. OECD (1977: 19 n).

[2] *Keizai Tōkei Geppō* 356: (November 1976): 131-4: Tables 90, 91V.

[3] *Oriental Economist* 45: 806 (December 1977): 44.

[4] *Nippon Tōkei Geppō* (Monthly Statistics of Japan) 198 (December 1977): 8: Table A-5.

[5] OECD (1977: 53, Table A).

oil and other imports. But this impressive achievement had—and continues to have—unfortunate consequences. Most of Japan's exports consist of a limited number of commodities, notably cars and transport equipment, electrical goods, steel and chemicals, and the successful Japanese penetration of foreign markets in these goods has caused resentment among Japan's trading partners, who are all too often her competitors. The resentment has been sharpened because Japanese imports of manufactured goods have not increased at a similar rate. To allay criticism and to forestall action against her, Japan has tried to reduce exports and encourage imports by the quickest possible means: the revaluation of the yen against other currencies. Since 1975 the yen has been allowed to appreciate against the United States dollar. The effect on trade has been disappointing, but within Japan large numbers of smaller companies have found themselves unable to compete on world markets and have gone bankrupt. The older and less educated people who worked in these smaller firms could be said to have contributed twice to the Japanese export effort: once in that the low wages they received when they were in employment enabled bigger firms to export fine goods at low prices; and once more in that by losing their jobs they have borne the brunt of the effects of the revaluation that the export drive made necessary. At all events, it has become clear that exports are not only diplomatically embarrassing, but are also the eventual cause of difficulties at home. The certain cure of previous recessions has come to have side effects which aggravate the disease.

In these circumstances, the recovery from the 1973–5 recession has been slow and uneven. While the economy as a whole grew at a respectable rate in 1976 and 1977, many industries were still in poor shape, and the unemployment rate and the number of bankruptcies continued to rise. It is very likely that from now on—and only partly because of the oil crisis[1]—Japan will grow more slowly. Certainly she will have great difficulty in achieving the very high growth rates of the 1960s, when she was able to buy superior foreign technology ready-made and, with her young and growing labour force, use it to make goods for sale on apparently limitless foreign markets. In the 1980s, having caught up with the most advanced nations, Japan will have to innovate for herself. Her labour force will be older. Foreign markets will not be so open. Already, it seems, Japanese industry has begun to accommodate itself to a more sedate pace. Firms are borrowing less and spending less on new plant and equipment; and they are not making such intensive use of plant they already possess.

[1] A good brief discussion is in OECD (1977: 26–7).

If there is no difficulty in predicting that the Japanese economy will grow more slowly from now on, it is very hard to say how slower growth will affect the organization of industry. It might have been thought, before the oil crisis, that the Japanese company system was predicated on success, and that it would be seriously disrupted by any lack of it. The precarious financial arrangements of so many Japanese companies and their extensive commitments to their employees, seemed sustainable only in a booming economy. Japan's was a bicycle trick, done at speed or not at all. The behaviour of the Japanese economy during and after the oil crisis has confounded such simple prophecies. If the company system has survived so fierce a jolt, it would be unwise to suppose that it will disintegrate merely because the going is harder and parts of the vehicle are in disrepair. It is more likely that slower growth will cause only gradual and superficial changes in the company system. If the recent fall in bank borrowing is indicative of permanent change, and Japanese companies do reduce their dependence on outside credit, then relations between companies may alter slightly. Bank groups may become even more fragile. Big firms may have slightly less control over small ones. If the economy as a whole is less active, then there will be less assurance that every type of business will do well, and more incentive, perhaps, for firms to diversify so as to be sure of representation in whatever industry is growing fastest. To the extent that in the past firms bought each others' shares in the knowledge that shares in no matter what industry would increase in value, then there may be one less justification for mutual shareholding in the future. But none of these changes is likely to occur precipitately or in revolutionary measure.

Nor is it probable that slower growth will of itself bring drastic alterations to the labour market. Larger Japanese employers responded to the 1973–5 recession, as to previous ones, by restricting overtime, cutting back on recruitment, and transferring workers to subsidiaries.[1] By these means they achieved as rapid a reduction of the actual number of working hours they paid for as American firms during the same period. But the Japanese firms, unlike the American ones, and in spite of the disheartening circumstances, still hesitated to dismiss regular employees. A survey of thirty-one large firms and seventy-four firms of intermediate size over 1974–6 showed that no large firm and only one or two smaller firms dismissed full employees in any year.[2] Even so, the number of regular

---

[1] Details are given in Haruo Shimada (1977), from which much of the material in this paragraph is drawn.

[2] Haruo Shimada (1977: 62, Table 9). A few firms did, however, solicit resignations. cf. p. 173 above.

9

employees in Japanese manufacturing industry did fall by about nine per cent. between September 1973, when the new oil prices were announced, and September 1976.[1] It is very possible that the proportion of workers enjoying some form of 'lifetime employment' will remain lower than it used to be. But there is no evidence that the employment system or the nature of the labour market has changed, or even that it is not entirely compatible with the new conditions.[2] It must not be forgotten that the slower growth predicted for Japan will not, after all, be very slow, either by comparison with the economic performances of other countries or in relation to the increase in the Japanese population. There is no reason why, simply because the company system worked impressively well when the growth rate was ten per cent. annually, it should not work at least moderately well when the growth rate is merely five or six per cent.

I have already discussed at some length the most important event that is causing the company to change by invalidating the logic of its arrangements. No other development poses as inexorable a threat to the company system as the ageing of the population. We have seen how it affected Marumaru, a company of modest size, in 1970–1. Today the shortage of young people and the growing number of old ones is a matter of the most serious concern to companies of far greater stature. I mentioned earlier that there are two obvious ways in which companies might adjust. They can abandon the 'traditional' Japanese system, by reducing the dependence of pay on age, and raising the age of retirement. The alternative is to preserve the 'traditional' system, by restricting the number of people who can benefit from it. The firm becomes, like construction companies in Japan and elsewhere, an organizing centre run by élite and privileged employees, co-ordinating the activities of dozens of associated companies and sub-contractors.

Either method of overcoming the demographic problem is likely to have important consequences for industry and society. If companies raise the age of retirement and keep their older workers, but at relatively lower salaries, then there may well be changes in the nature of authority within the firm and in the degree of labour mobility between companies. Within the firm, the association between age, status and authority will become weaker. Young managers will often have to command older workers who would previously have been superannuated, and, like the team leader at Marumaru with his older mid-career entrants, they may find it difficult to exercise their authority. The modification of the pay by age system is

---

[1] Calculated from figures given by Haruo Shimada (1977: 56–7, Table 5).
[2] Cf. Haruo Shimada's own conclusion (1977: 64).

likely to lead to changes in the labour market. If employees cannot expect their earnings to rise more or less automatically with age and length of service, they will be encouraged to look for better terms with new employers. If mobility increases so, surely, will the significance of skill. Employers will recruit workers with particular skills on the labour market, and will assign them to specialized jobs. On the other hand, if companies adopt the alternative course, and restrict the number of people to whom they offer 'lifetime employment', the organization of industry will change rather less. The drawback of this solution, however, is that it will perpetuate the present distribution of wealth and power in society. The middle-aged and better educated will continue to benefit at the expense of the less educated and the old. I shall return to the question in a moment, but it seems unlikely that such a state of affairs will be politically acceptable to a rather older population.

It is as yet too early to do more than speculate upon which of the two modes of adjustment will become more common. Big companies appear, according to a recent survey,[1] to be improvising various adaptations to the problem, without having devised a uniform solution. Some firms have resigned themselves to having to employ more older workers, and are making arrangements to use them more effectively. Nissan Motor, for example, is said to be spending between six and seven per cent. of its capital investment budget on equipment and reorganization aimed at improving the productivity of older workers. Companies like Hitachi and Ishikawajima-Harima have created project teams composed of older employees, and assigned them to tasks, such as design work or running sales campaigns, in which their age is no liability and their experience an asset. Other companies have created subsidiaries specifically to absorb older workers. Nippon Kōtsu Kōsha (the Japan Travel Bureau) encourages superannuated employees to join a subsidiary company which operates booths in department stores and hotels. Sony has a subsidiary called Max Seiki to which its employees over fifty may transfer. Chiyoda Chemical Engineering, Fujitsū, and Konishiroku Photo have all reduced the extent to which pay increases with age. At Chiyoda the salaries of those over the age of forty-two are now to be negotiated with the firm. Many companies, among them Mitsui & Co., Asahi Glass, and Sumitomo Metal Mining, tempt their employees to resign early by offering them larger separation allowances if they do.

Whether the average age of retirement rises or falls, there will still be

---

[1] *Nikkei Business*, 23 May 1977, pp. 36–49, 'Kōreika shakai Nippon no kōzu' (Design for an ageing society: Japan).

9*

an increasing proportion of the population beyond working age, or at least beyond the age when people can fully support themselves. Older men and women will have to rely on two sorts of income, state pensions and private annuities. The cost of increasing state pensions can be met simply by raising taxes, and there is no reason to think that a mere increase in taxation will upset the company system. In any case, personal and indirect taxes, which are at present low, will probably rise faster than taxes on industry. But people are unlikely to be content to depend entirely on the state. They will demand company pensions, and will contribute privately to endowment policies. The institutions which manage pension and insurance funds must surely, therefore, become larger and more powerful than they are now. Since their liabilities will be for the long term, they will have good reason to invest in the more durable assets, shares and land. In this they will behave quite differently from today's dominant financial institutions, the city banks, which borrow and lend for the short term. The demand for equities will rise, and there is every prospect, especially if a slower economic growth rate causes firms to borrow less money, of a change in the balance of debt and equity capital in industry. Companies will issue more shares, and, more important, they will have to pay more attention to their dividends; for the pension funds which will control much of their capital will have no other motive for holding shares than to secure income and capital gains. Management goals may therefore have to change. Profit and profitability, the rate of return on assets, may become much more significant; and if they do there will be some effect on social relations within the firm.

Another, rather less potent, threat to the logic of the company system comes from the new requirement that company accounts should be consolidated.[1] A company must incorporate the accounts of its subsidiaries (that is, companies in which it holds more than half the shares) with its own. Before this requirement passed into statute, a company could maintain high levels of profitability and productivity and so justify high wages by exploiting its subsidiaries, the accounts of which were quite separate. The parent company could buy in goods from its subsidiaries at artificially low prices, or require them to hold inordinately large amounts of stock on its behalf. The financial position of the parent company, which might be quoted on stock exchanges and so be bound to make its accounts public, would then appear rather better than it was. Now there is no advantage to a parent company in imposing on its subsidiary, for its subsidiaries'

---

[1] For a discussion of consolidation see Robert J. Ballon et al. (1976: 243-52).

sales, stocks, profits and wages must be counted with its own. But big firms can still maintain themselves at the expense of smaller associated companies, in which they own less than half the shares, and of small sub-contractors which may be wholly dependent on them but in which they may have no stake at all. Moreover, a parent company can always sell some of its shares in a subsidiary to bring its shareholding down to less than fifty per cent. of the whole, and so avoid unpleasant revelations.[1] Consolidation can hardly be said, therefore, to sound the knell of industrial gradation; but it does reduce the value to larger companies of maintaining that gradation, and it may yet have a levelling effect.

Consolidation may also induce companies to place more emphasis on financial measurements and less on market shares. One of the principal methods by which Japanese companies have kept themselves homo-geneous is by making their more successful specialized divisions into sub-sidiaries. An electrical company, for example, with a growing chemical division, may well establish that division as a separate chemical company. The management of the parent company can then continue to run an electrical company in the electrical industry, while the management of the subsidiary becomes the management of a chemical company in the chemical industry. The two companies will not, of course, be indepen-dent. Ultimate control over the subsidiary will rest with the parent com-pany, and the subsidiary will be dependent upon its parent for much of its business, and especially, perhaps its credit. The subsidiary will also receive many of its staff from the parent. Nevertheless, the frame of reference of the two companies will be different in many important ways. The managers of each can pursue quite separate aims. The employees will compare their salaries with those offered by 'other firms in the same industry'. Outsiders will distinguish the reputations of the two firms. With consolidation, however, the frame of reference of two companies becomes more nearly the same. The managements both of the parent and the subsidiary now have to bear in mind that the subsidiary is contributing to (or detracting from) the financial standing of the whole group. It would only be a limited consolation, to take an extreme instance, that the subsidiary doubled its sales, if in doing so it halved the profit of the whole group. And just as financial measurements may become more important within the consolidated group, so there may be a tendency to use them to compare one consolidated group with another.

Other, slightly more remote eventualities may upset the system. In

---

[1] Holger Kluge (1977: 25) notes that Mitsubishi Chemical recently reduced its sharehold-ing in an unprofitable subsidiary to avoid having to show poor consolidated results.

recent years, the federations of enterprise unions have joined together to conduct 'spring offensives' for higher wages and better conditions, as well as in support for demands for new government policies. These 'spring offensives' represent only a limited form of co-operation between unions; but if in the future unions were to draw closer together, and if at the same time the employees of smaller companies were to join unions in greater numbers, it might be more difficult for big companies to impose themselves on small ones, and easier for men to move between companies of all sizes.

There is potential for disruption, too, in the influence of foreigners. Foreign companies in Japan depend for their recruits on the secondary labour market, and they characteristically pay very much higher salaries than Japanese firms to men of given age and experience, and offer their employees greater responsibilities and more rapid promotion. So far, however, the influence of foreign-owned companies has been small. Only a tiny percentage of the working population has been in their employ. They have been unable to attract the kind of people they would have liked, in spite of their high salaries, because they were not well known. In addition, joining a foreign company, because it has meant working for foreigners, has been seen as something socially uncomfortable and mildly unpatriotic.

In the future, however, foreign companies may possibly employ a slightly higher proportion of the working population, though a lower one than in Britain or Germany. Foreign companies may also become better known. Even today IBM is as well known in Japan as its principal Japanese competitor, Fujitsū, and Japanese working for Nestlé or Shell need not fear obscurity. As more foreign-owned companies come to be staffed almost entirely by Japanese, and as the Japanese lose something of their commercial patriotism, the other objections to working for foreign companies may lessen. A time may come when major Japanese companies have to compete seriously with their Western rivals for recruits, and when the loss of middle managers and skilled workers to Western companies may be more than a minor irritant. If it does come, Japanese companies may have to make adjustments of considerable consequence. One of the first might be in the treatment of women. Even today foreign firms probably use their women employees more effectively and offer them better terms than Japanese companies do. Large numbers of well-educated and able Japanese girls already prefer to work for foreign companies. Although their loss to Japanese companies is presently accounted of no significance, an increase in the number and size of foreign firms, and a shortage of educated manpower in Japanese ones, might bring a change first of concern and then of policy.

There is the faint prospect of an even more rapid, because more direct, effect of foreign companies on the Japanese company system. If foreigners were able to buy smaller and less efficient Japanese companies in order to improve them and make them better able to compete with their large rivals, then industrial gradation would rapidly become less marked and the privileges of big firms less assured. Foreigners have in the past bought small Japanese firms, but infrequently and with great difficulty, because the risks to the purchaser are considerable and the administrative barriers to the acquisition of Japanese companies hard to surmount. It is unlikely that the Japanese government will make things much easier for foreigners in the future, in spite of full capital 'liberalization'.

In any case, although it might be exciting, especially to Westerners, to picture a struggle on Japanese soil between the opposing company systems of West and East, it is best not to overestimate the extent to which foreign companies in Japan will cause Japanese arrangements to change. Foreign firms no longer have the authority of superior performance. They themselves have a greater respect than before for Japanese practices, and are as likely to allow their Japanese subsidiaries to 'go native' as their Dutch or Canadian ones. Above all, they are made aware by a suspicious government and a vaguely hostile press that they are in Japan on sufferance, and that they must be careful to avoid giving offence or causing an upset.

There is also the possibility that the Japanese company may be altered as a result of its own operations abroad. It might be thought, for example, that the *ringi* system of decision-making would have to be modified, because it would appear cumbersome and even unintelligible to senior foreign employees. This sort of hypothesis underestimates the ability of foreigners to adapt to practices which, though superficially different, are in many ways analogous to their own. It also underestimates the ability of Japanese to preserve their customs. After all, firms like the trading companies and the Bank of Tokyo, which must surely employ as many foreigners as Japanese if all their subsidiaries and affiliates are taken into account, conduct their Japanese operations, at least, in a quintessentially Japanese manner.

The third set of reasons why the company may change concerns its position in society, and the degree of support the industrial order can claim from the population as a whole. Industry has demanded considerable sacrifices of the Japanese people in the past. Two circumstances make it unlikely that it will be able to do so in the future. Industry has diminished its role in Japanese affairs by the very success with which it has played it. The country has become so rich that one need not be so sure that what is good for Mitsubishi is good for Japan. The clearest sign of a change in attitudes is the success of the consumer movements,[1] which are frequently led, as one would expect, by women. The most effective of the many campaigns conducted by these movements is still, perhaps, that of Shufuren, the Housewives' Federation, against Matsushita Electric Industrial. When, in 1970-1, Matsushita, together with some of its chief rivals, appeared to be making inordinate profits on television sets in Japan, and to be selling them more cheaply in America than in the home market, Shufuren instituted a boycott of the company's products. After Matsushita's profits had fallen sharply, its management agreed to change its sales practices.[2] Similar campaigns have been directed against cosmetic manufacturers and banks; while property developers and construction companies have frequently been attacked for ignoring the rights and wishes of residents near the sites of their new buildings. The intense activity against pollution in recent years, too, is an indication of the ways attitudes to industry have been changing, as much as of the objective worsening of environmental conditions. Cases of pollution are not, after all, new to Japan. The first Minamata victims were struck down in the early 1950s. Then, however, pollution could be seen as an inevitable concomitant of economic growth, which was necessary for Japan's wellbeing; and industry could not be too severely censured for disturbing the environment when it was doing so much for the country. Today, however, the citizenry is, rightly, more concerned with the quality of life than with perennial industrial growth; and local communities are less likely to forgive a firm for the nuisances it commits simply because it is providing economic benefits.

The change in the relation between industry and society manifested in consumer movements and pollution campaigns may be accelerated because of a second circumstance. The ageing of the population, which is likely to have such profound consequences on the internal organization of industry, is also liable to affect industry's position in society. It will decrease the proportion of the population who benefit directly from the

---

[1] A good case study in English of one of these is Savitri Vishwanathan (1977).

[2] The chairman of Matsushita was later to remark that his company, too, had suffered from its own policy of 'dual pricing', and that he was glad that it had been forced to change its ways. *Asahi Shinbun*, 4 February 1971, p. 8, 'Zesei wa shōhisha no chikara'. (The correction was the power of the consumer).

success and prosperity of industry, and increase the proportion who benefit only indirectly, if at all. The percentage of the population over sixty-five years of age is expected to move from 7.04% in 1970 to 9.52% in 1985 and 11.98% in 1995.[1] This will mean a vast rise in the number of adults (and therefore voters) who are not being looked after by employers, and who have no immediate incentive to allow industry special privileges. Instead, the older people will probably demand better social services from the government, which will in turn no doubt look to industry for the money to provide them. The problem of looking after the older people will be acute, not only because so many of them will be growing old at the same time, but also because they will lack the independent financial resources they might have had, if the firms from which they retired had granted them better separation allowances and pensions. These new old, the burgeoning generations of an ageing Japan, are the very same people who gave their working lives to the economic rebirth of their nation. They will certainly be morally justified in calling for the repayment of the debt due to them. But that will not make it easier to pay, nor help industry to adjust to its new role as supporter of the community rather than its prodigal dependent, Japan's staff rather than her sword.

The political implications of the change in attitudes and in the composition of the electorate are already beginning to be apparent. As I remarked at the beginning of the book, the relations between government and industry, and between political parties and companies, have never been quite as close and harmonious as phrases like 'Japan, Inc.' imply. They have, however, been closer in the past than they are today. It is clear that the government, instead of closing its eyes to the peccadilloes of companies, is dissociating itself from them as quickly as possible. Cases of pollution, price fixing, or commercial conspiracy against the public interest, which ten years ago the government would have tut-tutted into oblivion, are now made the subject of dramatic enquiries. The most spectacular of these was the summoning to the Diet in 1974 of the presidents of the major trading companies, Mitsubishi, Mitsui, Marubeni, Sumitomo, C. Itoh, Nisshō-Iwai and Tōmen, and of three banks, the Bank of Tokyo, Dai-Ichi Kangyō, and Sumitomo Bank, to explain 'excess profits' and various irregularities, such as tax evasion.[2] There is little doubt that during the years of high inflation immediately after the oil crisis trading

---

[1] Ōbuchi Hiroshi* (1975: 233) and Yamaguchi Kiichi* (1972: 43–6).
[2] The proceedings took place from 25 February 1974, and accounts of them are to be found in all the major Japanese newspapers.

companies did increase their profit margins,[1] and that companies had in the previous few years been partly responsible for pushing up the prices of a number of commodities, from wool and timber to land. Yet the companies were scarcely the prime cause of the inflation. The blame for that lay with the oil-producing countries and, to some extent, with the Japanese government itself. It was evident from the nature of the Diet proceedings, in which the presidents were not indicted on specific charges nor placed under oath, that the session was what one might call a 'blackwash'. The greatest businessmen of the land were being arraigned not so much for the particular acts their companies had done, as in the role of scapegoats for ills which it was not in the government's power to cure.

Eventually, no doubt, the decreasing importance of industry to society will be reflected in the decreasing importance of the company to the employee. Where he works and what he does at work may become merely an aspect of a man's existence—of more concern, certainly, than his golf club or where he lives—but part of the whole nevertheless. Opinion polls already suggest that people are slowly coming to take a more casual view of their employers, and are less willing to place work above their families and their personal interests.[2] Just as the change in social attitudes to industry as a whole is most easily observable in the activities of those who gain least from industry, particularly women; so within the firm the young men and women whom the company rewards least are the first to detach themselves from it. We saw in the case of Marumaru how young shop floor workers were most interested in affairs outside the firm, and most inclined to think of Marumaru as a means to their particular ends. Young women, from whom the same degree of commitment to work has never been expected, are probably readier than ever to think of their employment as merely a way of getting enough

[1] Return on equity of the three biggest trading companies (parent company figures only) between 1970-4 was:

Six months to	Sept 1970	March 1971	Sept 1971	March 1972	Sept 1972	March 1973	Sept 1973	March 1974
Mitsubishi	15.1	15.3%	9.0%	14.3%	18.3%	18.5%	18.1%	17.4%
Mitsui	16.5%	15.8%	12.3%	14.5%	15.9%	14.1%	12.6%	15.2%
Marubeni	11.2%	11.7%	8.8%	10.2%	13.3%	16.2%	19.0%	17.9%

Source: Daiwa Securities Co., Ltd. *Analysts Guide, 1975.*

Note that Mitsui at least did not profit greatly from the oil crisis. It should also be recognized that much of the increase in profits came from 'stock profits', arising from the sale of stocks of goods bought at the lower prices prevailing before the oil crisis. 'Current cost' accounting methods would yield a much lower profit rate.

[2] Sepp Linhart (1975: 204-8).

money to marry or to spend a year in Europe. There are signs that companies are having to compete with wives, families and hobbies for the time and energy even of their older workers. Senior managers are constantly inveighing against 'my home-ism', as the Japanese call 'private life', using that same derogatory half-English in which they term an ephemeral singing star a 'talento'. Perhaps in the future industry and the company will lose the friendship even of the highly educated, who, in great contrast to their European and American counterparts, have been industry's most loyal allies. The cleverest graduates of the finest universities will no longer fight to enter banks, and industry will receive as little intellectual honour as in Britain and, increasingly, in America.

Yet though work and the company will surely preoccupy employees less, the change will probably take place only slowly, and may not go as far as in the West. For some time to come the commitment to work and the company will remain strong. Working hours will be long and holidays short. Men will still spend as much time after work with their colleagues as with their wives. It will take the Japanese some time to learn the use of leisure, as opposed to the drinking parties and mah-jong sessions in which they pursue work by other means—though the large number of poetry circles, chess and *go* clubs and bookshops, the packed attendances at musical performances and baseball games, and the enormous if temporary enthusiasm for fads such as bowling, all suggest that they are learning hard. Until government welfare expenditure is greatly increased the Japanese will need to work more than Europeans and Americans do, for less will be provided for them if they do not. They will also continue to be bound by sentiments and ideals which made a virtue of work when work was more necessary to them than it is today: by the community spirit so carefully fostered by Japanese companies, which disengagement from the firm must betray; and by the sense of purpose, progress and service which comes from respect for science, nationalism, and Confucian theory.

Convergence and the Search for Efficient Altruism

Will the result of all these changes be to bring the organization of the Japanese company closer to that of the Western one? Will the systems of West and East converge?

Indeed many considerations make it plausible that they will. The two systems are evidently coming to look alike in some respects. Japanese companies are recruiting from the labour market. Certain firms are making efforts to offer women careers more like those of men. Pay is gradually coming to depend less on age and more on skill and job content. Nor is it simply the Japanese who are changing, for Western companies are adopting Japanese arrangements. In Europe and America firms are offering more and more welfare benefits to their employees, partly because high marginal tax rates make salary rises pointless, and partly because state welfare schemes are proving to be of inadequate quality. Certain European countries have encouraged 'mensualization', the establishment of monthly pay and similar benefits on a uniform scale for employees of all types. Many companies in the West are ceasing to make the products they sell, and are relying on sub-contractors (often in Korea, Taiwan, or Japan itself) to manufacture goods for them to market under their own brand names. In the United States the recent decline in stock markets has caused companies to depend more on borrowed money and less on equity capital. The Joint Shop Stewards Committees in British factories have some of the characteristics of a Japanese enterprise union, in that they are confined to one firm, that their interests are opposed to those of the Committees of other firms, and that the shop stewards, like Japanese union leaders, hope for careers within the firm rather than within their unions, once their term of office is over.

In many cases the convergence of form is the result of the application of identical principles. Japanese companies are beginning to pay more attention to skill and job content partly because it is by reference to these attributes that it makes the best sense to employ mid-career entrants; and this is one of the chief reasons why Western firms rely so much on the idea of 'skill'. American companies have turned to sub-contracting for the same reasons as Japanese ones: to keep their market shares and pay high salaries at the same time. The British Joint Shop Stewards Committees are as much a recognition of the central importance of the corporation in fixing terms of employment as Japanese enterprise unions.

Yet there are many powerful reasons why a simple convergence seems most unlikely. It is not easy to find much justification in what has happened to Japanese industry in the past for a 'convergence hypothesis'. The organization of Japanese and Western industry was probably more similar in 1910 than in 1970. Many of the apparently exotic features of Japanese industry on that latter date—pay by age, 'lifetime employment', mutual shareholdings among companies, and so on—were not entirely or even largely historical residues which were slowly fading away. On the contrary, they were the results of relatively recent developments, which occurred when Japan had already had several decades of industrial experience and should, if convergence had been taking place, already have been half-way along the path to uniformity.

Next, in so far as there are Japanese and Western company systems (and the systems really exist as simplified extrapolations from an enormous variety of companies in different places and different industries, and of a multitude of sizes, qualities and shapes) the two are logically coherent and yet mutually incompatible. Similar forces acting on each of them do not have similar effects. Convergence between them, when it occurs, does not take the form of a steady progression. Instead it is discontinuous and desultory. Something may cause one aspect of the Japanese company to become more like an aspect of the Western company. As a result there may be further changes in the logically related aspects of the Japanese company. Some of these secondary changes, too, may be convergent, but others may be positively divergent because of the incompatibility of the two systems. It is possible to see this effect in the reactions of Japanese companies to the ageing of the working population. A firm can reduce the dependence of pay on age, and so bring its pay system closer to those in the West. Yet at the same time it can force its employees to transfer to subsidiaries at an early age, and so emphasize a Japanese organizational trait.

The third and perhaps most convincing argument against any idea of a general convergence in the future is that in Japan and in each of a dozen Western countries changes are taking place in quite separate directions. The British experiments with nationalization, and with the admission of trade unions to the councils of government, have not been repeated in the United States. The new rules for the administration and investment of American pension funds, which may in the long run have a considerable effect on the organization of industry, have no parallel in West Germany. The worker directors of that country do not have Japanese counterparts. Japanese statutory auditors, on whom great formal powers have been conferred by law, are not easily comparable with company officials anywhere else. It appears that developments in industry are no more conspicuously convergent than developments in politics, or broadcasting or literature. They have considerable relevance to what is going on in other societies, certainly, because of common preoccupations and much imitation; but they are at the same time conditioned by indigenous traditions, and prompted by forces and events different, and differently combined, from those in other nations.

Where does the future of the Japanese company lie, if not in simple convergence with the Western pattern? The forces for change are acting in two directions. Some are altering the nature of authority within the firm; others are affecting its position in society.

The Japanese company today represents an impressive solution to the problem of authority in industry. The employees, or more accurately male employees, of each company, matured by experience and chosen on merit, have exercised authority in a spirit of self-conscious harmony and public service. Their authority has been acceptable to those they commanded because their subordinates, given time and the acquisition of merit, could expect to have their own term in office; and because those in command used their authority in what was so obviously the best interests of those beneath them. In the future the ideological justification of authority may be less sure. There will be greater scope for debate about the nature of merit and the rightness of seniority. It will no longer be quite so plausible to talk of harmony or claim the privilege of public service. Some may even dispute the grounds on which men may rule women. The exercise of authority will also become more difficult, because it will no longer be so easy to arrange that everyone has a turn at the wheel, and because it will be harder to persuade subordinates that they are being disciplined for their own eventual benefit.

The position of the firm in society has been one of nearly unquestioned privilege. On the assumption that Japan must gain from it, the Japanese company has been allowed to pre-empt much of the wealth of the country and exert enormous influence; and it has been able to use that wealth and influence on behalf of its employees. From now on, the firm will surely have to give more to others and expect less for itself. It will have to pay pensions and support government programmes, and at the same time accept restrictions of law and public opinion.

The two sets of changes will be all the more disturbing because they call for almost irreconcilable adjustments. Firms have been well disciplined precisely because they have been selfish. The inner harmony of the company has depended on an opposition between each firm and others, and each firm and the rest of society. It will therefore be extremely difficult for the Japanese company to maintain its superb discipline, and at the same time learn to be charitable.

This difficulty is scarcely confined to Japan. No country has yet evolved what every advanced industrial society urgently needs: an association for production which is both efficient and altruistic. It must be efficient because it is only by the best possible use of materials and skills that rich nations can hope to stay rich. It must be altruistic because so many citizens cannot work for themselves. They are too old, too young, too preoccupied with education, or too weak to meet exacting standards, and they have therefore to be supported by others. Yet the common conditions of such societies make both efficiency and altruism hard to achieve. Educated workers, taught to think themselves every man's equal, will not have discipline thrust upon them. Money scarcely buys their acquiescence, certainly not their commitment. They must be persuaded or inspired into efficient order. At the same time, altruism is daunted by limitless needs and impersonal masses. People must give more and give willingly, but to an immensity of strangers. And everywhere efficiency and altruism seem to be counterpoised. One can only be had at the expense of the other. The conspiracies are well ordered, whether they are Japanese trading companies, American law firms, or British merchant banks. The instruments of service—schools, welfare bureaucracies, or nationalized industries—are poorly organized, confused in purpose, and often resented both by those who support them and those they are trying to aid.

By a happy set of circumstances, while the country was developing, and most of the population was young and at work, the Japanese company achieved a miracle of organizational alchemy. It was the efficient giver, the beneficial competitor, and the selfish philanthropist. It cannot be so in the future. To this extent there has been convergence, that Japan now shares the perplexity of other developed countries: how can wealth be created with energy and resolution, and yet distributed with compassion?

Starting from where they do, with their own talents and impediments, the Japanese are most unlikely to reproduce the particular compromises made in the West. We experiment with worker participation in the hope of achieving co-operative discipline, while trying to avoid licensing plots against the public interest. They have to organize kindness without copying our mistakes. They will strike their own balance, and we must hope that it will be successful. At any rate, they bring to the problem three great advantages. They have the opportunity and the ability to learn from others. They are ready to change, and yet have so far been able to resist utopian blandishments. They have, in the Japanese company, which has brought them so much so quickly, promising material to work upon.

References

References to *Japan Statistical Yearbook* and other handbooks, and to anonymous articles in newspapers and journals appear only in the Notes.

Abegglen, James C.
1958 *The Japanese factory: aspects of its social organization* Glencoe, Ill.: The Free Press

Adachi, Kazuo
1965 'Cost management in a special machinery company' *Keio Business Review* 4: 69–93

Adams, T. F. M.
1964 *A financial history of modern Japan* Tokyo: Research (Japan) Ltd.

Allen, G. C.
1940 'The concentration of economic control' In E. B. Schumpeter, ed., *The industrialization of Japan and Manchukuo* New York: The Macmillan Company
1962 *A short economic history of modern Japan* 2nd revised edition, London: George Allen & Unwin

Arisawa Hiromi and Naitō Masaru
1973 *Rōdō shijō no chōki tenbō* (The long-term prospects for the labour market), Tokyo: Tōyō Keizai Shinbunsha

Azumi, Koya
1969 *Higher education and business recruitment in Japan* New York: Teachers College Press, Teachers College, Columbia University

Ballon, Robert J., Iwao Tomita and Hajime Usami
1976 *Financial reporting in Japan* Tokyo: Kodansha International

Barber, Richard J.
1970 *The American corporation: its power, its money, its politics* New York: E. P. Dutton & Co. Inc.

Beed, C. S.
1966 'The separation of ownership from control' *Journal of Economic Studies* 1: 29–46

Bellah, Robert N.
1957 *Tokugawa religion: the values of pre-industrial Japan* Glencoe, Ill.: The Free Press

Bendix, Reinhard
1963 *Work and authority in industry* New York: Harper Torchbooks

Berle, Adolf A. and Gardiner C. Means
1967 *The modern corporation and private property* revised edition, New York: Harcourt Brace & World Inc.

Berry, Charles H.
1971 'Corporate growth and diversification' *Journal of Law and Economics* 14: 371–83

Bieda, K.
1970 *The structure and operation of the Japanese economy* Sydney: John Wiley and Sons

Bisson, T. A.
1954 *Zaibatsu dissolution in Japan* Berkeley: University of California Press

Blood, Robert O., Jr.
1967 *Love match and arranged marriage: a Tokyo–Detroit comparison* New York: The Free Press

Blumenthal, Tuvia
1976 'The Japanese shipbuilding industry' In Hugh Patrick, ed., *Japanese industrialization and its social consequences* Berkeley: University of California Press

Broadbridge, Seymour
1966 *Industrial dualism in Japan: a problem of economic growth and structural change* London: Frank Cass

Brown, William
1966 'Japanese management: the cultural background' *Monumenta Nipponica* 21: 47–60

Caves, Richard E. and Masu Uekusa
1976 *Industrial organization in Japan* Washington, D.C.: The Brookings Institution

Chan, Paul Timothy
1969 'The labor movement' In Robert J. Ballon, ed., *The Japanese employee* Tokyo: Sophia University Press

Clark, R. C.
1975 'Union-management conflict in a Japanese company' In W. G. Beasley, ed., *Modern Japan: aspects of history, literature and society* London: George Allen & Unwin

Cole, Robert E.
1970 'Japanese workers, unions and the Marxist appeal' *The Japan Interpreter* 6:2: 114–32
1971 *Japanese blue collar: the changing tradition* Berkeley: University of California Press
1972 'Permanent employment in Japan: facts and fantasies' *Industrial and Labor Relations Review* 26: 615–30
1976 'Changing labor force characteristics, and their impact on Japanese industrial relations' In Lewis Austin, ed., *Japan: the paradox of progress* New Haven: Yale University Press

Cook, Alice H.
1966 *An introduction to Japanese trade unionism* Ithaca, N.Y.: Cornell University Press

Curtis, G. L.
1975 'Big business and political influence' In E. F. Vogel, ed., *Modern Japanese organization and decision-making* Berkeley: University of California Press

Cyert, R. M. and J. G. March
1963 *A behavioral theory of the firm* Englewood Cliffs, N.J.: Prentice-Hall

Dahrendorf, Ralf
1959 *Class and class conflict in industrial society* London: Routledge & Kegan Paul

Daiwa Shōken Chōsabu
1977 'Kabunushi sōkai hakusho' (White paper on shareholders' general meetings), *Shōji Hōmu* 785 (Special Issue)

Dore, R. P.
1969 'The modernizer as a special case: Japanese factory legislation 1882–1911' *Comparative Studies in Society and History* 11: 433–50
1973 *British factory—Japanese factory: the origins of national diversity in industrial relations* Berkeley: University of California Press
1975 'The future of Japan's meritocracy' In Gianni Fodella, ed., *Social*

structures and economic dynamics in Japan up to 1980 Milan: Luigi Bocconi University, Institute of Economic and Social Studies for East Asia

Florence, P. Sargant
1972 *The logic of British and American industry* 3rd edition, London: Routledge & Kegan Paul

Fox, Alan
1971 *A sociology of work in industry* London: Collier-Macmillan

Galenson, Walter and Konosuke Odaka
1976 'The Japanese labor market' In Hugh Patrick and Henry Rosovsky, eds, *Asia's new giant: how the Japanese economy works* Washington, D.C.: The Brookings Institution

Giddens, Anthony
1973 *The class structure of the advanced societies* London: Hutchinson

Glazer, Herbert
1969 'The Japanese executive' In Robert J. Ballon, ed., *The Japanese employee* Tokyo: Sophia University Press

Glazer, Nathan
1976 'Social and cultural factors in Japanese economic growth' In Hugh Patrick and Henry Rosovsky, eds., *Asia's new giant: how the Japanese economy works* Washington, D.C.: The Brookings Institution

Goldsmith, R. W.
1958 *Financial intermediaries in the American economy since 1900* Princeton: Princeton University Press

Hadley, Eleanor M.
1970 *Antitrust in Japan* Princeton: Princeton University Press

Hara Kensaburō
1970 *Atarashi rōdō seisaku no kakuritsu* (The establishment of a new labour policy), Tokyo: Jiyūminshutō Kōhō Iinkai Shuppankyoku

Hazama Hiroshi
1963 *Nihonteki keiei no keifu* (The genealogy of Japanese-style management), Tokyo: Nōritsu Kyōkai
1971 *Nihonteki keiei: shūdanshugi no kōzai* (Japanese-style management: the merits and demerits of collectivism), Tokyo: Nihon Keizai Shinbunsha

Herendeen, James B.
1975 *The economics of the corporate economy* New York: Dunellen Publishing Co.

Hirschmeier, Johannes
1965 'Shibusawa Eiichi: industrial pioneer' In William W. Lockwood, ed., *The state and economic enterprise in Japan: essays in the political economy of growth* Princeton: Princeton University Press

Hirschmeier, Johannes and Tsunehiko Yūi
1975 *The development of Japanese business 1600–1973* London: George Allen & Unwin

Imuta Toshikatsu
1968 *'Kindai shinyōsei no keisei to kabushiki kaisha no fukyū.'* (The formation of a modern credit system and the spread of the joint-stock company), in Hazama Genzō, ed., *Kōza: Nihon shihonshugi hattenshiron* I. Tokyo: Nihon Hyōronsha.

Ishii, Ryōsuke, ed.
1958 *Japanese legislation in the Meiji period* Centenary Culture Council Series. Tokyo: Pan-Pacific Press

Jacquemin, Alexis P. and Henry W. de Jong
1977 *European Industrial Organization* London: Macmillan

Japanese National Commission for Unesco, ed.
1959 *History of industrial education in Japan 1868–1900* Tokyo
1966 *The role of education in the social and economic development of Japan* Tokyo: Institute for Democratic Education

Kanno Watarō
1961 *Bakumatsu ishin keizai-shi kenkyū* (Studies in the economic history of the late Tokugawa and Restoration periods), Kyoto: Mineruva Shobō

Kaplan, Eugene J.
1972 *Japan: the government–business relationship: a guide for the American businessman* Washington, D.C.: U.S. Department of Commerce: Bureau of International Commerce

Kawamoto, Ichirō and Ittoku Monma
1976 'Sokai-ya in Japan' *Hong Kong Law Journal* 6: 179–88

Kiefer, C. W.
1970 'The psychological interdependence of family, school, and bureaucracy in Japan' *American Anthropologist*, 72: 66–75

Kishimoto, Eitarō
1968 'Labour-management relations and the trade unions in post-war Japan' *The Kyoto University Economic Review* 38: 1–35

Kluge, Holger
1977 *Financial reporting in Japan: case study* Tokyo: Sophia University Socio-Economic Research Institute Bulletin No. 67

Kobayashi Takumi
1976 *Fujin rōdōsha no kenkyū* (A study of women workers), Tokyo: Jichōsha

Kōsei Torihiki Iinkai Jimukyoku (Office of the Fair Trade Commission)
1971 *Nihon no kigyō shūchū* (Business concentration in Japan), Tokyo: Ōkurashō Insatsukyoku

Large, Stephen S.
1972 *The rise of labor in Japan: the Yūaikai 1912–19* Tokyo: Sophia University Press

Legge, James
1861 *The Chinese Classics, Volume I: The Doctrine of the Mean* Hong Kong: The London Missionary Society

Levine, Solomon B.
1958 *Industrial relations in postwar Japan* Urbana, Ill: University of Illinois Press
1967 'Postwar trade unionism, collective bargaining, and Japanese social structure' In R. P. Dore, ed., *Aspects of social change in modern Japan* Princeton: Princeton University Press

Linhart, Sepp
1975 'The use and meaning of leisure in present-day Japan' In W. G. Beasley, ed., *Modern Japan: aspects of history, literature and society* London: George Allen & Unwin

Lockwood, William W.
1954 *The economic development of Japan: growth and structural change 1868–1938* Princeton: Princeton University Press

Lockwood, William W., ed.
1965 *The state and economic enterprise in Japan: essays in the political economy of growth* Princeton: Princeton University Press

Machlup, Fritz
1967 'Theories of the firm, marginalist, behavioural, managerial' *American Economic Review* 57: 1: 1–33

Mannari, Hiroshi
1974 *The Japanese business leaders* Tokyo: University of Tokyo Press

Marsh, Robert M. and Hiroshi Mannari
1971 'Lifetime commitment in Japan: roles, norms and values' *American Journal of Sociology* 76: 795–812
1972 'A new look at "lifetime commitment" in Japanese industry.' *Economic Development and Cultural Change* 20: 611–30
1976 *Modernization and the Japanese factory* Princeton: Princeton University Press

Marshall, Byron K.
1967 *Capitalism and nationalism in prewar Japan: the ideology of the business elite 1868–1941* Stanford: Stanford University Press

Marx, Karl
1909 *Capital* Volume III (edited by Frederick Engels). Chicago: Charles H. Kerr & Company

Masaki Hisashi
1973 *Nippon no kabushiki kaisha kinyū* (Japanese joint-stock company finance), Kyoto: Mineruva Shobō

Matsushima Shizuo
1967 '*Keiei kanri no Nihonteki tokushitsu*' (Japanese style characteristics of management and administration), in Mannari Hiroshi and Sugi Masataka, eds., *Sangyō shakaigaku* Tokyo: Yūhikaku

Mito Kō, Masaki Hisashi and Haruyama Hideo
1973 *Daikigyō ni okeru shoyū to shihai* (Ownership and control in large enterprises), Tokyo: Miraisha

Nakamura, James I.
1965 'Growth of Japanese agriculture, 1875–1920' In William W. Lockwood, ed., *The state and economic enterprise in Japan: essays in the political economy of growth* Princeton: Princeton University Press

Nakane, Chie
1970 *Japanese society* London: Weidenfeld and Nicolson

Nakano Takashi
1962 '*Shōka ni okeru dōzoku no henka*' (Changes in the extended family among the merchants), *Shaikaigaku Hyōron* 12: 2: 23–36

Noda, Kazuo
1975 'Big business organization' In E. F. Vogel, ed., *Modern Japanese organization and decision-making* Berkeley: University of California Press

OECD
1977 *OECD Economic Surveys: Japan, July 1977*

Ōbata, Kyūgorō
1937 *An interpretation of the life of Viscount Shibusawa* Tokyo: Diamondo Jigyō Kabushiki Kaisha

Ōbuchi Hiroshi
1975 '*Kongo no keizai hatten to jinkō yōin*' (Future economic growth and population factors), in Minami Ryōzaburō and Ueda Masao, eds., *Nihon no jinkō hendō to keizai hatten* Tokyo: Sensō Shobō

Ōhashi Ryūken, ed.
1975 *Nihon no kaikyū kōsei* (The class composition of Japan), 6th edition, Tokyo: Iwanami Shoten

Okamoto Hideaki
1971 '*Shakai hendō to rōdō ishiki*' (Social change and worker consciousness), *Nihon Rōdō Kyōkai Zasshi* 142: 1: 14–29

Ōkochi, Kazuo
1958 *Labor in modern Japan* Tokyo: The Science Council of Japan

Okumura Hiroshi
1975 *Hōjin shihonshugi no kōzō: Nihon no kabushiki shoyū* (The structure of corporate capitalism: share ownership in Japan), Tokyo: Nihon Hyōronsha

Oshima, Harry T.
1965 'Meiji fiscal policy and economic progress' In William W. Lockwood, ed. *The state and economic enterprise in Japan: essays in the political economy of growth* Princeton: Princeton University Press

Pechman, Joseph A. and Keimei Kaizuka
1976 'Taxation' In Hugh Patrick and Henry Rosovsky, eds., *Asia's new giant: how the Japanese economy works* Washington, D.C.: The Brookings Institution

Pressnell, L. S., ed.
1973 *Money and banking in Japan* London: Macmillan

Roberts, John G.
1973 *Mitsui: three centuries of Japanese business* New York: Weatherhill

Rohlen, Thomas P.
1974 *For harmony and strength: Japanese white-collar organization in anthropological perspective* Berkeley: University of California Press
1977 'Is Japanese education becoming less egalitarian? Notes on high school stratification and reform' *The Journal of Japanese Studies* 3: 1: 37–70

Runciman, W. G.

1974 'The class structure of the advanced societies' *British Journal of Sociology* 25: 108–11

Sano Yōko

1972 *Joshi rōdō no keizaigaku* (The economics of female labour), Tokyo: Nihon Rōdō Kyōkai

Sethi, S. Prakash

1975 *Japanese business and social conflict: a comparative analysis of response patterns with American business* Cambridge, Mass.: Ballinger Publishing Company

Sheldon, C. D.

1973 *The rise of the merchant class in Tokugawa Japan 1600–1868: an introductory survey* New York: Russell & Russell

Shibusawa, Eiichi

1909 'Joint-stock enterprise in Japan' In Shigenobu Ōkuma, ed., *Fifty years of new Japan* Volume I, London: Smith, Elder & Co.

Shimada, Haruo

1977 'The Japanese labor market after the oil crisis: a factual report (I)' *Keiō Economic Studies* 14: 1: 49–65

Shinohara, Miyohei

1970 *Structural changes in Japan's economic development* (Economic Research Series No. 11. The Institute of Economic Research, Hitotsubashi University) Tokyo: Kinokuniya

Shirai Taishirō

1971 '*Rōdō kumiai to kōgai mondai*' (Labour unions and pollution problems), *Nihon Rōdō Kyōkai Zasshi* 142: 1: 4–13

Smith, Thomas C.

1955 *Political change and industrial development in Japan: government enterprise 1868–80* Stanford: Stanford University Press

1967 ' "Merit" as ideology in the Tokugawa period' In R. P. Dore, ed., *Aspects of Social Change in Modern Japan* Princeton: Princeton University Press

Soviak, Eugene

1971 'On the nature of Western progress: the journal of the Iwakura Embassy' In Donald H. Shively, ed., *Tradition and modernization in Japanese culture* Princeton: Princeton University Press

Taira, Kōji
1970 *Economic development and the labor market in Japan* New York: Columbia University Press

Takamiya, Susumu
1970 'Background, characteristics and recent trends in Japanese management' In British Institute of Management, ed., *Modern Japanese management* London

Tominaga, Ken'ichi
1962 'Occupational mobility in Japanese society: analysis of labor market in Japan' *The Journal of Economic Behaviour* 2: 2: 1–37

Trezise, Philip H. and Yukio Suzuki
1976 'Politics, government, and economic growth in Japan' In Hugh Patrick and Henry Rosovsky, eds., *Asia's new giant: how the Japanese economy works* Washington, D.C.: The Brookings Institution

Vishwanathan, Savitri
1977 'Citizen movements against industrial pollution: case study of Fuji City, Japan' *Annals of the Institute of Social Science* (University of Tokyo) 18: 1–62

Vogl, Frank
1973 *German business after the economic miracle* London: Macmillan

Wadaki, Matsutarō, Ryūei Shimizu, Mitsuo Fujimori and Hirokuni Sogawa
1972 'Decision-making by top-management and business performance in firms of Japan' *Keiō Business Review* 11: 1–27

Wakō Shōken Chōsabu, ed.
1972 *Kigyō no fukumi shisan* (The hidden assets of enterprises), Tokyo: Nihon Keizai Shinbunsha

Wigmore, J. H.
1969 *Law and justice in Tokugawa Japan: Part 1* Tokyo: University of Tokyo Press

Winsbury, Rex
1970 'The managers of Japan' In British Institute of Management, ed., *Modern Japanese Management* London

Wray, Donald
1949 'Marginal men of industry: the foreman' *American Journal of Sociology* 54: 298–301

Yamaguchi Kiichi
1972 '*Waga kuni jinkō nenrei kōzō no hendō to kokusai hikaku*' (Changes in the age structure of Japan and some international comparisons) *Jinkō Mondai Kenkyū* 124: 17–49

Yamamura, Kōzō
1974 *A study of samurai income and entrepreneurship* Cambridge, Mass.: Harvard University Press

Yanaga, Chitoshi
1968 *Big business in Japanese politics* New Haven: Yale University Press

Yasuba, Yasukichi
1976 'The evolution of dualistic wage structure' In Hugh Patrick, ed., *Japanese industrialization and its social consequences* Berkeley: University of California Press

Yasuda Saburō, ed.
1973 *Gendai Nihon no kaikyū ishiki* (Class consciousness in modern Japan), Tokyo: Yūzankaku

Yoshino, M. Y.
1968 *Japan's managerial system: tradition and innovation* Cambridge, Mass.: M.I.T. Press
1971 *The Japanese marketing system: adaptations and innovations* Cambridge, Mass.: M.I.T. Press
1976 *Japan's multinational enterprises* Cambridge, Mass.: Harvard University Press

Yūi Tsunehiko
1977 '*Kabushiki kaisha no seisei to teichaku*' (The formation and establishment of joint-stock companies), *Chūō Kōron Keiei Mondai* 61: 326–33

Index

Abegglen, James C., 38n, 45n, 126n, 140, 141, 172, 174, 193n
ability
  and promotion, 114–7, 125, 166, 215
  definition, 115, 117, 216
absenteeism, 219
Adachi, Kazuo, 135n
Adams, T. F. M., 32n, 33n, 34n
'administrative guidance', 7, 8
advertising, 54, 164
age
  and seniority, 112–9
  and mobility, 151–2, 186–7
  and distribution of wealth, 236–7
ageing of population
  and company organization, 5, 177–8, 225, 248–50, 259
  and recruitment at Marumaru, 137, 156
  and labour market, 147–9, 154–5
  political implications, 254–5
agriculture
  Meiji, 19–20
  mergers among firms engaged in, 59t
  price regulation, 229
Allen, G. C., 23n, 32n, 42n, 75n
Alps Electric Co., Ltd., 173
altruism, 260–1
Amagasaki Iron & Steel Mfg. Co., Ltd., 78n
Amano Corp., 62
apprenticeship, 15–7
Arisawa Hiromi and Naitō Masaru, 142n
articles of association, 2, 98, 99
artisans, 13, 16, 25
Asahi Breweries, Ltd., 52t
Asahi Chemical Industry Co., Ltd., 61
Asahi Glass Co., Ltd, 75t, 249
Asahi National Lighting Co., Ltd., 81t
Asahi Nenkan, 233n
Asahi Optical Co., Ltd., 52t
Asahi Organic Chemicals Industry Co., Ltd., 61
Asahi Shinbun, 229, 231n, 254n
Asano Sōichirō, 23
assets, balance sheet valuation of, 77–8, 86

attendance prizes, 188
auditors, statutory, 99, 101, 259
authority, managerial
  ideological justification, 37, 125, 138, 212–6
  practical support for, 96, 139, 212, 216–8
  and mobility, 141, 210–20
  and immobile employees, 186, 203
  and private life, 203
  and labour unions, 203, 218
  representation in media, 203–4
  and mobile employees, 207–8, 217–8
  possible changes in, 219–20, 248, 260
Azumi, Koya, 72n

Ballon, Robert J., Iwao Tomita and Hajime Usami, 250n
bank groups, 73, 77–80, 247
Bank of Japan, 21, 230n
Bank of Tokyo, Ltd., The, 253, 255
bankruptcies, 244, 245, 246
banks
  predominance among early companies, 32–3, 34–5
  in *zaibatsu*, 42, 73
  types of, 71
  influence on industry, 71, 77–80, 244
  and gradation, 71–3
  lending restrictions on, 80
  and flow of funds, 226–9
Barber, Richard J., 85n
bars, 206–7
Beed, C. S., 85n
beer industry, 52t
Bellah, Robert N., 26n
Bendix, Reinhard, 37n, 85n, 213n
Berle, Adolf A. and Gardiner C. Means, 85n
Berry, Charles H., 55n
Bieda, K., 67n
Bisson, T. A., 43n
Blood, Robert O., Jr., 209n
Blumenthal, Tuvia, 62n